D0389015

DRESS CODES

DRESS CODES

OF THREE
GIRLHOODS—
MY MOTHER'S,
MY FATHER'S,
AND MINE

Noelle Howey

PICADOR USA
NEW YORK

The names and other identifying characteristics of some of the people depicted in this memoir have been changed.

Picador® is a U.S. registered trademark and is used by St. Martin's Press under license from Pan Books Limited.

Endpaper photos courtesy of Chris Howey and Dinah Howey-Mouat. Top row, left to right: Dick, age 3; Dinah, age 9; Grandma and Noelle, 1979; Noelle, age 6. Middle row, left to right: Dinah and Dick, high school graduation; Dinah and Dick getting married; Dinah and Dick, 1980s; Chris, first cross-dresser meeting, 1987. Bottom row, left to right: Dick and baby Noelle, 1973; Dinah, Noelle, Dick, and Grandma H., 1977; Chris wins beauty pageant; Dad Christine, Noelle, and her mom.

Library of Congress Cataloging-in-Publication Data

Howey, Noelle.
    Dress Codes : of three girlhoods—my mother's, my father's, and mine / Noell Howey.—1st ed.
        p. cm.
    ISBN 0-312-42258-X
    1. Children of gay parents—United States. 2. Gay fathers—United States—Family relationships. I. Title.

HQ777.8 .H68 2002
306.874—dc21   2001059060

Second Picador USA Edition: November 2002

10 9 8 7 6 5 4 3 2 1

FOR CHRISTOPHER

CONTENTS

PREFACE   Spring, 1984   *xi*

PROLOGUE   The Spoiler   *xiii*

PART ONE   *Foundation Garments*   *1*

1   Coming Out, 1986   *3*

2   Portrait of My Father as a Young Man   *8*

3   Sugar, Spice, Everything Nice   *13*

4   Snips, Snails, Puppy Dogs' Tails   *36*

5   Mythologies   *53*

6   An Ordinary Girl, an Ordinary Life   *57*

7   Cross-dressing: A Primer   *68*

8   Checklists   *86*

9   Coming Out, 1962   *106*

10   Coming Out, 1983   *114*

11   Typecasting   *117*

12   Makeovers   *135*

13   Something Old, Something New   *156*

PART TWO   *Fabrications*   *171*

14   Clothes Lines   *173*

15   Phasing Out   *176*

16 Closet Cases   *195*

17 Larvae   *213*

18 Losing It, 1989   *227*

19 Girls Get Emotional   *230*

20 Coming Out, 1990   *252*

21 She Thing   *258*

22 Schisms   *280*

23 Vagina Monologue   *298*

24 Snapshots from My Trip   *314*

ACKNOWLEDGMENTS   *331*

One is not born a woman—one becomes one.

—SIMONE DE BEAUVOIR, *THE SECOND SEX*

Spring, 1984

It is just about my favorite game in seventh grade, second only to Hooker Barbie and Pimp Ken.

I sneak one of Mom's teddies—ideally the gold one with snaps on the bottom—out of Dad's dresser (for some reason, she keeps them in his underwear drawer), snag one of the *Playboy* magazines stacked beneath an old *Newsweek* in the linen closet, and lock my bedroom door. I tape the shades to the window and position the record needle on Madonna's "Love Don't Live Here Anymore." I glide on cherry Lip Smacker and sky-blue eye shadow, and try to keep the teddy—exactly ten sizes too big—from falling off. I keep an ear out for Mom or Dad coming up the stairs.

"I know you want it," I whisper.

I crook my leg around the doorframe and glide my crotch up and down against the edge. "Harder," I growl, as my hot breath forms small, moist circles on the painted wood.

I pretend the doorframe is named Jake, and that he is a tall, sexy ninth grader. When I am ready to have sex with Jake, it feels like I have to pee, and I hold myself like when I can't unlock the door fast enough to get in the house.

Before I put everything away, I squat on the bathroom sink in front of the mirrored medicine cabinet and run my hands down my hairless legs, unsnap the teddy bottom, and arch my privates

up toward the mirror like I'm about to do the crab walk. I hum
" 'cause I'm a woman" from the Enjoli commercial quietly so no
one can hear. I squint into the mirror, in the hopes that through
my curtain of eyelashes I will see an image that reflects my soft-
focus dreams.

While I am playing, Dad is down in the basement, a place that it
seems all dads like to be. It's cold, and made of blue concrete,
like a swimming pool that's been emptied out. Despite the fact
that the basement floods every April when the spring storms hit
northeastern Ohio, we keep all 150 square feet packed with what
I think of as boy stuff: a sawhorse, a toolbox, an extra fridge
packed with vodka and Budweiser, that sort of thing. Just before
he headed downstairs, my dad mumbled that he was working on
a project.

My father has tucked himself in the windowless back room of
the basement. He takes out the portable makeup mirror from
behind the solvents, a cache of dresses from under the camping
equipment. He leans into the mirror, slicks on Ruby Red Max
Factor and puckers. When he hears a creak on the stairs, he frantically starts unscrewing his jar of cold cream. It's the cat. "Jesus
Christ," he mutters, and slips into a green hausfrau number. He
imagines himself done up in a frilly floral apron, merrily folding
laundry for the whole clan. In the dim watery light of the basement, he can barely see his stubble or Adam's apple. He runs his
hands over the padded bra, trying to ignore the stray wiry chest
hairs.

This is ridiculous, he thinks. Stoically, he wipes all traces of the
cosmetics from his face. He goes upstairs and barks at me to get
away from the TV because it's time for the PGA championship.
When my mother comes home from the grocery store, he tells
her he spent the afternoon refinishing the end table.

The Spoiler

I'm about to ruin the surprise.

In case you missed it way back when, maybe because it looked a little dour, like just another one of those interminable art movies about Mother Ireland, here's the big secret of *The Crying Game*.

Dil, the sexy club singer who sings in that throaty, melancholy way, has a penis. If you watched the movie, you learned this fact about an hour or so into the film, at which point you may have gasped and turned in awe to your boyfriend or girlfriend and scrutinized Dil for the rest of the movie, trying to detect any nascent signs of masculinity. Of course, if you were my father, you simply shrugged, downed another handful of buttered popcorn, and sighed "I knew it all along. Look at those wrists."

Of course, my father had a cheat sheet: she, like Dil, is transgendered, transsexual, gender dysphoric, gender-conflicted, a she-male, a chick with a dick.

In *The Crying Game* and the handful or so of other movies on transgendered folk, the climax of the story occurs when our hero or heroine comes out. It's neither pretty nor uplifting. It doesn't involve a heartfelt confession at the dinner table: *"Mom . . . Dad . . . I'm gay."* Our gender-confused protagonists tend to come out quite literally, after being coaxed or downright forced to drop their skivvies or unwrap a mummified bosom to the shock of their locker-room pals and oblivious sex partners. Vomiting ensues. The hot babe tearfully reveals her angry inch; the cutie-pie boy reluctantly exposes his B-cups. We in the audience ache with empathy for our hero. He (or she) is tragic in a Greek sense: Like Oedipus, he is destined to defile all society holds dear and be exiled for it. Like Pandora, she just can't keep her trap shut. And like the Chorus, we watch, we weep.

Make no mistake: drag à la Hollywood is often just that. A drag.

Since my father came out ten years ago, everyone from party guests to my college professors have wanted to know how I discovered the truth. They want to know how I found out that my dad liked to wear women's clothes, or maybe how I learned he actually wanted to become a female. I'm not sure what they expect to hear, though given their soft, dulcet tones of voice, their hands placed gently upon my shoulder, I think they are expecting something rather apocalyptic.

Not that I can blame them. Since the long-ago moment when a sideburned, white-suited Phil Donahue ushered his first crossdresser onto the talk show stage, coming out as transgender has become virtually a national spectator sport, albeit closer to the carnival freak show atmosphere of pro wrestling than the soporific, George Will–sanctioned world of baseball.

Marla (formerly Mark) or less often, Lance (formerly Laura), waits quietly in the backstage area until his or her loved ones are assembled onstage. The sour ex-wife confesses that Mark has always been a little limp-wristed; the aggrieved mother recalls how Laura always liked dodgeball more than the average Brownie. The doorbell rings. The theme music blares. Mark sashays out in a cut-away number, stopping to flip up his skirt to reveal his ruffled panties. Laura struts out, bowlegged with machismo, wearing mirrored sunglasses and a scowl.

"Did you know Mark wanted to be a woman?" the host presses.

"No, I mean . . . not like this," his ex-wife weeps, just before being ushered out on the arm of a pop psychologist.

The real-life, untelevised coming out moment is rarely that dramatic. Nor does it happen just once. In our particular case, my
father rather uncinematically came out at least three or four times
to my mother and me.

Dad first came out to my mom, his high-school sweetheart,
during a casual phone chat in late 1962. My dad said he liked to
wear fuzzy sweaters. Giggling, my mom said she did, too, and
uncomfortable with the silence, asked whether he thought their
teacher wore a hairpiece. Twenty-four years later, my mom told
me that my father was a cross-dresser just after we bought jeans
at a mall. Unlike my mother, I knew just how freakish this behavior must be. Thanks to the alienating power of that knowledge,
the next coming out didn't happen for three years. I was seventeen by the time I finally saw my father actually *dressed* like a
woman. She looked more like Suzanne Pleshette than Boy
George.

Do you hear the strings swelling to crescendo in the foreground?
You shouldn't. Let's be real here: Nobody died. I was never in-
stitutionalized or impoverished. I have been on Prozac, but suffered only a little water retention as a side effect. My parents
never escaped from anything: jail, the military, the Khmer Rouge.
They didn't even bother to go to Woodstock. "Yeah, I think we
had a barbecue that weekend at Avon Lake," my mother mumbles
now. "At Mr. Reinker's. You know, he had a boat." They are
normal, in the way Ohioans respectfully refer to each other. *Normal*, in the way New Yorkers mean when they are feeling sorry
for those people who live in the middle of nowhere.

This isn't a tragedy. It's just nonfiction.

Still, I have a girl for a dad, and that's news, even today when
everyone and his brother has some newfangled family structure.
I have two female parents. Not all that unusual in the scheme of
"nontraditional families," except that only one is a lesbian, and
only one gets to be called my mother—and they're not the same

person. In a world in which 90 percent of the five thousand books about fatherhood in the library are really about *man*hood, that's still a real mind-blower.

I have a dad who is a woman much like me, but with better legs. And when he was still male, I had a dad possibly like yours: sullen, sporadically hostile, frequently vacant. I had a dad who became a woman in order to be *nice*.

I have a family that survived a life in the closet by employing humor, tinted car windows, and thousands of dollars' worth of therapy. A family that gave its patriarch Chanel No. 5 for Father's Day. A traditional family—loving father, supportive mother, doting child—that would probably be the right wing's worst nightmare.

I am a different person because my father was a man, then a girl, then a woman. I watched her go through puberty right after I did, putting on too much makeup before going for the "natural look"; wearing three-inch heels before deciding that flats had better arch support.

And as punishment for embracing her womanhood, she—once among the most highly compensated advertising creative directors in Ohio—lost many friends, and gradually plummeted toward the poverty level. In the meantime, I was congratulated for continuing to love her, for being willing to know her. No one would have blamed me, I was reminded, if I had turned my back.

When my mother told me the secret about my father, nothing actually changed, but change was finally made possible. The secret, once revealed, sliced through the hazy inertia of our average, dissatisfied, suburban lives. Like most real-life coming outs, the event itself didn't need to be harrowing or humiliating to be life-altering. My father's coming out was not the crowning climactic moment of my life; it was a beginning, a point of departure.

PART ONE

Foundation Garments

ONE

Coming Out, 1986

My mother's hatchback was parked in Section B, Aisle 12, between a small pile of beer cans and a battered Plymouth that looked as though it belonged on cement blocks. We were quiet.

I don't remember whether we left the house in the late morning or the early afternoon; I don't know if it was a Saturday or a Sunday. I can't say what we discussed in the car on the way to the mall, or whether we simply drove in silence. I didn't ask why we were going shopping all of a sudden, though I assumed we were trying to get out of my father's way. He looked pretty tired.

I watched the raindrops meander, forging crooked, loosely braided paths up the windshield. I had always been mesmerized and perplexed by the way rain crawls up car windows.

"Honey, are you listening? Do you understand what I'm saying?" my mother asked.

It was cold, even for late autumn, even for Cleveland.

"Yes, of course," I scoffed, buttoning my jacket.

My mother twisted in her bucket seat to face me as head-on as possible. That couldn't have been comfortable.

"I think you're not quite taking this in," she said.

Today, out of nowhere, right after our usual bowls of cornflakes, my mother decided that I needed socks, underwear, scrunchies—

immediately. She hustled me into the car. "We're going to Penney's over at Randall," she said. "I'm not spending ten dollars so you can tell Debbie that you have socks from the Gap."

Randall Park was a strip mall behemoth with mud-streaked red carpeting, dry fountains, and third-tier retail establishments: Spencer Gifts instead of Papyrus, Frederick's of Hollywood instead of Victoria's Secret. I usually went elsewhere; thanks to purported gang activity, kids under sixteen weren't supposed to loiter in Randall without a chaperone. Anyway, I preferred the mall in Beachwood, or Bitchwood, as everyone called it, which had gleaming tile floors, perfectly squeegied skylights, a food court teeming with exotic boys from neighboring high schools.

We bought a whole armload of socks, and a plastic tube stuffed with panties in various\pastel shades—a distant second choice after my mother rejected the thongs. She seemed anxious, fiddling with her keys, clucking her tongue.

While the clerk wrapped my panties in tissue paper, she asked my mother, "Honey, how's the weather out there? You know I hate not being able to see the outside from this place. It could be snowing for all I'd know!" My mother normally would've chuckled, "Oh boy, I just love windows, too. Well, it's raining right now . . ." And three minutes later, she and the cashier—named Wanda, apparently, originally from Kentucky—would be laughing and patting each other's hands like long-lost childhood friends. My mother, the former speech therapist, would have instinctively started mimicking Wanda's phrases, her pauses, the places where her sentences would drift off. But today the clerk got no response. My mom simply smiled, weakly, and handed over her credit card.

Before we left the store, I ran over to the Misses section to ogle a pair of size zero side-zipper Guess jeans. My mother lingered in the aisle watching me, warily. "Well, we bought cheap so-ocks," I pleaded, elongating my syllables preciously. This poor-me-buy-me-expensive-clothes bit never worked, but I always gave it a shot.

My mother didn't even blink. "Okay, okay," she sighed. "Get whatever you want."

Mom walked slowly back to the car in the rain. I practically skipped ahead, clutching my bag of jeans to my heart like found treasure. Debbie will *die*, I thought gleefully.

"Come on," I yelled. "You're getting wet."

She tossed the remaining bags in the hatchback between the lawn fertilizer and her golf clubs. We got back in the car, and I flipped on the radio. *". . . easy lover, she'll take your heart but you won't feel it."*

"Um, can I change it?" I asked tentatively, realizing that having been gifted with designer loot, I should probably tread lightly with my requests.

"Actually, can you turn it off?" Mom said.

She stared straight out the windshield, tapping her fingers against the steering wheel. *Uh-oh.* It's work. She's been fired. Suddenly my heart lifted. It's Dad. Maybe he's dying! No, that's terrible. I take it back. I'm sorry, God. Or whoever. I take it back. Make him just sick. Maybe they're getting divorced. Or he's moving. Far, far away.

"It's Dad. There's something I need to tell you."

My mother said one of the following things:

a) "Your dad likes to wear women's clothes."

b) "Noelle, your dad is different from other dads in that he likes to wear girls' clothes, and he wants to do it all the time."

c) "You know how you like fuzzy sweaters? Your dad likes them, too. Girl sweaters, I mean."

My mom doesn't know what she said either.

In truth, it doesn't matter. I remember exactly what I thought:

You have got to be kidding me. There's no news like hearing irrefutable proof that you're not the sole cause of your parents' woes, your father's drinking, your unshakable feeling that you're not put together quite right and finding out the problem all along was your father's unrequited yearning for *angora*.

My mother was looking at me very intently and quizzically. "You understand, Dad has been doing this for many, many years. And he doesn't want to have to hide it from you anymore."

"It's a big secret that he likes to wear girls' sweaters?" I retorted, trying to keep my voice steady and fierce.

"Well"—my mother sighed—"yes. And we wanted you to know." I supposed I was scripted to weep, to riddle my mother with questions. *Tough*. I was not going to be upset about this. I had decided not to care about my father years ago. With that resolution firmly in mind, I immediately burst into tears.

"So, it's not my fault? That he's so . . . like the way he is? He doesn't hate me?" I sobbed. "It's not my fault?" My mother says I repeated that same sentence twenty times. Despite my resolve not to crack, not to betray the fact that I actually, maybe, loved my father, once I started crying I couldn't stop. Nor could I stop feeling an overpowering sense of relief engulf my entire body, causing an almost anesthetizing effect. I blew my nose and wiped my face with my mother's sleeve.

"We're trusting you with this really important information, okay? You need to not tell anyone about this. You can talk about it with me, or your dad, or the therapist we've been seeing, if you want. She's really nice. But don't tell anyone about your dad. That means Debbie, too, okay? Dad could lose his job, we could lose the house, you could get teased at school. We need you to be an adult here, and keep this a secret."

My mother forced a grim smile. Her eyes were shot, her freckled face sunken and pallid, almost the color of jellyfish. For the first time, I realized my father wasn't coming out to me himself. My mother—kisser of paper cuts, attendee of parent-teacher functions, purchaser of produce—was on cleanup duty again. Of all the tasks not to push off on your wife, one might imagine coming out would be right up there.

"Sweetie," my mother said, registering surprise, "I told you your dad loved you. I always told you that."

"I know," I said, still exhaling. "*You* told me."

Had my mother or father told me the truth when I was sixteen, or twenty-five, I might have been beyond tears, and even beyond caring whether I was to blame for his obvious unhappiness. My father came out just in time.

TWO

Portrait of My Father as a Young Man

By the time I hit my mid-twenties, in the defensive manner typical of those urban apartment dwellers who shell out half their take-home pay to live in an overheated box with no bathroom sink, I would come to grouse about the suburbs. I would disparage their ubiquitous wood-chip-and-pebble landscaping, and the flags of neon watermelon slices flapping over every front door as though to announce, "We claim this land for Home Depot!" Yet in doing so, I'd play loose with the fact that the 'burb where I lived from zero to fourteen—the 2300 block of Edgerton Road in University Heights, Ohio—is perhaps the most diverse place I ever encountered: teeming with African-American and white and Asian families, Italians and Jews, stockbrokers and plumbers and welfare recipients. On our block lived Mrs. Barnes, a jovial old gal who walked three miles every day, blizzards be damned, from her fake Tudor to the bowling alley; the Creightons, a black family whose son, Omar, secretly played Malibu Ken to my Japanese Barbie; the Filipino Durans with their two daughters, gorgeous in plum red lipstick and open-toed pumps; and the two anonymous, inseparable men in the brick house, who everyone figured were brothers or cousins.

I will also have to ignore the plain truth of my childhood, which is that I adored my suburb. Far from being a homogenous petri dish, University Heights seemed magical to me beneath its veneer of the everyday mundane. It's not simply that I was prone to a wild imagination, wherein a routine trip to the grocery store could be recast in my mind as a quest to find sustenance for the brood. My neighborhood encompassed the universe, both real and make-believe. That's surely no different from virtually any child, for whom the entire world exists just below the height of the kitchen counter, for whom anything farther than twenty minutes away by car is unfathomably foreign. But my block, where I was permitted to wander, unobserved, without a sitter, was also a refuge. The loose lumber for a playhouse that never got built was a place to hide when my father's car rumbled up the driveway. The baby-soft patch of grass behind the garage where the blades never sliced, no matter which way you rubbed them, was a place to curl up after he fell asleep, head slung back with mouth agape against the cushion of his threadbare recliner. I was never the kind of kid who'd get worked up about seeing a yellow-bellied thrush, but when my father was around, I was thankful to have a backyard, and by extension, a place to disappear.

My father, Richard, who—in one of those wincing ironies you couldn't get away with in fiction—was nicknamed Dick, was the shadow in the corner of the living room. He was a brilliant advertising writer, a talented part-time actor, and in seemingly desperate need of a few different twelve-step programs. Although I knew he and my mother had been high-school sweethearts, I couldn't picture them meeting cute over homework and exchanging phone numbers with a wink and a blush. Mom, Joanie; Dad, Chachi? I was a creative kid, but my imagination wasn't that good.

As far as I could tell, after coming home, he'd mix up a twelve-consonant vodka and orange juice (three cubes, two stirs, leaving the spoon on the counter), and then sleep, watch TV, drink, and sleep again. Occasionally, he'd shake up the routine by eating a salad. Other times he'd even speak, grunting a sigh of agreement with a curmudgeon columnist, or scowling at inferior full-page ads crafted by big-name New York firms. Since day one, I tried to stay as far away from my father as possible, and the avoidance seemed mutual.

He wasn't an overwhelmingly menacing presence. Physically, he was slight, five-ten with a baby face, a gut as pasty and rounded as proofed yeast, and a ten-hair comb-over. But boy, could he give you a look. The Stare, as my mother and I later dubbed it, was obtained by narrowing his eyes into slits while the rest of his face remained immobile granite. He didn't seem irritated or angry. His eyes simply went dead—as hard and unreflecting as milk glass. Thanks to his ability to conjure that stare, I was certain that my father merely tolerated me.

My mother was an optimist, but beyond that, she believed religiously in the power of rational thinking. If a behavior seemed explicable via any type of -*ology*, then it must be fixable. Logically, she knew that my father loved me, and, therefore, if we were forced together often enough, he would get better at showing his affection, until my father and I were happily do-si-doing at Girl Scout father-daughter square dances.

"Go sit on Daddy's lap," Mom would whisper, sitting next to me in the kitchen while my father lubricated himself into a half-drunk stupor in the den. "Noooo," I'd whine. "Noelle," my mother would say, "he loves you so much. Daddy just has some problems. He doesn't know how to reach out to you." She would explain to me that although his mother, my Grandma Howey, drowned me in affection, she had not been nearly as close to my father.

Mom went on to explain that my father was handicapped, emotionally, in the same way that some people can't walk or see. "You are so mature, Noelle," she told me. "You can help out your dad."

"Okay." I sighed. I *did* know—my mother often gave me this missionary pep speech. "Honey, give it a try. Come on," she would say, as she pulled me to my feet and, perhaps trying to lighten the mood, playfully patted my butt with an unspoken *skedaddle*. Finally, I would give in and plod with a Dead Man Walking gait to my father's recliner in the den, certain that I was going to disappoint my mother again by having failed to transform my father into Super Dad.

I was four. Or six. Or nine. It doesn't matter what age I was; the plot remains the same. I lurched to sit on my father's lap. He never moved. It was like sitting on the Lincoln Memorial. I leaned back and tried to nuzzle under his chin. Nothing. I twisted sideways in order to throw my arms around him. I could smell him, that trademark musk of Vitalis and Dial soap. Then he rustled the newspaper, trying to pull it from under my bottom without touching. "Can't you see I'm reading, Noelle?" He sighed. "Can we do this later?"

Later wasn't meant literally. He would fall asleep or, without a word, drive off to rehearsal. He acted in a local repertory company, and always played the part of the conniving bastard: Goebbels, a wife-beater, Nixon. After he left for the evening, my mother, in her usual sad way, would apologize for my father's behavior for the ten-thousandth time.

"He loves you, baby, he really does," my mother said, cradling me tightly. In kindergarten and first grade, I cried. In later years, I was able to hold myself together by counting things—kitchen tiles, blue posies on the wallpaper, lines on my mother's hands—until I got bored with being sad. The two of us would go to my parents' bedroom, where I watched TV while my mother pulled out a two-thousand-piece jigsaw or her crossword puzzle book, focusing her attentions on puzzles with easily obtainable solutions.

Now, in case it appears that I am seguing into a disclosure of brutality involving large metal belt buckles or having to clean bathrooms with a toothbrush, I should make a disclaimer: namely, that while my father was fairly unpleasant, he was by no means the worst around. My father could hardly compete with Jenny's dad, who whipped his kids daily, or Michael J's dad, who ended up in the state pen.

He even had interludes in which he was as gentle and wisdom-imparting as any TV father. These were called Christmas, Valentine's Day, and Easter. He would lavish gifts upon my mother and me, always grand gestures: the turquoise ring, the framed paean to fatherly love, the bicycle with training wheels. Better still were the fleeting, spontaneous moments when my father became the tickle monster, coming toward me on all fours while I giggled madly, or when we played keep-it-up with a half-deflated balloon in the dining room.

Yet these random acts of kindness could be more upsetting than when he was an out-and-out creep. Were it not for those occasional, wonderful moments, my mother would have packed our luggage and moved us out. I might have been able to distance myself from him and stay that way, instead of tumbling back, accidentally and in spite of myself, into caring about him again. My father was inconsistent, and inconsistency bred hope. So, despite wanting to hate him, I lay in bed at night devising ways to become more beautiful, more gifted, simply *more*, so that he could stay in his holiday spirit all year long.

THREE

Sugar, Spice, Everything Nice

The basic Female Body comes with the following accessories: garter belt, panty girdle, crinoline, camisole, bustle, brassiere, stomacher, chemise, virgin zone, spike heels, nose ring, veil, kid gloves, fishnet stockings, fichu, bandeau, Merry Widow, weepers, chokers, barrettes, bangles, beads, lorgnette, feather boa, basic black, compact, Lycra stretch one-piece with modesty panel, designer peignoir, flannel nightie, lace teddy, bed, head.
—Margaret Atwood

In the beginning, there was a tutu.

Or rather, a strip of shiny nylon loosely stitched to mosquito netting in robin's-egg blue. I'd wanted a pink tutu to match the ballerina wallpaper I had begged for since filing out of the Colony Theater after a revival matinee of *The Red Shoes.* Blue was a boy's color, even if it made a good crayon, and it wouldn't have been my first choice. Nonetheless, that's what Grandma Howey could find on the remaindered table at the fabric store, so there it was. At six, it was my favorite costume.

If my "other grandmother," Grandma Schultz, had made the tutu, it would have been a perfectly constructed confection of pink crinoline with embroidered cabbage roses. Grudgingly, I would have found it acceptable. But I thought my ugly, itchy knee-length tutu was perfect because, like all good things, it came from Grandma H.

I wore that tutu with my matching leotard just about everywhere except, well, ballet class, where such froufrou attire would never have been tolerated. But at home, I leapt around the house in it the rest of the week, pretending the kitchen counter was my barre and that the middle of the living room was Lincoln Center (the New York City Ballet of my imagination was surprisingly fond of setting its performances to *Saturday Night Fever*).

At first ballet was easy. I was skinny and flexible as warm taffy, and Mrs. Green, an elderly rabbi's wife who taught what she affectedly called "la danse russe" in her converted basement rec room, was thrilled with my potential. As she coached us through the five positions, I applied myself to ballet with compulsive vigor, mouthing the strange French words for everything. I practiced constantly, always trying to keep my leg straighter, my arm more delicately curved.

Dancing in recitals made me feel as ethereal as the delicate figurine in a music box, and I eagerly soaked up the praise— something I would never get in gym class, where poor eye-hand coordination and a pathological fear of the ball rendered me last pick on every team, every time. Plus, when I was dancing, neither of my parents ever missed a show.

Of course, the downside was that ballet hurt, especially once I started dancing en pointe and left the comfort of Mrs. Green's basement with its steaming, leaky radiator and water-damaged parquet floors for a ballet academy held in its own building. As the pain grew, I schooled myself to think of ballet class as romantic. I associated my aching abdominal muscles and oozing toe blisters with unfortunate but necessary hardships in the pursuit of beauty, like the days when women laced up in rib-crunching corsets or had their feet hammered into bindings. And so the eight aspiring prima ballerinas in my class balanced on our tailbones in perfect V's, with legs quivering unbended in the air and arms gracefully akimbo for ten minutes straight. Our Russian instructor, snarly as a cold-war-propaganda-film villain, hovered over us with a cherry red yardstick, ready to smack anyone who fell backward. After a few months of this torment, I was thoroughly over the romance of ballet and ready to consign myself to a completely sedentary life. Unfortunately, I liked to have an excuse for an audience, and Grandma H. was so proud of me for sticking with dance. She said it made me look poised and graceful, she boasted, "like a little lady."

In the K through six years, Grandma H., my father's mother, was my own personal goddess. She had a helmet of yellow hair, which intentionally matched her compact car; a softly wrinkled face caked with department store foundation and powder; a closet jammed full of tasteful clothes and drawers laden with designer scarves, shawls, wraps, cashmere throws and their corresponding brooches, pins, and pendants. A divorcée since the late fifties, my Grandma H. was a hottie: the bottle blond envy of the Greater Cleveland AARP chapter.

I was not impervious to her beauty; I spent hours feasting on the photo of her in homecoming court, not long before her ill-fated marriage to my grandfather. She was stunning in an Ava Gardner sort of way, with lustrous dark hair cascading down her back as in a shampoo commercial, wide brown eyes and a fashionable hourglass figure. What rendered her even more exotic, at least to me, was the whiff of Southern belle she gave off, thanks to early years growing up amidst the flowering dogwoods of rural Alabama. The South didn't linger in her accent, an unforgiving nasal newscaster drone that was unmistakably northern Ohio, but you could glimpse it in her demurely folded hands, her way of shooing away and simultaneously basking in a compliment, her ability to fawn over people she disdained. Without hesitation, I yearned for an ounce of my grandmother's chilly etiquette and the sumptuous beauty of her youth.

Back in my early grade-school days, I was aware that I was cute: pug-nosed and dappled with freckles in the summertime and vaguely reminiscent of the wholesome fraulein on the Swiss Miss package when I wore my blond hair in braids. However, the distinction between cute and beautiful wasn't lost on me. Cute meant mediocre—worth a grin at most—but beautiful caught your breath, turned your head, stopped your heart, or traffic. Ever since my first entrance, coming butt backward into the world with my umbilical cord wrapped around my neck like a pearl choker, causing a bit of frenzy in the delivery room, I wanted to make people stop and look at me.

Unfortunately, they always wanted to talk, too, and that's where things got complicated. Although I clamored for attention, I was painfully shy with strangers, and spent every gathering cowering behind my mother's back, clasping desperately to the untucked tail of her blouse. "Say hello, Noelle," she commanded, urging me out yet again. "Hello," I whispered, mournfully, to her thigh. "Can you look up, Noelle?" my mother asked. Gradually, I craned my head upward, red-faced and apologetic. "Um, sorry," I murmured dolefully, to the bemusement of the grown-ups and relief of my mother.

I realized early on that my mother, the quintessential producer who always preferred a backstage role both personally and professionally, would not be the one to teach me how to commandeer the spotlight. Grandma H., on the other hand, knew all about upstaging, about playing both the ingenue and the grande dame to the *nth* degree. To my delight and my mother's annoyance, she was fully prepared to instruct me on how to do the same.

By the time I was six and three-quarters, Grandma H. decided that I was ready for more than one costume. She decided to create an entire dress-up box out of cardboard and gold wrapping paper. "Now you can pretend to be someone else whenever you want," she gushed. "You can *liberate* your imagination."

The so-called Liberation of the Imagination was a concept that endlessly intrigued and plagued Grandma H. She owned well over twenty books with titles like *Recapturing Your Childhood Spark*, or *The 10% Life: A Guide to Waking up Your Latent Mind*. (At the time, I thought she was reading them to better understand me, but over time, I came to realize that she was less concerned with relating to a child's world than inhabiting it herself.) She studied these various tomes, taking longhand notes on legal pads after reading each chapter and typing up her conclusions on her manual typewriter. Sometimes she would refer to the notes while she was painting in the corner of the living room. She specialized in gigantic neon still lifes of fruit and flowers, like a bouquet of daisies against a yellow canvas as loud as Las Vegas. You couldn't stare at it too long because, like the sun, it would cause you to see dark spots everywhere for the next thirty seconds.

Grandma H. didn't seem to like being a grown-up; but personally, I couldn't wait. In second grade, we were assigned to write a paragraph about our favorite age. I wrote about being thirty. My teacher, Mrs. Gotwald, took me aside and pointed out to me that she meant an age I had already *been*. That made no sense to me; childhood was just a limbo period before you really got to have fun, like getting a job, buying furnishings, making babies, and filling out forms like the 1040.

Although I didn't understand why my grandmother didn't want to be an adult, I had to admit she made a great kid. Routinely, after we arrived at her apartment, she'd change out of her elegant designer cashmere into her "play clothes." From then on, she was insatiable, speeding Hot Wheels cars (with *vroom* sound effects) under the desk or transforming the windowsill into a dance floor for paper dolls. I almost always tired of games hours before she did. "Can we stop yet?" I once groaned, after playing Strawberry Shortcake & Friends Live in the Bread Box for three straight hours. "Oh . . ." Grandma said forlornly. "Well . . . okay. I mean, sure. If you want to . . ."

I shrugged. "All right, Grandma, but only a little longer." Longer stretched into five more hours, as my grandma refused to read, make dinner, or do anything else that detracted from our busy work renovating the bread box into a franchise of the Berry Bake Shop. "Here, see," she giggled, tapping me on the shoulder, again reinforcing why I would someday refer to her as a hybrid of Martha Stewart and Mr. Rogers. "I made Strawberry Shortcake an oven out of Wonder Bread and pipe cleaners!" I rubbed my eyes. "That's great, Grandma"—I smiled tenderly—"but can we stop? Please?" That night, before we went to sleep in her big double bed, I read *Ballet Shoes*, the story of Pauline, Petrova, and Posy, while Grandma hunched over her desk, studying how better to perfect her childlike ways.

My grandmother got custody of me on most weekends, but I spent Monday thru Friday nights with at least one of my parents. Most of the time, especially in the summers, we were all at home in the evenings. But during the theater season—coinciding precisely with the school year—my father was frequently in rehearsal, while my mother worked the box office or ran the lights in the hopes of obtaining a few minutes of quality time with him.

It worked. My parents never seemed more like married people than during the rehearsal phase of a play. Dad would run his lines onstage, during breaks, and Mom would sit in the third row, munching on butter cookies from the green room and making notes on her legal pad. Ironically, when he was playing a bona fide role, she could always tell when he was being honest, when his motivations were clear, and whether he was communicating with the audience. Though averse to performing herself, she understood the art of connection and helped him learn how to reach out to hundreds of people whose faces he could barely see. On the occasions when the sitter would fall through, I had the privilege of watching them work together, butting heads intellectually like people who loved and respected one another—a perspective on them that I never saw quite often enough. My mother worried when I was holed up in the theater with them: *Noelle will miss her bedtime. Noelle won't get all her homework done.* But I never complained.

Dobama Theater was a dive. Located in the basement of a classic prewar on a block my father called Firetrap Row, Dobama smelled perpetually musty; the dank floors were never quite dry; the thrust stage, if left to nature, would probably grow moss; the green room was carpeted in coffee rings and dust bunnies. It was also prone to clichés: framed photographs, presumably deep, hung in the whitewashed gallery area; a man strummed acoustic peace anthems at intermission. I wanted to spend every waking moment there.

The darkness, the solitude, the free-floating angst of that place was seductive, especially to a little girl who was beginning to fancy herself as tragically misunderstood. I could be wistful for hours at a time without anyone telling me to turn my frown upside down or look alive. It was the world of adults; since I felt so ill suited for the universe of the playground, that world enticed me—promising a haven where, someday, I might belong. After that period of blessed moping and another of watching actors behind the curtains feverishly mouthing their lines while pacing back and forth, we'd all go to the Mad Greek restaurant. The cast would inhale plate after plate of gyros and grape leaves while I happily fell asleep on my mother's lap.

My father was universally acknowledged as one of the theater's major talents. He rarely got even a mediocre review, and had a solid fan base among the season subscribers. All the other actors—especially those who were accountants and lawyers by day—seemed a bit awed and frightened by his fiery intensity. They did this acting thing for fun, to let off a little steam, to have a creative outlet. Dad, on the other hand, was not engaged in a hobby. He so fully embodied whichever murderous, sadistic, seductive, wantonly cruel character he was assigned at the moment that the others would actually forget he was acting until he started drinking beer and cracking jokes at the Greek later on. "Damn, he's good," I'd hear them whisper to each other. "Fucking scary," someone might add.

My mother and I were never happier than when my father was playing a cretin. He'd spend hours a week screaming and mock-stabbing, and then on his night off, perhaps due to exhaustion, he'd be unusually relaxed and attentive. On those nights, he often asked me to run lines with him. I tried to impress him by reading without any stutters or mispronunciations.

"I want another baby," I read aloud to him, slowly.

"We already have a baby," my father said back, his voice rising, the copy of A. R. Gurney's *Scenes from an American Life* sitting on his chest for easy access.

"They're not babies, and they're not mine. I want to have my own baby before I dry up completely."

"Get out of the car, bitch," he shouted.

"Daddy?"

"Is that the line?"

"No, Daddy, I have a question. When you yell, you're not yelling at me, right? You're not mad at me?"

"No, Noelle"—he sighed—"I'm yelling at your character." I'd nod, and vow not to ask any stupid questions like that the next time.

Grandma H. gave me another item for my shiny new costume box on my eighth birthday. Much like the tutu, it wrapped around my middle and tied with a bow in the back. But this was an apron, and it was pink-and-orange plaid with a kangaroo pouch in the middle for carrying spoons and other relevant objects. I was less excited about the apron than the tutu, but I had to admit it made a fabulous accessory for playing housewife: a short game that mainly consisted of heating chocolate patty-cakes by the light of my Easy Bake oven's hundred-watt bulb. When I waddled into Grandma H.'s living room, beaming, gingerly holding my coaster-sized disc of cake between two latch-hooked potholders that matched my apron, she looked ready to cry. "You . . . look . . . so . . . *coordinated,*" she said slowly, with utter delight, and propped me up against the couch. "Where in the blankety-blank is the Polaroid?"

On hearing that her mother-in-law had given me an apron, my mom laughed so hard that she almost dropped a lit cigarette in her coffee. "Oh boy," she said, wiping her nose. "Noelle, the apron is fine. Just do us all a favor. Don't let Ella Mae teach you how to cook."

I didn't get that at all. I vastly preferred eating at Grandma H.'s airy little apartment in Shaker Heights to trekking over to Grandma Schultz's flat one-story in what I thought of as the country because the mailbox wasn't attached to the house. Grandma H. served food as good as Burger King on bright purple TV trays: Stouffer's potatoes au gratin; Peter Pan and Smucker's grape on Roman Meal, cut into fours; Stouffer's Salisbury steak; Chef Boyardee beef ravioli; Stouffer's macaroni and cheese. And always vanilla ice cream with sticky clumps of hot fudge sauce scraped off the bottom of the saucepan for dessert.

In Grandma Schultz's dimly lit kitchen, on the other hand, adults spoke of Ullman's drinking and cousin Beatrice's divorce over a smorgasbord: fluffy scrambled eggs, rye toast with apple butter, fresh raspberries that Grandma sold roadside, salted beefsteak tomatoes, a half pound of crinkled brown bacon on a paper towel, cantaloupe that dripped down your chin, chicory coffee that percolated in an urn. I was disturbed by the lack of brand names. We didn't watch TV during breakfast. The grown-ups talked and listened to the radio. *AM* radio.

It took me several more years to comprehend that Grandma H. could not cook, or sew, or clean, or do just about anything that women of her particular generation were allegedly schooled in. She only cooked from scratch once a year, on Easter, and that special recipe was for meat loaf: a block of defrosted ground

round baked in a bread tin until it was completely moisture-free, with canned gravy the color of mercury dribbled over the top. Easter dinner at Grandma's was the only time I saw my parents hide food in their napkins. Grandma H. applied the exact same level of perfectionism to her cleaning and other housekeeping details: "dusting" with an elegant, pearl-handled duster that had lost nearly all its feathers; "scrubbing" the floor with a wad of dry toilet paper wedged between her toes. Nonetheless, despite all of this unabashed mediocrity in the domestic sphere, back in the fifties, my grandmother had somehow managed to get herself written up in the *Cleveland Press* as an "outstanding House Wife," with several recipes (adopted nearly verbatim from the *Joy of Cooking*) quoted alongside a photo of her, shiny and lipsticked in an immaculate kerchief and sundress holding up my sailor-suited father in midair as though he was a product she was touting.

My grandmother raised two sons—my uncle, an acting teacher; and my father, a copywriter and thespian—who learned from the best, for her truest talent was in marketing. Magically, she transformed herself from a homecoming princess to a noteworthy housewife and by the time I showed up, a retired executive and third-tier local celebrity—that is, she might rate a caption in an article about a local society event, but she wasn't an automatic invite. She brilliantly reinvented herself, every image honed to a polish for each decade of her life. And I was madly in love with her.

The worshipful gaze with which I beheld Grandma H. was not much encouraged or shared by either of my parents. My father went through the motions—opening doors for her, pulling out chairs, saying hello—but not without emitting irritated sighs at regular intervals or otherwise conveying the unmistakable sentiment that he would rather be flossing than dealing with her, thank you very much.

My mother was more subtle, but the fact that she disliked

Grandma H. slowly seeped into my consciousness. My grandma, in her dry-clean-only crepe de chine and pancake powder, and my mom, with her casual wear and ruddy, freckled face, couldn't have been farther apart in taste or style. But their differences went far beyond accessories.

My mother was a former teacher and bleeding-heart liberal, raised by God-eschewing, registered Communists to be cynical of government. She initiated me into the whole personal-is-political concept, insisting I skip the birthday party across the street when they didn't invite my black friends to come; explaining to me that sex was a good thing when it was consensual and between mature people. My grandmother was a Reagan voter, who mostly saw political events as a fine opportunity to meet wealthy people in equally well-tailored business suits. In later years, she kept a framed copy of the *Vanity Fair* cover with Ron and Nancy waltzing in evening finery tucked in her nightstand drawer. "They remind me romance is still possible, even when you're as ancient as me," she told me once, only half-joking.

Grandma H. was not satisfied with my mother. She was not rich, not blond, not sleek, not fashionable, not subtle. Grandma H. thought I had potential to be all of those things—despite my public-school pedigree, I still might be schooled into an eighteenth-century dilettante, with all the arts of song, dance, and wordplay worthy of a Jane Austen heroine. Thanks to having sons she had missed out on the chance to play amateur image consultant and thereby mold a young girl into a heightened, idealized version of herself.

Her drive to mold me, after a fashion, wasn't entirely solipsistic. Occasionally, she would recall, still seething, how she was shoved out of a PR position two months before qualifying for her pension—largely, she thought, because she wouldn't get an adjoining hotel room to her new boss at a convention. The only reason, she explained to me, that she stayed afloat, and eventually attained affluence after her divorce from my long-since-deceased grand-father, was simple: survival skills. She wanted me to know how to flirt, to cajole, to play hardball, and when the going got rough, to get out.

About a week before the Christmas of 1980, my mother, Grandma H., and I readied the house for the ensuing festivities. We had an assembly-line level of efficiency. By 9 A.M., my mom was on all fours, scrubbing the kitchen linoleum while apple, pumpkin, and sour cherry pies bubbled to a golden brown in the oven. My father spent the day doing heaven knows what, only showing up around 4 P.M. to run a quick vacuum and ask my frazzled mother, arm deep in silver polisher, whether he could help. Grandma H. and I were assigned to decorating duty. "I have no eye for that interior design stuff." My mom shrugged, quizzically watching Grandma and me twist fluffy cotton boas around porcelain Santa Clauses and stuffed reindeer.

With relish, Grandma and I displayed my fancy-pants dollhouse with functioning electricity on a side table. We assembled mini-ature garlands and tied microscopic ribbons around thimble-sized presents to put under the tiny tree. We wrapped the arms of the brown-haired father in his business suit around the brown-haired wife in her apron, carefully situating them in a corner. The chil-dren—a boy in blue footie pj's and a girl in a pink nightie—were placed in front of the fireplace. Grandma, in her nightcap and spectacles, and Gramps, with his cane, sat on the porch swing in the fake snow. It was a perfect Christmas tableau, as we all agreed. "What a great job," my mother said, wiping sweat off her forehead with her shirt. "Oh boy, do I need a shower. Noelle, keep an eye on the ham for me?"

By the time the party started, my mother was dressed and gingerly made up—with a hint of blush and clashing pink lipstick, perhaps left over from college. She'd keep blotting her lips until she looked like her normal self again. My father set out the alcohol, loosened his tie, and sat in front of the television until he heard a car pull up. Grandma, already pinned and curled and powdered, helped me get dressed. "No, not the plaid dress—it looks homemade," Grandma scowled, nixing the green-and-red dress my other grandmother had sewed. "Try this one," she said, holding out a pink velour sweater and matching skirt. After vetting my clothes, she gathered my long braid tied with a satin ribbon. She didn't let me put on makeup, though. "No way, José," Grandma said, picking up the phrase she heard me say a million times. "You're too little for that. Maybe when you're nine."

Soon, filing into our newly festive home were multitudes of thirtyish men in beards and brown tweed coats, their wives in psychedelic muumuus dropping cigarette ashes on the carpeting, people from the local theater and my father's ad agency and the schools where my parents once taught. My job was to carry their thick, damp winter coats upstairs to pile on top of my parents' bed. That lasted about a half hour. Then, finally, I weaved through the crowd, past the hip pockets and chain belts, to the coffee table. It was crammed to overflowing with baked Brie wheels, chocolate fondue, Christmas cookies, cashews, forgotten tumblers of Bloody Marys, and Mom's specialty—water chestnuts and a chunk of Dole pineapple encircled with bacon and drenched in maple syrup. I pulled out a toothpick and stabbed every canapé, filling my "Merry Xmas!" paper plate high with goodies, and retreated to the corner to perch on the warm radiator and watch my father.

As at any typical party, he was in the center of the room, gesticulating madly with a wild smile on his face. "You know why I voted for Anderson?" he laughed. "Carter made his family walk to the White House instead of taking the limo at his inauguration, and he sold the presidential yacht. At that rate, if he'd gotten another term, he'd have abandoned all forms of modern transportation and would be floating in an inner tube to Europe for the NATO meetings . . . with Billy feeding him Goobers and beer from a rowboat." He took a slug from his drink, exchanged barbs with a few other men, and left the circle of people around him who were stooped over in red-faced laughter. "You kill me, Dick!" a woman choked. "My stomach hurts, you bastard!" Another woman grinned and planted a lipsticked smooch on his cheek. "Don't get me started on Reagan," Dad snorted. "Jesus H. Christ." My father shot a giddy grin at me once or twice, but after a few more cocktails, he seemed not to see me at all.

After the guests left, my mother wrapped herself around him, flushed with afterglow. "You had fun tonight?" she asked, breathlessly. My father was slowly coming down, his adrenaline almost visibly slowing to a trickle in the sudden silence of the room.

"You did a great job on the food, Dinah," my father said, and the two of them huddled on the sofa, each giving color commentary on the night's events. I curled up on the carpeting right near them, not so much listening to what they were saying as absorbing the music of their exchange—soft banter dotted by intermittent, chest-clutching laughter.

The next morning, my father slept until noon, and woke up with red eyes and a foul mood. "Dad," I whispered, "are you okay?"

"Please," he'd growl. "Keep it down. Don't you have somewhere you need to be?"

After Grandma H. gave me the apron, contrary to my mother's expectations, she never tried to teach me her boil-stir-and-serve approach to cookery. "Good grief, you don't want to wear that anywhere near the kitchen!" she exclaimed, when I asked if I could help heat the Beefaroni. "Noelle," she said, "the apron is just for show."

Around that time, my mother started working at a local bookstore, and several days a week I would accompany her there. I lounged on their indoor-outdoor carpeting with my head resting on a pile of fabric-covered books for babies, and perused the young adult offerings that, technically, I wasn't supposed to be ready for: *Give Us an A . . . for Allison*, and *Cheerleaders Rule!* These books were peopled by girls with thick hair the color of corn, sweaters pulled tight over full bosoms, and handsome boys with grown men's voices who asked them to wear ID bracelets when they went steady. It all sounded dreamy, and so unlike the scowling teen-agers who flicked pop tops from their car windows onto our lawn.

Cheerleading seemed like the solution to all my worries. I had lost interest in ballet; I wasn't all that jazzed by the way my toes bled every night, and even more disturbing was the realization— foisted on me by a PBS special—that prima ballerinas tended not to develop big breasts. In fact, the dancers' hope was that their breasts would stay small forever, or they wouldn't have much of a career. That cinched my decision to ditch the toe shoes.

I figured I needed all the help I could get. I was becoming horribly ugly—or "awkward," in hushed adult parlance—and comments from classmates only seemed to confirm this unpleas-ant development. By third grade, my teeth were starting to grow out and apart, enough so I could slurp spaghetti through the gap. Mitchell Johnson started calling me "Bucky" and "No-Hell," which made me fume because it was a swear. I was so desperate to miss the pranks and teasing of recess in the school yard that I stayed inside to help grade papers, scrape gum off desks, and write pensive, florid "fiction" about wallflower girls on Holly Hob-bie stationery. This did not win me any popularity contests. LaTanya Richman got dozens of those "Garfield says: You're the Cat's Meow!" valentines and hordes of chocolate hearts on Feb-ruary 14, just because she wore a bra already (she had been held back), while I got a handful of hard candy and cards from those kids whose moms made them write a note to everybody.

I did make a few halfhearted attempts to break out of the nerdy girl role I could feel myself slipping into and which, if I wasn't careful, might be my unwelcome niche for all eternity. I tried undoing the top button of my oxford shirts, which made me feel like a wild woman. No one noticed. I wore a Michael Jackson T-shirt to school. "He sucks," one of the boys informed me. I started reading soap opera magazines and teenybopper rags ("The real Andy Gibb! At home with Scott Baio!") conspicuously during free time, holding the magazine open directly at eye level, trying to telegraph my coolness to the entire classroom. If anyone suddenly thought, *Wow, she's hipper than I thought!*, they kept that little morsel of flattery well hidden from me. What I never tried—and might actually have worked—was *speaking* to the other kids. I still couldn't bring myself to talk comfortably to anyone other than my mom, grandparents, and a handful of friends. So I grudgingly accepted my current dork status, and started to work assiduously to make myself popular in the future by becoming the perkiest cheerleader this side of Dallas.

In fourth grade, I enrolled in the community center's after-school Cheerleading Class. I showed up in my costume at a local basketball court and stood in line next to five preteen girls who adopted me as their mascot. Our teacher was a sixteen-year-old blond, busty, blue-eyed incarnation who signed her name, Ashleigh, with a heart after it, and was quite obviously perfect. She doted on me, bringing me stuffed bears and introducing me to her quarterback boyfriend, a barely verbal mass of hormones she called "The Rod Man." She was a fount of knowledge. She taught me how to apply violet mascara in no fewer than five coats. Based on her own experience transforming from Ashley to Ashleigh, she advised me on how to "exotify" my name. "Put those two dots over the first 'o,' " she said, "and it looks French. Which is a major turn-on. Seriously." But even Ashleigh couldn't teach me how to do cartwheels. The closest I got was a round-off, which is actually just a cartwheel in which you fall over halfway through.

She broke the news to me on the last day of class. "Sweetie," she said, gently, "you can't cheer if you can't do a cartwheel. But hey, you have time. You're just a little thing, still." I nodded and said I understood. I went home and threw away all my cheerleading books.

My father caught me tossing them, one by one, into the trash can in the garage. "Hey, what's wrong?" he asked. His brown eyes, so much like mine, looked warm and concerned.

"I can't be a cheerleader. I'm not good enough," I muttered, looking down, realizing that I was reinforcing everything he probably already thought. I could just hear the thoughts buzzing through his mind: *Can't catch a ball, can't cartwheel, buck teeth. We should have had more children.*

"Noelle, you're always good enough for Mom and me. It doesn't matter whether you're good at cheerleading or not," he said, and scooped me up in his arms. I wanted to spend the rest of the evening like that, with my face buried in his neck, breathing in his smell. For a moment, it seemed like he wanted that, too. Then he froze. I could feel his body slowly tense, and without an ounce of the tenderness that had been evident a moment earlier, he mechanically set me down on the floor.

Suddenly, he was cross. "Now, could you stop feeling sorry for yourself, and get these books out of the trash?" he admonished. "You think we're made of money?"

Sometime during that school year, my father solemnly announced that we needed to eat "together, as a family."

My mother looked amused. "We," she said, motioning to herself and me, "do just that. You're the one always watching *Escape from Alcatraz* or something." (My father's predilection for prison movies was the stuff of family legend even if it now makes for rather heavy metaphor.)

"Well, that's all going to change," my father said, staring at me. "I want to know what your mother is letting you get away with."

He laughed, no doubt intending to lighten the mood. Nonetheless, I was scared. On the occasional Sunday that we had to eat with the good silverware and cloth napkins, I often got so rattled from sitting next to him that I would spill my milk.

What agitated me so was his obsession with table manners. Don't put your elbows on the table. Don't play with your food. Don't talk with your mouth open. Granted, none of these faux pas was particularly egregious for him to point out. But the Emily Post in him didn't stop there. He screamed for five minutes after the time that I ate my mashed potatoes with a spoon. He was livid if I turned a spoon upside down, even if it was already in my mouth. Once I was caught blowing bubbles in my milk; I thought he was going to collapse a lung.

Unforgivably, he even brought boys into the whole mess. Again and again, he'd say, "Someday you'll thank me when you want to eat at a boyfriend's house and not embarrass yourself." Or after catching me eat with my mouth open, he'd admonish: "Why would boys think you're pretty if you do that?" Personally, I didn't get that. At recess, booger-snorting contests were all the rage; it was hard to imagine one of these boys getting enraged at me for using the salad fork for my main course.

I couldn't possibly put up with the pressure of eating with Dad every night, I confessed to my mother. It sucked up most of my energy to talk to him for two minutes, let alone twenty. Even with cheerleading class over, I could barely deal with the stresses I already had: There was homework to be done without error, and of course, most taxing of all, there was popularity to plan. My mother shrugged. "He's trying," she told me. When I still looked aghast, she added, "Don't worry. It's just a phase anyway."

As it turned out, perhaps because she had preemptively threatened him to be nice, she was right. That night, my father visibly tensed when I ate my tomato soup with a teaspoon instead of the big one, but he didn't say anything. He made pleasant conversation about work and what rock band I liked these days. And within a week, to my mother's and my mutual relief, he was back in the living room.

Grandma H. only took about three minutes to recover from the disappointment that I would never be head cheerleader. She ran to the linen closet and pulled out a long cylinder wrapped in tissue paper.

"I was going to save this, but here you go," she said, with barely repressed glee.

I tore open the paper to reveal a shiny silver baton.

"Being a majorette is this close to being a cheerleader," Grandma said, showing me her index and middle finger pressed tightly together.

"Great," I said, unconvincingly. My inability to do cartwheels (and futile attempts to learn) had already made me seem comical to the other girls at school. Karen Longsworth, a girl with forty-five friendship pins attached to her shoelaces, had informed me one day during gym that since every girl could do a cartwheel, then I must be a boy. Never good with a comeback, I simply sneered "Oh yeah?"—before doing a full about-face and running away. I couldn't imagine heading back out to the playground with a baton, and opening myself up to even more ridicule.

I didn't want to let Grandma H. down yet. She had given me so much love and attention that I felt I owed it to her to try and become the adorable young lady she wanted.

"Thanks, Grandma." I grinned, and tossed the baton up in the air, nearly taking out a music box on the way down.

"Just work on it." She smiled.

My father began encouraging my mother to take on more responsibility at the bookstore. In some of his gentler, lucid moments, he told her that she sold herself too short and should capitalize on her abilities, particularly her organizational zeal and empathetic manner. "If everyone else if going to get ahead on the Peter Principle," he reasoned to her, "why shouldn't you be promoted on the basis of, say, intelligence and warmth?" (While my father may have planted numerous other self-esteem ills in my mother, fortunately, a fear of professional inadequacy was not one he ever nurtured.) Nudged along by his approval, she pursued and was promoted to a full-time managerial position. She helped open a café at the store, called Epilogue, which got written up on the front page of the *Wall Street Journal* (they were very impressed with the notion of putting a coffee bar *in* a bookstore). She was working long hours scheduling hammered dulcimer performances and coordinating publicity for their crossword puzzle contests. I still went to the store sometimes, but more and more often, I came home by myself after school.

I considered this an excellent development, mostly because I now had unfettered access to *General Hospital*. I also realized, thanks to *Seventeen* magazine, that carrying a key around your neck made you a "latchkey kid," and "one of a growing number of preteens *who have to let themselves in the house.*" The article, written in a sonorous tone, told the stories of girls with asterisks after their names who felt abandoned by their working moms. I read the article with relish. I had never been disadvantaged before! Let alone one of a growing number of preteens! This was very exciting.

The only downside of staying home was that I started to see my father—who arrived home before my mother—a great deal more. I was expected to interact with him for at least a minute or two.

"Did, uh, school, uh, go well?"

"Are you, uh, liking the new teacher? Oh, same one? Do you like her? Him?"

As soon as the so-called pleasantries were dispensed with, I would scurry upstairs to my room, not to emerge until I heard Mom's car pull into the driveway.

"Hello!" she'd chirp, unloading bags from whichever errand she'd run onto the kitchen counter.

"Mom!" I'd shriek, and run into her open arms. My father, watching television in the adjacent room, wouldn't say a word.

"Hi, Dick," she'd say, almost sheepishly.

"I'm watching this," he'd respond, often without so much as a sideways glance.

My mother would withdraw, disappointed but unsurprised, into the kitchen, where she'd bounce me on her leg and I would over-compensate for both of us by kissing and hugging her until she had to forcibly remove me so that she could brown the pork chops and mash the potatoes.

In those days, she would often look hopeless, when she wasn't looking furious. I'd ask her if she was happy sometimes, and she'd kiss me, and say "You make me the happiest mom in the world," which wasn't exactly a straight answer. Later, I learned she was briefly seeing a counselor after an argument during which my father refused to have another child (too terrified they might have an XY this time). The Ph.D., a chubby, bearded young man whose eyes lit up at the thought of counseling a transsexual, encouraged my mother to get her husband in for an appointment. As for her own mental health, he told her she seemed to be doing quite well and to hang in there. Marriage, he said, was about compromise.

Later that night, while my father stayed downstairs, my mother and I huddled on her bed eating apples she had peeled and quartered, and fanning each other with magazines. She flipped through Silhouette Romance paperbacks, and I filled out *Yes & Know* booklets with invisible ink pens, while the PBS fund drive flickered on the old black-and-white.

She changed into a satiny nightgown in front of me, and as usual, I was fascinated by her body: so pillow-soft and white, with ripples of flesh like the ancient women in museum paintings, and a mammoth doughy bosom that seemed impossible to attain my-self. I curled close to my mother's voluminous breast, and she stroked my hair, reassuring me that yes, Little Pooh, Big Pooh loved us both, not realizing I had been hoping that he would go away and leave us as peaceful as we were this moment. Even now, at age nine, I regarded her desperation to make it all work as utterly futile, and I promised myself that my life, at least, would not hinge on placating my father.

That year, my grandmother had a brilliant idea. Suddenly, after reading one of her creativity books, she realized that my parents should send me to Hathaway Brown School for fourth grade, one of the private schools nearby, rather than public school, which she refused to see as anything other than a dreadful way to get mixed up with people whose parents weren't white-collar.

Her son was a case in point. After all but flunking out of the preppy all-boys' school where he sat near Strobe Talbot in English, my father was forced to attend a local public high where he met my mother, daughter of a Russian Communist truck driver and an R.N. from Kentucky. And where my grandmother's grand plan to keep my father in wool argyles, golfing with Mitty, and wed to Pitty-Pat fell irretrievably apart.

She had a chance to avoid that fate with me, her bubbly baton-dropping granddaughter. So one day, as my father was catatonic on the sofa, leaving my mother to make conversation about cold fronts with Grandma H., she began her lobbying effort.

"So," she said, a smile curling over her lips, "I think Noelle would benefit from a private school education." I immediately buried my head in an *Archie* comic.

"Who's paying for it?" my mother asked dryly.

"Well, I've heard it's not too expensive," my grandmother demurred.

"Ha," my monosyllabic father snorted from the corner. All three of us looked at him, quizzically, as though the cat had just spoken.

"Ain't gonna happen," said my mother, sliding into the sassy, slangy voice she used to irritate hoity-toity types.

"Now, Dinah," my grandmother said, testily, "be reasonable."

"Ella Mae, Noelle likes her school, she has good teachers, friends from different backgrounds. I see no need to spend thousands of dollars on another school." My mother tried to keep her voice even, to my relief. I tried to concentrate on reading about Veronica's sporty new convertible. "I'm her mother, Ella Mae," she said firmly.

"Dinah," Grandma H. said, pursing her lips in dismay and staring reproachfully at my mother, "that is not the issue."

"No," my mother said, glancing with fury at my silent father, "that's precisely the issue."

My mother stormed out of the room, while my father buried himself in the paper and my grandma rolled her eyes. I sat there frozen in place trying not to betray any emotion, yet sensing for the first time that I might no longer be on my grandmother's side.

FOUR

Snips, Snails, Puppy Dogs' Tails

It is really funny how different two brothers can be. His brother was so anxious, eager, and insistent when he was Dick's age. Dick is awful bright, but boy, wouldn't I love to be able to hear his thoughts for a minute, just to figure out what's going on in that mysterious head of his.
                              —Ella Mae's journal, October 1955

Two boys in denim dungarees and Cleveland Indians jerseys were playing in the backyard. Two ten-year-old boys getting ready for a fight.

The olive-skinned one with the helmet of shiny black hair was small, and sturdy as a traffic cone. His name was Bruce. He sidled back and forth, jockeying for position in the same herky-jerky way that made him the local thumb-wrestling champ. The other boy, slim-hipped with hair as blond-white as a cirrus cloud, made quick, jagged staccato motions, to the right and the left. His name was Dick. He tried to jog back and forth like the olive-skinned boy, but didn't do it right. He stepped back and forth, almost tripping over himself, as though he was trying to do the box step on a muscle relaxant.

The boys were not alone. The two Older Brothers, the ones who set this whole thing up, perched on crates right behind "the ring," a shady dirt patch beside the garage where the grass wouldn't grow. Their skinny arms were spackled with crusty pink calamine circles; a Magic Marker tattoo of a lightning bolt front and center on each of their naked rib cages. The scowling, dark-haired one known as "Big Bill"—so-called because, at age thirteen, he towered mightily over his diminutive brother—punched his buddy, Roger, on the shoulder.

"Ow!" Roger yelled, more loudly than necessary, and blew a fart noise on his hand in Big Bill's general direction. Bill ignored him. The fight was getting good.

Dick's head was tucked under Bruce's arm as though it were a kickball, and Dick was squealing like a little girl. That's what Roger jeered, anyway, as he flicked splintered pieces of a broken Popsicle stick at Dick's butt. Big Bill counted to ten. "Ding ding!" he yelled, and he and Roger both whooped. As usual, they both bet on Bruce.

"Okay, Dick," Bill told his little brother, "hand over your Bazooka."

"But Bill," Dick insisted, "I never said I would win."

"No one likes a sore loser," Bill said, snapping his fingers.

The vanquished, if reluctant, fighter nodded in deference to his big brother's point and handed over his gum. He did not, *would not cry.*

"You're too easy," Bruce sneered at Dick. "I don't wanna fight you no more." Bruce tried to storm away, but Roger yoked him by his back belt loop. "You'll fight whoever I want whenever I want." Roger laughed, and turned to Bill. "So how's tomorrow at two? This time, for . . ."

"Jawbreakers," Bill said triumphantly. "And hey, Dick, do you think that Bruce'll really break your jaw?"

Dick blushed. He didn't mean to; it was an accident. As soon as he felt his cheeks get hot, he immediately pressed his fingers against them, operating under the sunburn principle that applying pressure makes even maroon skin fade back to normal—at least for a few seconds. Big Bill was watching him. Nervous, Dick interlaced his hands in front of him. Wrong move. He put his hands on his hips. Oh Jesus, not that. Finally, he plopped his bony butt down in the dirt with a thud, too exhausted to stand anymore.

Big Bill pinched his nose. "You stink. You better toughen up, or they'll beat your butt for real in junior high."

Four months later, Dick wrote out his annual List for Santa. He sat at his desk, pens neatly lined up according to their position on the color wheel, and in loopy cursive, listed (in descending order of importance) what he wanted for Christmas. 1. Mouseketeer hat, 2. Turtleneck: to go with Mouseketeer hat, 3. Coonskin cap, 4. Roy Rogers costume, 5. Pez. Heart pounding, he officiously presented the list to his mother, snapping the paper with a bit of a royal flourish. He was ready to announce rationales for every gift choice. "Every boy in school has a coonskin!" "Dad told me that Roy Rogers was his favorite, too!" His mother put down her ironing and sat down on her bed to examine the list.

"Well, goodness, Dick," she exclaimed, "all you want are clothes? Don't you want any toys? Bill asked for a scooter and a bunch of new comic books. Do you want that, honey?"

Dick jumped up and down. "I want to play Mouseketeer the most," he said, still bouncing. His mother kissed him on the top of his head.

"If you want to know, I already think you're ten times more handsome than Cubby."

Dick said nothing, before galloping downstairs into the living room, where his dad put the new TV. While it was warming up, in time for the *Mickey Mouse Club*, he sucked down a Lickem Aid, glittery sugar that came in an envelope at the drugstore. Once the show started, like most boys, he kept his eyes fixed on Annette Funicello. She and the other Mouseketeers all dressed alike, even the boys. This was very convenient, because there weren't many outfits that boys and girls both wore. He knew a boy who came to school one day wearing a pink shirt, and he was sent home with a bloody lip. So, if he could only get his hands on those mouse ears and turtleneck, no one would even realize he was playing Annette. Dick was impressed with this clever plan.

On Christmas morning, he paced around his bedroom from four to six, staring at the clock, willing the minute hand to speed up. It was snowing and silent except for Big Bill's snoring in the next room. Their father, Jack, got home late last night thanks to the annual "Xmas Midnight Madness" sale at his furniture store. "We had a run on those avocado recliners," he'd grumbled to Ella Mae. "People want their whole damn living rooms to look like pea soup."

"Now, come on," she had stage-whispered. "We need to do the stockings."

The stockings were always the best part, once you got past the new underwear. Mom crammed them with striped peppermints, peanut clusters wrapped in tissue paper, windup cars, and little odd boxes for what she called "thises and thats," although Dick rarely had anything small enough to put in them. It did not bother Dick one iota that Santa was not responsible for the boxers or the boxes. He had a plenty fervid imagination all by himself, willing himself into the lineup of the *Mickey Mouse Club*, onto Dale Evans's horse, or into the neighbor girl's slumber parties, where she and similarly pink-pajamaed females probably stayed up late exchanging secrets.

That morning, at 10 A.M., once Jack stumbled bleary-eyed downstairs and grabbed a mug of coffee, Dick and Bill both attacked the mound of carefully wrapped presents with nails and teeth, like feral animals. With frantic fumbling fingers, Dick ripped open present after present. Two pairs of blue jeans with the plaid flannel lining stiff as gypsum board. A Santa Pez dispenser. A Roy Rogers hat. Mom had started from the wrong end on the Xmas list.

Dick curled up into a ball on a pile of crumpled reindeer gift wrap. "Sweetie, I know you're disappointed, but you said you didn't want toys," his mother said breezily. "Next time you should probably give that a little more thought."

From the very beginning, Dick wanted to be like the other boys. The boys who skinned their knees and made car-crashing noises in school assemblies. Then, of course, he wanted to emulate his role model par excellence: his dad.

Jack Howey, a frustrated artist, elegant storyteller, and inept businessman, was six-five, with shoulders as sturdy and broad as shelving units. He was tall enough that he had to cant forward to fit through average-sized doorframes, and when he took his wife out, he looked like he was wearing her on his belt. Thanks to premature baldness, excellent teeth, and a pale, almost ghostly complexion, his head tended to look enormous and white, like a cue ball. This makes him sound not quite handsome, which was true, but he wasn't unattractive either. He looked like a solid, healthy young man—perhaps deceptively so.

Jack's father was a furniture magnate who recklessly—albeit without malice—eponymously named his store and therefore expected his eldest son to take over the business, which Jack did with little complaint. Except for having a taste for single malts and tales told by the dim bug lanterns in a smoky mom-and-pop tavern, Jack was a good man. He married Ella Mae a few years after she graduated high school, and figured he had done fine. She didn't have much money, but she was quick-witted and beautiful. He loved her, or figured he did, never having felt anything in the past by means of comparison.

Jack sold sofas in aqua and goldenrod. Wrought-iron lamps and chandeliers. Speckled Formica countertops with monikers like "Diamond Dust." He thought his customers had terrible taste. During lunch break, he took his coffee and leftover pot roast into the receiving dock where he'd sketch faces: wrinkled old farmers, plump African warriors. Then he'd whittle their figures from blocks of wood sawed from remaindered end tables. He hung his art on the walls of his house, an otherwise unremarkable two-story in Cleveland Heights that he purchased with the profits from a flush 1952 when just about everyone wanted to toss out their oak furniture for fancy plastic. Sometimes, after a bad day at work, or abandoning an unsuccessful art project, he would come home and insult everyone's table manners. Afterward, he skulked into the living room and remained mute and motionless until the kids were asleep.

After better days, he'd head home for dinner, and—every now and then—to pick up Dick, his favorite little bar buddy. Over his wife's weak protestations, he'd take Dick to his favorite tavern, where they'd both clamber onto bar stools. Jack would throw back a Scotch and water, while Dick sat straight up, feeling quite important as he sipped his Shirley Temple from a frosted stein. For the next several hours, Jack would buy a few rounds and tell stories of the wife, the store, the antics of the dog, that straddled the line between nonfiction and fiction. The stories may have been largely for the benefit of his boisterous compatriots, but also seemed to be for Dick, who laughed the hardest, who wept the longest, who wrapped his skinny arm around his huge father's waist as far as it would reach.

A half-drunk Jack would drive home slowly, with both hands on the steering wheel while Dick slept with his head jostling lightly against the passenger-side window. Jack would carry him upstairs to bed and kiss him good night. Sometimes Jack would sit on the edge of the bed for hours watching Dick sleep, with a patience Ella Mae rarely had. She could parse out her affection, as though she was storing some up for the future, as though she was afraid she might run out. But Jack's love, for both of his sons, was bountiful, almost painful. His love for them inspired him to whittle for hours as he worked up special birthday gifts. But at least in the beginning, their needs for food and shelter and Pez dispensers also seemed to ensure that he would remain tethered to the store.

That year, Jack had his first heart attack. He was at work, convincing a newly married couple to invest in a Naugahyde sofa, when he suddenly collapsed. Ella Mae got the call from the hospital at home two hours later, having just returned from her garden club meeting. She told Bill to watch Dick and ran out of the house, a handkerchief pressed to her mouth. For the next week, she told the kids that Jack was going to be fine as they dined on the casseroles left on their doorstep by Bruce and Roger's mother and other neighbors.

"I heard your dad's in the hospital," Bruce shouted to Dick, as they walked to school on opposite sides of the street. "Is he going to die?"

"You're stupid," Dick yelled back, and sped forward as fast as his stiff blue jeans would allow him.

As it turned out, Jack *was* fine. He arrived home, his arms filled with several bouquets of well-wishers' flowers, which he placed in a giant vase on the table just outside of Dick's room. That night, he didn't go to the bar (the doctor had told him to cut down). He played a gentle game of catch with Bill and Dick, and sat downstairs on the couch with his wife. Later, he kissed her hair while she cried, quietly so as not to wake the children.

Dick didn't hear a thing. He had filched two daisies out of the vase and pressed them between the pages of a *Superman* comic book.

The girl across the street always had flowers in her window. Different kinds each week: ruby red begonias, yellow roses, pink carnations. Each bouquet was framed by yellow curtains emblazoned with giant sunflowers. Dick's were of race cars.

He liked flowers. It wasn't like wanting to cheat on tests, or stealing licorice from the drugstore. It wasn't a crime. Okay, it was a little feminine, but not like taking tap dancing or playing jump rope or something *really bad*. Still, he didn't think he should tell anyone. They would think he was strange.

So he sneaked his mother's cache of gardening books up to his bedroom and hid them under his bed, the same place where Big Bill might have hidden pictures of Marilyn Monroe and Lana Turner. Every night, Dick pulled out one of the books with both hands and wrote page after page in longhand in a notebook. "Mosslined baskets filled with begonias and coleus . . . black-eyed Susan's . . . violas, candytufts and daffodils . . . hot pink primroses . . . raspberry colored moss roses and the lavender of Canterbury bells." Later, he would type all the information on the Royal typewriter in the dining room, stack each three-hole-punched page neatly on top of one another and put them all into a binder. A thick black notebook, jammed full of flowers, that he kept with the other botanical contraband under his bed.

During the summer after fifth grade, to everyone's surprise, Dick signed up for Little League tryouts down at the high school. It was a conscious decision, made with approximately the same amount of enthusiasm as choosing between toothpaste flavors. The males at his school were beginning to identify themselves as certain kinds of boys: that is, a Scout, a Little Leaguer, or a Juvenile Delinquent. (There was no fourth choice, short of becoming a bookworm—also a club of sorts, but not necessarily one into which you'd willingly enroll, especially since you were always paying dues to the Delinquents.) Dick couldn't see himself on the Boy Scout campouts—he chafed at thinking of all the initiation rituals involving bug-eating or various permutations of wrestling that must be involved. He certainly wasn't cut out to be a Juvie. He didn't have the grades.

His mother was thrilled, if vaguely stunned. She thought it might do Dick good to get out more: out of the house, out of his books, out of his head. She also believed ballplaying would increase his confidence, routinely shot down by Bill's orchestrated fights and teasing. Bill had been granted a sojourn at overnight camp, and it would be a wonderful change of pace, Ella Mae thought, to get *both* kids out of her hair for a little while.

For two weeks before the tryouts, Dick and Jack played catch in the cool eaves of their backyard maples after dinner, smacking mosquitoes off their arms and tossing the baseball back and forth—first only five feet away and then backing up to all of twenty feet away, until Jack was almost in the street. Jack was endlessly encouraging every time his son was able to catch the ball, rather than watching it fly between his legs or over his head. "Ooh, boy, you made my hand hurt with that one," Jack cried, when Dick tossed the ball back. "No, Dick, no, not underhand. Throw it from the top. Attaboy."

Tryouts came on July 1. School had been out for three weeks, and the parking lot at Cleveland Heights High School was filled with mothers in Buicks and Fords, their throats hoarse from telling their sons to stop misbehaving. They climbed up the metal bleachers in their flowered sundresses and slightly disheveled head kerchiefs, exchanged pleasantries and mints, and affixed their eyes upon their sons. *If John doesn't make the team, I'll never get the painting done*, one haggard mother told Ella Mae, who nodded and smiled.

The boys, all fifty of them vying for thirty spots, lined up. A coach slapped Dick on the back and sent him out to third base, where he proceeded to forget everything he had ever been taught. After not catching the ball over a period of five minutes, Dick was told he could run on home. The other boys smirked until a coach blew a whistle and told them not to make another sound, it would be their turn soon enough. Dick ran into his mother's arms, blinking his eyes as fast as possible to keep from crying.

"It's all over," he moaned in the car on the way home. "I'm going to be a loser."

Ella Mae grew testy. "Dick," she said, exasperated, "I'm sorry, but getting all worked up isn't going to change anything."

"Uh-huh," Dick murmured, thinking about how obviously his failure would prove to his father that, once again, he did not keep his eye on the ball. Or that he had thrown like a girl. Now, the next time he went with his father to the bar (Jack's abstinence had lasted approximately twenty-two days), his dad would just introduce him as "my son Dick" again, not "may I introduce the next Herb Score, ladies and fleas, starting pitcher Dick Howey!"

"If you want this badly enough," his mother sighed, "you can try harder and make it next year. Einstein said that success is more about perspiration than inspiration, and you should remember that. Give it your all, and everything will work out in the end."

Two days later, on his bed, Dick found a poster rolled up with rubber bands on his bed. Herb Score. A note tucked inside read "Never mind—you're still my favorite ballplayer! Love, your dad."

That night Dick slept soundly, his small fists curled tightly around his new poster.

One day that summer, Ella Mae left Dick at home while she went to her doctor's appointment.

"Can you hear this?" Dr. Mann asked, while a metal instrument made beeping noises in her ear.

Sitting with her hands pursed, in a neatly starched dress, she answered yes. "Hear this?"

"Yes."

"And this?"

"Yes."

"And this?"

"Yes."

"Hmm." The doctor furrowed his brow. "I didn't make any noise that time."

Ella Mae burst into tears.

After a battery of tests, the doctor informed her that she was losing her hearing, and had a 50 percent chance of total deafness by the time she was forty-five. She was in her late thirties. She was still on the young side, sexy, the ideal housewife—and was on the verge of becoming handicapped.

Blind men in literature grow prophetic, able to "see" the truth once their vision is gone. When Ella Mae began to lose her hearing, she did not magically start to understand everyone with crystal clarity, as though she could finally hear the subtext beneath their spoken words. Instead, she began to place walls between herself and everyone else, including her sons and husband. Not that she was in denial. She told Jack. She told the family. She read every pamphlet, every book on hearing loss. She studied the new technology of hearing aids and went to see her ear doctor once a month. She even looked up hearing loss experts in New York and scheduled meetings with them. But she smiled less easily, less often. She patted Dick on the head more instead of kissing him. Something had shut down inside.

Sometimes I thought I would have to get away to maintain perspective or I would go stark raving mad. One morning I went into Sonotone Hearing Aid Company. I only went in to get my mind on something else and to exchange some ideas. I talked to the Director of Advertising and Promotion. So I started spouting off telling him what was wrong with the industry. He listened and would bring out ads and say what do you think of that? I would tear it to shreds and tell him why. I didn't know what kind of impression I was making. Later, he called and asked me to write a pamphlet. I was very excited. This is so much more interesting than making sandwiches all day.

— Ella Mae, October 1956

Crepe scarves in mauve, lavender, and kelly green. A tailored nautical suit with white piping. A satiny green nightgown from Sears. *I was just looking for my Roy Rogers hat. Did you see it?*

A gold lamé gown, now two sizes too small. Navy blue pumps. Beige silk stockings, still damp from the wash. *I needed something to use as a Batman cape.* Each item was hung on a wire hanger. The whole closet smelled of laundry soap and mothballs. Dick's tiny hand ran down the length of the gold lamé, twisted the scarf around and around his sweaty palm. *Oh, hi . . . Mom. I was just looking for you.*

Dick never got caught in his mother's closet, breathing in the close, fragrant air, stealthily slipping his foot in and out of a giant high-heeled shoe. He never got caught running into his room and pulling out his notebook—the one chock-full of flowers—to scribble the initials I.W.T.B.A.G. and cross them out, pressing the pen hard into the paper from both sides so no one could decipher the code. I.W.T.B.A.G. I.W.T.B.A.G.

By January of 1957, Ella Mae had been put on retainer with the Sonotone Company. Every two weeks, she would get a check in the mail that was made out just to her. Once she saved up $100, she opened up a bank account in her name alone. Jack joked about it, asking her if she was hoarding the dough so she could afford to leave him. She laughed that she wanted to have something saved away just in case he spent their life's savings on a bender. "Look, kids, she's pretty *and* funny," he responded.

More and more, Jack worked late, or went straight to the bar—doctor's orders be damned. He didn't take Dick along with him anymore. Jack was worried that Dick might get himself into some sort of trouble if he blacked out.

"Your mother doesn't think kids belong at bars," he informed Dick, while Ella Mae fumed.

"Why, Jack, I didn't know you were listening," she retorted, as Dick stormed past her up to his room.

While Jack went out, Ella Mae spent the evening with her two sulky sons, and pored over a stack of library books—all recommended by her doctor—about preparing yourself for deafness.

After the kids went to bed, she turned the volume of the TV down to inaudible and crouched a few feet away from the screen, doing her best to read Imogene Coca's lips.

She didn't wait up.

Several months after Dick turned twelve, his father had another heart attack. He was sent to specialists in Newark, New Jersey, which seemed like thousands of miles away. Ella Mae went with him, staying in a nearby hotel and writing letters home about the "myocardial infarction" to Dick and Bill. At fifteen, the elder was off cavorting in a used car with his girlfriend. It was left to Dick and their grandmother, who took care of the two boys, to deal with the endless army of people from the neighborhood and the church who once again brought over various wrapped dishes and gifts of catcher's mitts and blowing bubbles intended to distract the boys.

Dick had a difficult time understanding why any church committee should care whether the Howey family was supplied with pantry staples and diversions. As far as he could ascertain, when they actually attended services on the various holidays, no one seemed to notice them, but once the specter of death invaded their household, the Ladies' Service Club showed up on their doorstep with a year's worth of jam. This perplexed him, as it was just one more way that religion seemed inscrutable.

The first time he realized that religion made no sense was upon observing the sign in front of his church's driveway and crosswalk that read "Presbyterian X-ing." Dick thought that must mean that only Presbyterians were allowed to cross the street there. Yet he saw Episcopalians and Catholics do it all the time as they walked home from school. Thus, he discerned that perhaps religious rules were not always strictly followed. Even after he learned that he had ever-so-slightly misunderstood the sign, he still never put much stock in the whole pray-and-repent routine—except when his father was sick.

In the autumn during his father's second serious illness, he walked into the whitewashed nave of the church, bent his head in front of the altar, and made a couple of solid promises. "God," he whispered, "I promise I'll be good. I promise I'll be normal. I'll pray all the time." He clenched his hands together tightly.

The next day Dick went to school and played football at recess, even knocking over one of the other boys. He made fun of the girl with a harelip. He spat a wad of paper into someone's hair, although they didn't notice, and he was too shy to say what he had done. A teacher told him to behave, and to Dick's mind, everything was going splendidly.

Then a week later, his grandmother got the Western Union that Dad was okay and that he and Mom would be back by Thanksgiving. Overwhelmed with relief, he pulled out his notebook and scribbled the letters once again that made him feel so soothed. I.W.T.B.A.G. I.W.T.B.A.G. I want to be a girl.

Dick informed me that he had tried the "not being afraid" feeling and it helped a little. He said he wished he was Davy Crockett who sings in his song that he is not afraid of anything. I told Dick that it was fear that was his worst enemy. And when he would protest I would say that as long as he had fear there would be something to be afraid of in the neighborhood or school or somewhere.

—Ella Mae, December 1957

Surgery changed Jack, although no one could articulate exactly how. He was moodier, though not cross; more distant, although not vacant. He lost the business, although that wasn't all his fault. One of his employees apparently embezzled nearly the entire holdings of the store during the three months Jack was in the hospital, and the store was forced to file for bankruptcy. They sold off all the goods in one final "midnight madness" sale and boarded up the storefront.

Now at home all the time, Dick and Bill uncharacteristically started avoiding their father, who no longer had the energy for catch and a few jokes, much less the patience. At first, he would occasionally pull out his knife to chisel away at a block of wood, but less and less so over time. Eventually, he took every last piece of his art off the walls, the mantel, the shelves—now he was calling them "tschotchkes"—and packed them away with all of his supplies in a cardboard box, which he taped shut as though to provide an extra deterrent to fiddling with them again. When Dick asked his father why he was putting the art away, Jack growled that he'd rather be in an all-white room than look at all that crap. Dick said that sounded like a hospital room or something. Jack said, "That's fine with me. I'll be back in one of those soon, anyway."

Jack wasn't much more attentive to his wife. Gone were the romantic gestures: the little pecks; an occasional bouquet; the gentle jests and compliments. When the boys were going to be out for a full afternoon, Ella Mae didn't even bother to haul out the negligee anymore. Why bother? Jack didn't really look at her anymore. Had the heart attack killed his libido? Did he think of her as defective, now that she might lose her hearing? Was he really at work until midnight all those times? Ella Mae didn't know. Increasingly, she didn't care.

"You know," she said quietly one night, as he lay back on one of the store's leftover recliners, "I could have run that place."

"Ella Mae, we're not going to talk about this." He glared at her. "I'm a sick man."

"Yes. You're right. You are," she responded, in a contemplative manner, as though she had just come to this conclusion. "And you're going to kill yourself." It wasn't a question. "That's a nice privilege to have, Jack. Some of us—" She steadied her voice. "For some of us, getting sick isn't a choice."

Jack whipped forward in his chair. "Ella Mae," he said deliberately, "I never do anything I want to do."

"So that's it," she said, dabbing at her eyes. "You're going to kill yourself."

Jack reluctantly lifted himself out of the chair and offered his handkerchief. She blew her nose on the monogram. "I'm scared," she said. "Bill keeps getting into trouble. Dick is so quiet; it's not normal. You don't talk to me anymore. You don't even pay attention to the boys."

He didn't hold her. He stood there and watched her cry, as though she was a character on the TV. "Now, now," he muttered, sounding a little impatient, as he sat back down in his chair. "It's all going to be fine. You go on to bed."

"Aren't you coming?" she asked.

"I'm in no rush," he replied.

He spent the night sprawled on the recliner, and soon enough, he was sleeping elsewhere altogether. With Ginny, the receptionist at the heart doctor's office. With Kim, the cocktail waitress. Maybe it was a misguided—if unoriginal—attempt to prove he wasn't a middle-aged man with a heart condition. Or perhaps he had been having affairs all along, and Ella Mae only suspected once she was emotionally distant enough to accept it.

Regardless, she had grown sick of playing housewife to a man who was no longer willing to play doting husband and dutiful businessman. Her writing was garnering some notice, and she had even been asked to apply for some public relations jobs. No matter how many cigarettes she smoked or carrots she chewed on between lunch and dinnertime, she was getting banana rolls under her stomach and soon enough, she would be losing her hearing. She was going to be damaged goods, no longer able to ride on a dazzling smile and a Junior League membership. Not that they'd be able to afford that much longer, anyhow. Shortly before the end of Dick's seventh-grade year, she asked Jack for a divorce. He said, "You bet." And within a month had moved into a new apartment with Bill—who had been ready to bolt for New York City if his mother grounded him one more time.

Dick stayed at the playground the entire day that his father and brother moved out. He didn't want to watch the men load their boxes into trucks, reminding him of what was being taken away and what would be left. He sat on the jungle gym, watching the girls play house—always the same way, with a father, and mother, and a boy, and a girl. *That's the way it should have been with us,* he thought, sadly, before running over to a bunch of boys who were playing with race cars in the sand.

FIVE

Mythologies

During the long, lazy afternoons at my mother's bookstore, I'd often arm myself with giant, illustrated books about gods and goddesses, and my favorite was D'Aulaires' *Greek Myths*. I spent hours paging back and forth between the goddesses, studying their golden hair, their simple togas so much like the Princess Leia costume I constructed out of an old sheet and a curtain pull.

I liked Aphrodite, of course, the obvious choice; besides the fact that she was the most beautiful and most desired, she had big boobs. I knew I was supposed to like Athena, because she was the smart one, but she was rather dull and humorless. Besides, I had gone to summer camp with Athena Michael, a cranky girl who liked to blow milk out her nose, so that sort of ruined the name for me. Regardless, no one came close to Artemis in my book. She was lithe, tall, fierce, and, unlike Aphrodite, didn't give it away for free. Around fourth or fifth grade, I whiled away an extraordinary amount of time reading and rereading the myth where she was spotted bathing by Actaeon, and furious at being seen in her panties, turned him into a stag as punishment. I was only a few years past the days I could run topless through a sprinkler in my front yard, and yet still several shy of sprouting breasts that needed to be hidden from a boy's prying eyes. Artemis was the ultimate sex symbol; smoldering and powerful, and still, remarkably, good.

I tended to skip over Hercules in the Greek myth books. The man gods were all violent and boring, anyway, like prehistoric action figures. Herc, that angular macho head, was the worst. So I never read the story of what happened to Hercules once he was enslaved to Queen Omphale.

Back in 1953, my father read that exact tale every night before he went to sleep. It didn't take long. The whole saga comprised a mere two sentences of the thick *Bulfinch's Mythology* that Jack had once given him as a gift. Dick committed that short passage to memory, until he could whisper it to himself while trudging through snow on the way to school or as a means of getting through any other unpleasant situation that might arise.

"While in this service the hero's nature seemed changed. He lived effeminately, wearing at times the dress of a woman, and spinning wool with the hand-maidens of Omphale, while the queen wore his lion's skin."

The myth was too short for Dick's liking, and far too vague. What kind of dress? A dress like my mother's? he wondered. Like a movie star's? And what did they mean by effeminate? He looked it up in the dictionary, but that wasn't much help. It said effeminate meant "in the manner or style of a woman." But which woman? Which style?

Despite the gaps in information, Dick still somehow felt comforted by the story. And late at night, when he couldn't fall asleep, he would close his eyes and imagine himself garbed in a dress of butter-soft chamois, his fingers expertly looping and threading raw silk into the spinning wheel, while the girls from the local Campfire Girls troop smiled at him like he belonged.

My mother, Dinah, was made of different stuff than my father and I.

She was utterly disinterested in beauty icons, whether of Greek legend or modern-day celluloid. She did not read books or see movies, then lie back on the bed as I did, staring at the ceiling while transposing herself into fictional bodies.

Dinah was, above all, pragmatic. She was taught by her mother, a dutiful worker bee, to value common sense, courtesy, and the hours in a day. She was expected to prepare a "home-cooked meal"—meaning no cans allowed—every evening and watch over her younger sister every afternoon. Perhaps as a result, Dinah became one of those girls referred to as "down-to-earth" and "having both her feet on the ground." She was plodding, methodical; she looked side to side to see the world. Not up, and rarely inward.

She was intellectually curious, but generally about other people—never herself. For fun, she'd try to piece together clues to the curious behaviors of her friends and parents as though they were the befuddled figures in a mathematics story problem. Her passionate, melancholy dad, in particular, fascinated her because his extreme emotions seemed so excessive, so cinematic, so foreign to an even-tempered, get-along kind of gal like herself. After all, she had determined early on that she would be nothing special. That may sound like low self-esteem, but actually it was an aspiration. She had already ascertained that being average was her greatest talent.

Bypassing sexy icons like Betty and Veronica, Dinah inadvertently modeled herself on a much more accessible female. She had decided to be Midge. In the *Archie* comics Dinah perused by the candy rack of the corner drugstore, Midge—a peripheral character—was neither desired nor reviled. In her mind, she was moderately attractive, though not as beautiful as Veronica; smart, though not as clever as Betty. She was included in the gang's outings to the soda fountain, and had a boyfriend, a big sweet lug named Moose. Midge was not singled out, but she was not left out, either.

Midge was the perfect template for a girl who never theorized about what Prince Charming would say, or planned the topper she'd put on her wedding cake. "Eeeww," Dinah said about such stuff, wrinkling her nose beneath thick horn-rimmed glasses. Those fantasies were for silly girls who held hands with imaginary friends at three and talked to animals at four, in preparation for fictional marriages with celebrity bridegrooms by nine. Those girls could barely wait for adolescence to bequeath the ritual event of First Love, which would—as the story goes—make them whole. Dinah, in her refusal to daydream about future romance, was something of an accidental feminist. Unfortunately, she would later learn, if you don't ever fantasize about an ideal, you may not realize when you're being disappointed.

SIX

An Ordinary Girl, an Ordinary Life

If my mother, Dinah, had her druthers, you would skip this chapter. "I'm boring," she asserts to me, while laying out cards for a game of solitaire. "There's nothing much to say about me." She has all the hard-won trappings of normalcy: a two-story aluminum-sided house with a vegetable garden, a 401(K), a minivan. Her friends are middle-aged, middle-of-the-road women, round-cheeked and thoughtful, who wear Santa sweatshirts at Christmas and always help wash the dishes after supper. And, in the way that we all reconstruct our lives in reverse, altering our own anecdotes and stories year after year in order to make them more congruent with our present-day selves, so, too, has my mother recast her own childhood.

She speaks of those preteen years as though her life was a seamless mélange of heaping pots of sauerkraut, picnics at Lake Erie, and acing times tests. It sounds like Everychildhood, fodder for a folksy Jean Shepherd vignette. Certainly, there were days, and weeks, every bit as delightfully average as she claims. But even those days were threaded through with doubt and fear, of the kind I can barely imagine. At my mother's happiest moments—or perhaps, especially then—there was always the hovering feeling that *this life might not last.*

※　※　※

"If anyone asks you a question about your parents, just tell them 'I don't know,'" her mother, Glenn, distractedly scolded, while trying to work a dark, translucent circle of bacon grease out of her starched white uniform.

Who would be asking? What's there to know? Dinah wondered. Once the baking soda solution had worked its magic, her perpetually harried mother bustled off to the second shift at the hospital. Meanwhile, Dinah washed up the lunch dishes, placed them in the drying rack, and walked the six blocks back to school, swerving from sidewalk to curb in order to avoid passing next to a high hedge, in case anyone was hiding within.

My mother's father, William Schultz, the child of devout Catholic Czech immigrants, was a hell-raiser who renounced the church and capitalism and grew up to be a local union leader. My mother's mother, Glenn Herrell Schultz, was a slip-through-the-back-door rebel, the youngest of twelve, who escaped her restrictive family from the boondocks of Kentucky in order to become a professional nurse—and, in the process, a Yankee. Although Dinah was not a troublemaker as a child, she was a perfect product of her environment. The daughter of an organizer and a nurse, she herself grew up to be the consummate organizer and nurse.

At age seven, in the scraggly backyard of the four-family house they shared with a German family on welfare and their fourteen cats, Dinah would line up the kids on the block in no particular order and assign them to various roles. Carol would play the Sky King from the TV show; Darlene would play Penny, his dull niece; Barb, the fiendish rancher who stole the Sky King's ponies; and Dinah would play the sheriff or the mother. Technically, neither of those roles was big, but she was no dummy; she knew who was really in charge.

Yet no one saw Dinah as a bossy threat. Maybe it was because she seemed so innocuous: an adorably round little kewpie with red cheeks, downy dark hair, stubby fingers like sausage links, and thin lips curled into a constant grin. It was her lisp—hers was not nearly as cloying as when people mimic children's lisps—that made her seem the farthest thing from intimidating. She had a very short neck, which made her shoulders look raised, as though she was huddling with the shivers. That made people want to hug her, which they often did.

Because she was so genial and approachable, all the kids on Auburn Avenue, even Frank (the requisite local menace), accepted that Dinah was the best choice for neighborhood social director. She took her role seriously, showing up at Carol's front door with a basket of metal toy guns and shot caps on Monday afternoon; toting aprons and spatulas so everyone could play house on Tuesday; and on Thursday, collecting a handful of trash can lids to create an abbreviated diamond for a game of "baseball" played with a volleyball and forearms as bats. Perhaps with the exception of that one unfortunate day when an enraged five-year-old Dinah was pulled into a biting fight with two other kids—after which all three went home bloodied on the chest and arms and a gnaw or two away from infection—she wielded her power kindly.

The aforementioned Frank was a detested kid, whose favorite pastime was baiting Charles, the only other boy on the block. Chuck was a gentle soul, who would have gladly spent all day rearranging the china cabinet in Dinah's backyard playhouse, were it not for Frank sneering from the bushes.

A typical interaction went something like this: "Doubbba bededa sissie," Frank muttered in his usual garbled speech, through the pink-curtained window.

"Shut up!" Chuck whined, not needing to understand the words to know that Frank was mocking him.

"Yeah, Frank," Dinah echoed. "Leave Chuck alone." Frank sneered, flipped them the bird, and left, but Dinah didn't feel any better. It affronted her that Frank didn't like her, didn't seem to need her help. Until she thought, *Maybe that's just it. Maybe he doesn't like me because I* could *help him.* From then on, she worried about Frank more and more all the time.

In fifth grade, Dinah's elementary school couldn't afford clean erasers or textbooks that weren't bound together with rubber bands. But somehow, magically, the Cleveland school system sent them Mrs. Jones. This magical lady, in her tailored blue suit, sensible brown heels, and hair teetering in a tall bouffant, wasn't as dowdy as Dinah's regular teachers. She was professional, with a vaguely scientific aura about her. She pulled the kids out of the class, one by one, to go into the hallway and practice tongue twisters.

"Sally sells seashells by the seashore."

"Thally thelleth . . ."

"Okay, now try making the 's' sound. Put your tongue right at the back of your front teeth. 'Sssss,'" she whispered to Dinah. "Hear it?"

Dinah nodded gleefully, gazing at this amazingly smart woman, and deciding on the spot she wanted to be that glamorous someday, decked out in two-inch pumps and a prim librarian blouse, administering important tests to children and changing their lives.

Over the next year, Dinah worked with the speech therapist, sharpening her "s's" until they could cut glass. In the meantime, her sympathy for the loathsome Frank and his speech impediment grew deeper.

"Underneath all that mean stuff," she yammered to her mother over ham sandwiches, "I'll bet Frank is really nice. He's probably mad because he can't talk. His school should have someone like Mrs. Jones."

"Um-hmm," Glenn said. "I'm sure you're right."

Dinah chewed her sandwich thoughtfully, convinced that even the most wretched people like Frank, who seemed to inflict pain for want of a better hobby, could be saved. If they could just talk about their problems, maybe she could solve them.

Letting it out, expressing oneself, talking about it: These were not lessons that Dinah learned from her parents. Glenn, for one, could be as stubbornly stoic as Charlton Heston's Ben-Hur. Even when prompted, she spoke as little as possible about her feelings or opinions.

"Mom, when did you know you loved Daddy?" Dinah once asked.

"What kind of question is that?" Glenn tsked. "Now help me with these dishes."

"Mom, do you like the president?" Dinah asked, another time.

"My goodness, what you think up!" Glenn sighed. "Now help me with these dishes."

Perhaps her years of enforced silence at the dinner table back in Frankfort kept her quiet well into her adulthood. Dwarfed by her husband's charisma and ideological fervor, she might have decided that they would have a division of labor: She would keep the floors mopped, the clothes folded, the pies baked, and the bills paid on time; he would tend to the children's need for affection and attention. In that sense, she was the organizer, and he was the nurse.

That said, William had his own communication deficit. Despite a general nature most described as affable, he was prone to bouts of deep melancholia that could stretch for days at a time, during which his children fled his presence and his wife worked extra hours at the hospital. Had he lived to see the advent of Prozac and Zoloft, he would likely have been prescribed a mandatory twenty milligrams a day.

The cause for his periodic funks was obvious, although not so easily remedied. Throughout the early to midfifties, he dashed from CIO union organization meetings to Communist Party meetings of a nature so secret that his family could not know any of his friends; followed by harrowing shifts as a truck driver at General Electric; and of course, weekly fights with the other Schultzes—not all of whom had forsaken their orthodox roots— over Jesus and Eisenhower. His mood swung between giddy idealism (after a good meeting), pensive anger (after a bad one), and panic—after glimpsing another dark sedan, too quiet and elegant not to be an FBI-issued vehicle, lurking halfway down the block from their home.

For most of his life, he did not speak to his children or even his wife about this omnipresent, sickening fear. He shoved it down deep and sat like a lump. Dinah and her sister, Rose, would tiptoe around the house, pointing at themselves and each other. "You made him mad!" "No, you did!" Eventually, his mood would pass, and he would passionately scoop his wife around her waist and plant a kiss on her neck while she giggled "William—not in front of the children." Dinah worshiped her father, who told her again and again that she could do anything. She basked in his praise but feared down deep that he was wrong. She couldn't keep him safe.

The neighborhood girls wanted to play dress-up. "I'll be the princess," said Darlene, "and Carol—you be Miss America. Dinah, you can be the movie star."

Dinah didn't care for costumes. Besides, the dress-up game was actually about pretending you had breasts. "Look at my big boobs like Jayne Mansfield," Carol cried, squeezing her flat chest in toward the center until it rippled. "Like Marilyn Monroe."

"They're blond," Darlene retorted. "You're a redhead."

"At least I'm not ugly like you . . . ugly," Carol taunted back.

Dinah was not happy to be preening in her mother's cocktail dress. She was displeased that it almost fit in the hips, and that she didn't have to squeeze her chest together in order to make breasts. She would have rather been back in her play clothes, which hung more loosely.

"I can't wait to be in high school," Carol moaned.

"And go to prom!" Darlene added breathlessly.

"I can," Dinah said, maybe because she couldn't picture herself being whirled around a dance floor like Grace Kelly, or romanced by someone like Rock Hudson. Unlike the other girls, when she looked in the mirror, she only saw herself.

Several years after Glenn moved to Cleveland, her sister Effie followed. Their father had died; the family was breaking up. There wasn't much reason for Effie to stay home. Like Lenny in *Of Mice and Men,* she was well-meaning but slow and just this side of retarded. Having no prospects for marriage or a job, she took a small apartment near William and Glenn and became a convenient baby-sitter for the busy parents. Dinah and Rose agreed on virtually nothing—creamy vs. chunky or Ricky Nelson vs. Marlon Brando—except the ineptitude of their aunt.

"Heeeellllloooo, sugars," Effie called, slamming the screen door.

"Hi, Aunt Effie," Dinah and Rose replied, in unison monotone.

"Well, goodness, aren't you two almost ready for bed?" Effie cried. "It's nearly eight."

Dinah bristled and swiveled away from the TV. "I go to bed at ten. Mom said."

"Sweet thing," Effie smiled, absently. "Now I need to call Paul and let him know I'm here, in case he needs me. Then I'll heat up the water for a bath. Okey-dokey? I'll be back."

"Goody," Dinah muttered, as Rose curled into a ball on the couch.

The girls rolled their eyes, hearing Effie on the phone with her strange new boyfriend, Paul. He was ridiculously tall, and wore a suit, even to Sunday breakfast, which struck everyone as plain weird. Her father especially didn't seem to like him, Dinah had noticed. He was always asking Paul pointed questions about where he worked, and what he thought of the president. But Paul didn't seem like such a bad guy: He laughed at her father's jokes, and seemed very intent on learning all about him. He also put up with the well-meaning babblings of Aunt Effie, who could try the patience of everyone.

"Nighty-night!" Effie shouted into the phone. "I love . . . oh, okay, bye then." She then wandered into Glenn and William's bedroom to "rest my eyes for a spell," to the children's delight. They eventually fell asleep, too, right there in front of the TV during the national anthem, having evaded a lukewarm bath in the basin in the attic, a wet kiss, and a tuck-in.

Paul and Effie didn't seem particularly romantic. When Glenn asked them how their six-month anniversary went, Paul replied that "every day with Effie is special" and patted her brusquely on the shoulder. He didn't look at his girlfriend; his eyes were fixed on William.

"Time for beddie-bye," Effie cried, clapping her hands.

Dinah plunged her cherry sucker back into her mouth and glared at the television. "My show's not even over yet," she retorted, without looking at her aunt.

"What'd I say?" Effie asked. "It's time for bed. Paul will be here soon."

Paul. Paul. Paul. Thanks to Effie's boyfriend, Dinah's bedtime had been moved up by fifteen minutes. She trudged over to her bedroom, slowly, as though her slippers were padded with lead.

"Alrighty, sugar," Effie soothed, pulling the five heavy blankets up to Dinah's chin and tucking them all around her body.

"Now you know what happens if you don't fall asleep right away?" Effie said, with a sudden look of concern. Dinah narrowed her eyes.

"The knocker'll come and get you," Effie whispered.

"What?" Dinah looked alarmed.

"The knocker wants you to go to sleep. And if you're not, he'll knock—knock—knock on your window like this"—Effie rapped softly on the wall behind Dinah's head—"and he'll come take you away."

Dinah's face fell, no longer the mask of sullen indifference from the living room. "What if Mom and Dad are here?" she asked quietly.

"They can't protect you, Dinah. No one can."

"Now go to sleep, sweet thing," she said, in her usual absent way, as she walked out the room and down the hall. "I need to call my honey."

There are men in dark suits who take Daddy away. Daddy is crying. Mom is crying. They never cry. Daddy goes to jail. Or they put him in a little room where they stick pins under his nails and make him tell everything. Except there's nothing to tell. Dinah is yelling at the men: "My daddy is good. Why don't you like him? Why do you want to hurt him?" They never answer. They never have a good reason.

There is a man who knocks at the window. He really wants Dinah to be asleep. He wants it so badly that he's willing to kill her and her parents if she isn't. She doesn't know who he is. Maybe he's that scary drunk man who wanders around on the street. Or a man in a dark suit. Either way, Dinah has to be asleep. Go to sleep, Dinah tells herself. Go to sleep!

Eventually, a few months down the line, William got wind that Paul had been assigned to another case. He had come up empty.

"You'd think they'd tell him to take off the goddamn uniform for goddamn undercover work," William scoffed, huddled next to his wife in bed. Incompetence riled him, even in his enemies.

"You'd think he could've been nicer to Effie," Glenn whispered. "She's got nothing to do with all this."

"I'm surprised he didn't think she was a spy"—William laughed—"cleverly disguising her vast knowledge of national security behind all that talk of Frankie Avalon."

Paul abruptly broke up with Effie, who subsequently spent a week locked in her apartment refusing to eat anything other than cream of tomato soup. "That man never really liked me," she said, once she was able to come out of her apartment again. "Oh, Paul, what did I do wrong?"

❖   ❖   ❖

"Dinah, the principal would like to see you in her office, please," my mother's fifth-grade teacher told her.

"Oooohh," the class echoed.

"What did you do?" one of the boys yelled out. "Did you get a B or something?"

Dinah rolled her eyes at the boy. "If that's supposed to make me feel bad, it doesn't," she informed him. But honestly, she wanted to know what she did, too. Was it that tutoring session she had to skip because of accordion practice? Was the principal mad because she told Tommy M. that she would be happy to teach him "stick-to-it-iveness" after he ducked out of the gym aide program? She wiped her hands on her blue skirt, and took a deep breath.

"Hello, Mrs. Williams," she said, lowering her eyes.

"Hello, Dinah," Mrs. Williams said. "Please come in." There were two men in dark suits sitting next to her desk, a large metal square usually covered in stacks of paper but now cleaned, wiped down.

"How are you, Dinah?" she asked, in a clipped manner, and without waiting for an answer, told her to sit down, please. Mrs. Williams must be in a bad mood, Dinah thought. Usually she smiled and gave Dinah a hug. She would praise Dinah's recent tutoring with the lower-grade kids, or congratulate her on winning another accordion competition.

Mrs. Williams sat behind her desk and tapped her pencil against the edge. "Dinah, these are two men who'd like to talk with you. This is—"

"Mr. So-and-so," the grey one said.

"Mr. Something-or-other," the blond one added.

"Hi," Dinah whispered.

"They're with the Federal Bureau of Investigation, Dinah," Mrs. Williams intoned. "The FBI. They'd like to ask you a few questions about your parents."

If anyone asks, just tell them 'I don't know.'

"Okay." Dinah nodded. *It was snowing outside. Maybe they could go sledding later.*

"Do you know this man?" the grey one held up a picture.

"I don't know," Dinah said. *Rose's mittens were still wet from the snowball fight yesterday, but she could borrow a pair.*

"Okay. Do you know this woman?" the blond one asked.

"I don't know," Dinah said.

"What do you mean 'you don't know'?" snapped Mrs. Williams, rising to her feet. "Yes or no?"

Dinah stared at Mrs. Williams. Had she forgotten who Dinah was? About the volunteering, and the As? Had she forgotten about the hugs? "No," Dinah said. "I don't know her."

"Fine. What do your parents do for a living?" The grey one was back.

"My daddy is a truck driver and my mom's a nurse."

"Is that all?"

"Yes," Dinah said. "That's all."

Dinah left the office two hours later, having offered as little information as in the first two minutes. She never once lied: She truly knew as little as she said she did. Never again did she look her principal in the face.

Still, those FBI agents accomplished more than they might have imagined. Had Dinah been a teenager, perhaps she would have gotten angry and immediately started chaining herself to various federal buildings in protest. Had she been a small child like her sister, perhaps she would have let the whole incident waft by her, as though it were a barely realized dream.

But Dinah was ten years old. She was a straight-A student. Obedient to a fault, she learned a doozy of a lesson that day: *Get along. Say your piece, but keep you and yours safe. And don't step over the line, or you might lose what you're fighting for.* It was a lesson that would not be forgotten.

SEVEN

Cross-dressing: A Primer

Time was running out for Grandma Howey. I was already in fourth grade. My efforts at cheerleading were a bust; baton twirling hadn't taken. My own meager achievements—a poem in *Cricket* magazine, a science olympiad medal—did not fully realize my potential. My golden hair was deepening into motor oil brown, and had been cut shapelessly boy-short. And I proudly wore white terry socks with high-heeled sandals—a fashion statement I can no longer comprehend.

My grandmother—who had graduated from books on Your Lost Childhood to books that numerically listed abstract ways to become a better person (*The 7 Secrets of Success, The 25 Best Things You Can Do Today*)—was an optimist (perhaps the only attribute she had in common with my mother). Grandma H.'s other descendants, Bill's two teenage twins and the baby, were a world away in Los Angeles, growing up on too much citrus and baking their skin brown in the noonday sun. They would be fine. But I was local, and for the most part, in the callused hands of a mother who refused to get manicures.

Grandma H. may have felt that, if she doted on me sufficiently and hung around us all enough, my father might eventually dole out some affection her way. If so, it was a misguided hope.

"Hi, Mom," Dad would say, aloof as always, hugging without touching her and kissing the air. Then he'd sit back down in his armchair. My grandmother would stare at the back of his head before blinking back tears and heading into the kitchen to patronize my mother. Later, Mom would bear the responsibility of telling her how much we all loved her and sending her off with Tupperware containers of stuffed cabbage; at most, as Grandma left, Dad would yell, "Later," without budging from his chair.

On a more cynical note, maybe she thought that if she pleased my father, he might be more willing to lend a financial hand. Contrary to appearances, she was utterly broke. She made a pittance at the Cleveland Public Library, where she ran the fundraising arm, and being social was expensive. She had unsuccessfully run the primary campaign for a local Republican judge, and the uniform required for such a hobby—a tailored red suit with complementary Hermès scarf—didn't come cheap. But everyone tittered over canapés, saying that Ella Mae really, *really*, looked like a younger Nancy Reagan when she wore it, which was reason enough to pay for expressing it from New York City. Unfortunately, then she'd be hard up for rent and would turn to her son for a few hundred dollars. He'd scowl, and write a check without a word. Grandma H. sought that unpleasant parent-child reversal out as often as she could get away with it. She didn't mind appearing helpless if it meant she would get a check; that sign of love. Where my father was concerned, she may have had little else to go on.

When I was younger, I used to pose in front of the mirror in various generic guises. *Now I'm Noelle, a gorgeous ballerina. Now I'm Noelle, the exquisite fairy.* Around age nine or so, I started to pretend I was other people altogether, and that when I looked in the mirror, I saw their faces staring back. *Now I'm Princess Leia. Now I'm Rapunzel.* My grandmother had given me a prom dress for my dress-up box, a "just 'cause" present as she called it, but I wasn't that interested. The tiara itched my scalp, and the dress, as brittle and pink a confection as if Mattel had manufactured it, was equally likely to induce a rash. To Grandma's dismay, I stopped wearing the prom dress almost immediately, and bought a cheap plastic princess costume from the drugstore. A pink vinyl cape, a white felt dress, an assembly-line scepter, and a plastic mask with an airhole punched between the lips. Square in the center of the chest was a giant picture of a princess with big blue eyes and wavy blond hair. Princess Cupcake.

"But how are you supposed to be Princess Cupcake—whoever that is—if she's pictured right on the costume?" Grandma asked, with some irritation.

"Grandma, everyone has a costume like this."

"Well, it seems silly to me," she scolded. "You're much prettier than this Princess Cupcake." I rolled my eyes.

I took Princess Cupcake home and put her in my dress-up box, alongside all my other homemade costumes. It quickly became my favorite, as I loved nothing more than plastic. Plastic costumes, plastic toys, food shrink-wrapped in plastic or frozen in waxy cardboard.

After school, I'd head upstairs to play Princess Cupcake. It was a quiet game. I'd lie on the floor in full regalia, eyes closed, and pretend I was being kissed and hugged by John Travolta. "Oh, Princess Cupcake," he'd murmur in a British accent like Dick Van Dyke in *Mary Poppins.* "You're so lovely. Like a flower you are."

One Saturday, while I was playing Princess Cupcake up in my room, and my father was blistering his skin on a lawn chair in the middle of the black-tar driveway, my mother called up to tell me I had a visitor.

It was Tyler Herman, arguably the ugliest boy in the world. He was chubby, with ruddy cheeks and hangdog jowls, and an unappealing tendency to mope around the neighborhood crying. I might not have been the center of social circles at Canterbury Elementary School, where I occupied the role of mousy girl who grades papers at lunch and sucks at dodgeball, but Tyler was an out-and-out pariah. I felt a little sorry for him, but hoped with far greater intensity that no one had seen him come in the house.

I propped myself up in front of the Barbie town house. Tyler loped in, looking absolutely gleeful. "Hiya, liah!" he said and stuck his tongue out.

"Um, hi, Tyler," I said, taking off my mask. "What's up?"

"You've got ants in your pants, so you do the dirty dance," he said.

Oh, we're rhyming, I thought, with a sense of doom.

"I've got something for you, and it's not shampoo." Tyler stuck out his tongue again.

"You do?" Get this stupid boy out of the room, I thought. He's an evil clown from the horror movies.

"Just look down, and you'll never frown." He giggled.

"Okay, fine," I said, looking down.

Poking out of Tyler's striped corduroys was one of the weirdest things I had ever seen. It was purple and red and . . . moving.

"What are you doing?" I shrieked. "Get that out of here."

"I can make it move. Do you like it?" Tyler was giggling like a maniac. In his excitement, he forgot to rhyme.

"Put it away!" I squeezed my eyes shut, and started to cry.

"Noelle, are you okay?" my mother called from the foot of the stairs.

"Yeah, Mom," I answered automatically. No way could she see this. I felt suddenly ashamed, and blushed in spite of myself.

"You go away!" I hissed sharply at Tyler, and pressed my hands to my cheeks. "Tyler has to go home," I shouted down to my mother. He shrugged, zipped himself up, and walked out. "See you at school," he said.

After he left, I ripped off the Princess Cupcake costume and stuffed it under the cheerleading uniform in the bottom of my dress-up box. I didn't want to play that game anymore.

*   *   *

Sometime during my fourth-grade year, Mom announced to me that a big change was in the works. We're finally leaving Dad, I thought, and started drawing floor plans for my new bedroom. I pictured evenings with just Mom and me, in front of a fire playing board games and eating bowls of popcorn, with no fear of my father coming in and casting a pall over the whole room. I also dreamed of a new stepfather, one who would kiss my mother when he got home from work and compliment—or at least eat— her cooking. This new guy would embrace me, hold me on his lap until his legs ached, bring me chicken noodle soup when I was sick, smooch my forehead when I did well in school.

"I'm leaving the bookstore," Mom informed me.

"No way!" I shouted, and burst into tears. This was her huge life change?

"Honey, I need a new challenge," Mom said. "I'm going to work at an ad agency, like your dad."

No more free books. No lazy afternoons spent huddled in the corner of the store, munching on an oversize Rice Krispies Treat and reading new releases. Worse, Dad wasn't about to head for the Best Western anytime soon.

"I can't believe you would do this to me," I pouted. "I hate you."

"Hey, hey," my mother admonished. "You don't get to talk like that. Now I know you're disappointed, but that's life. You'll still have plenty of books."

I glared at my mother, her eyes narrowed and stern behind octagonal frames. This year, my mother bought a new dining room set; she upgraded to a Japanese car and got a stylish new perm. She was apparently toying with a diet, too. I could tell because her middle had gotten less comfy to curl against. She couldn't, however, seem to change the only thing that truly mattered. She couldn't make Dad into a pleasant human being, and she couldn't—or wouldn't—make him leave.

❁ ❁ ❁

Within weeks, my mother was organizing large amounts of paper and sitting on a very cool swivel chair in a concertedly funky office with exposed brick walls and white-on-white paintings. In the meanwhile, I was discovering the joys of unfettered access to books.

While my mom worked at the bookstore, she generally oversaw the content of my reading material. She tended to be fairly liberal with my entertainment selections. She let me watch *Three's Company*, even though it made her grimace as though she had smelled bad cheese. She encouraged me to read one of those question mark books about puberty, like *Why is My Body Changing?* and hippie health tomes like *Our Bodies, Ourselves*. She even let me pilfer the *Joy of Sex* from her nightstand, perhaps intuiting that the pencil sketches of wicked ugly hirsute people in a clinch would hardly serve as an aphrodisiac. However, she had her limits. She gave a definite ixnay on anything that was violent: no scary movies or scary young adult novels.

So after school one day, I walked to the library and got out a scary young adult novel with an illustration of a pretty blond girl on the phone looking like she was on the verge of tears, and devoured the whole thing in one sitting. It was called *Are You in the House Alone?* and it was about a teen girl who was baby-sitting when she started to get creepy phone calls. Finally, a guy friend of hers showed up, making her feel really relieved. But of course, *he* was making the calls in the first place. He knocked her down with a fireplace poker and then he did something to her that I had never heard of, never imagined possible. He put his penis in her, while she was crying and screaming. The scene wasn't all soft and squishy and "between two people who respect and care for each other," like in the *Joy of Sex* or even the *World Book Encyclopedia*—whose definition of sex I had trusted without reservation. Still, it made sense on a certain level. Girls were always being warned in movies, in after-school specials, and in classes not to trust boys. Boys wanted it, they were going to get it. Like keep-away, the object of the game was to keep them going after it, but to make sure that they never actually got ahold of it. And it—this "it" everyone was always talking about—was you.

I closed the book, with a shudder, and after looking both ways down the library aisle, placed it spine backward on the shelf. I felt a weird rush of relief that I didn't look like that girl on the cover. I traced my tongue over the retainer that stretched across my teeth, as I often did when I was bored at school. But this time with a sense of urgency, as though the trappings of preteen awkwardness might protect me for a while from an evil I hadn't known existed.

Clue was boring, and I always lost. Monopoly took forever. I didn't even know what Banana Tree was, but the side of the box suggested players should be ages three through nine. I was ten. It was that kind of Saturday. Mindy refused to play Barbies; I didn't want to play Matchbox cars. Mindy slouched in the corner, chewing on her braid because her mother wasn't around to tell her to take her hair out of her mouth. After a few minutes, she suddenly perked up. I thought of a new game, she said. *Love Boat*. I stopped fiddling with the snap on Ken's pants. This sounded promising. My dress-up box wasn't quite up to the task, so we pulled stray items out of my Mom and Dad's closet: rayon blouse with a satin tie, corduroy blazer, wool skirt, and fringy brown suede boots. Anything grown-up-seeming.

Two hours later, Mindy, as Myrna, and I, as Phil, met on the bow of the ship just outside of the second-floor bathroom. It was love at first sight. Did you have fun at the shuffleboard contest? Positively. Shall we take a stroll around Puerto Vallarta tomorrow? Oh, but how wonderful. As "Rapture" played softly in the background, Phil moved in for the kiss. As soon as Phil felt Myrna's moist lips pressing sweetly, nervously against his, he closed her eyes. He felt like he'd caught a sudden chill. A moment later,

Myrna pulled back and shoved a braid into her mouth. Her eyes darted around the room, looking anywhere but at Phil. "I want to play Banana Tree," she said.

It wasn't the first time I had thought of playing the game which came to be known as Boy-Girl. But it was a game that demanded the right playmate: namely, someone female. When we were back in third grade, Jason Johnson had suggested something really similar—*Fantasy Island*, where he would play Mr. Roarke. I'd play a bikini-clad visitor, and he'd "lei me and make my dreams come true." But Jason was a boy, from his Mork suspenders to his habit of making booger sculptures on his desk. Between my father, who still intimidated the bejesus out of me, and my recent foray into forbidden books, I had become terrified of boys.

This fear manifested itself mostly at night. I was generally okay while my parents were downstairs, with ambient TV noise drifting up the stairs and at least the possibility that my father would rouse himself enough to thwart a criminal. But once my dad stumbled up the stairs, pulled the cord to switch off the bathroom light, and shut the door—while mine remained open, just a crack—I was entirely alone. As tired as my parents were (they slept *all the time*: during movies, in the middle of the afternoon, and again once the clock struck 10 P.M.), I was convinced they would never hear the faint shattering of a basement window, or the cautious, hedged footsteps of a man coming to stand in the doorframe of my bedroom. I saw him every night, his silhouette just visible from the pale light of the streetlamp that filtered in through the blinds. He was a hulking masculine shadow, with a gun and a veiled threat who was fixated on raping or killing me, if I moved or turned on the light, or if I fell asleep. After using me for his twisted pleasure, he would shoot a bullet into each finger, each limb, each organ. I would beg him to go across the street where a much prettier teenage girl lived, but he never listened. Every now and then, I got the guts to flip on the lights and take him on, hurtling down the hallway and peering into each room to see where he had hidden himself. Usually I made quiet deals with God, in whom I occasionally believed. I wished on stray eyelashes and blew them across my bedspread. *Please let me live until I get my period. Until I go to prom. Until Dad leaves.* Then I fell asleep, until the next bedtime, when it would start all over again.

The Boy-Girl games with Mindy continued with even greater frequency, although we soon dropped the Pacific Princess backdrop and pretty much cut to the chase. Sometimes my Phil brought her Myrna flowers in a pot from the downstairs porch or Oreos from the pantry. For recompense, he'd say, he wanted a thank-you kiss. Myrna, in reply, was unimpressed. She would launch into a giggle fit, which would lead to the hiccups, and then there'd be no kissing at all. So Phil, feeling that he obviously needed to be a tad more manly in his pursuit, got serious. He started pinning Myrna's soft pink arms to the Holly Hobbie sheet until she begged for a kiss. That got her attention. He used his old black ballet tights to tie her hands together and make her whimper. It all seemed very dramatic, very *Gone With the Wind*, so much so that the area between Phil's legs would be damp by the time Myrna was ready to go home for supper. When Phil perched atop Myrna's small body like a flag on undeclared land, his scalp came alive with electricity. His whole body felt alit from within: tingly and goose pimply, strong and powerful. *This must be what it's like to be a boy*, Phil thought. *Well, then, no wonder.*

On the afternoons Mindy wasn't allowed to come over, I had to fend for myself, mostly by squishing my lips against my closet doorframe for the entire duration of my album of K-Tel Love Songs. When I grew bored of that or my legs got tired, I'd play the game wherein Barbie et al. would act out the prostitute story line from Studs Terkel's *Working*, one of the baddest, coolest books I'd ever discovered on my parents' bookshelf.

"You got a trick for me, baby? I can turn it around," whispered Barbie.

"The John's in the Buick. Move your shit," whispered Ken.

Once my mom came home and asked me Gee Whiz questions about whether Sara Mitchell was still trying to make me eat snow, or how I was doing with fractions, I felt like a fraud. My mother still thought I was the angel I always had been; like most adults, she probably thought that children didn't have sexual feelings. How many after-school specials had I seen in which some girl who was really old—sixteen or seventeen—would be talking about whether she was ready to do it or not? Here I was, all of ten years old, tying my friend to a bedpost and tickling her privates with the pink hair of my Strawberry Shortcake doll. This was a secret. I had never had a secret before, and I wasn't sure if I could keep it. My incentive, however, was clear: My mom may have let me watch movies with sex scenes, but she sure didn't know I was already acting on them. I didn't want her to be disappointed in me, and give me that *see-what-you've-done* look that would make me cry. Of course, I also didn't want her to make it stop.

Grandma H. always seemed to have more free time in the summers. Maybe the offices were "sleepy" after the spring push for new friends of the library, or maybe she was playing hooky, but either way she tended to show up a lot at the house just after I'd get off the 3 P.M. bus from Girl Scout camp. Sometimes it was nice to have her there. She was always more excited about the new fire-building or first-aid badge I'd earned than my mother was, and she nodded appreciatively at all two zillion lanyards I made in the hobby shop. But more and more, as my fifth-grade summer progressed, she became needy. What disturbed me the most was that she seemed unwilling to notice that I was growing up.

One afternoon, I had plopped on the floor of our porch in my mint green "Juniors" uniform, replete with knee-high socks and a sash quilted with badges for selling thin mints and trefoils to all of my parents' coworkers. I was buried in a book when my grandmother came up behind me with a surprise.

"I've got something new for you to wear," she said, in a sing-song voice. "Something you've really wanted . . ."

I let out a squeal and jumped up in one motion. "Jordache jeans!" I hollered.

Grandma's eyes widened. "Jord-what? Huh? No, sweetie, look." She had made me another costume for my dress-up box. It was a saffron-colored poodle skirt with bobby sox and Mary Janes. "Because you love *Grease* so much," she said, "now you can be one of those fifties gals, going to the dances with John Travolta and all that."

Hadn't she noticed I was getting a little old to be dressing in costumes all the time? I wondered, fiddling with the hem on my uniform. Grandma was looking older herself, although she still seemed younger than everyone else's grandparents. Her crow's-feet were becoming more etched in her face, and she had lost large tufts of hair, after decades of peroxide abuse. She looked tired, and I wasn't going to make it worse.

"It's perfect," I said, watching her face relax into a smile. "I love you." With that simple exchange, our relationship changed. Once I began to pity her instead of relentlessly trying to please, I had the upper hand; it wasn't a happy switch for me, nor can I imagine, for her. It was, however, permanent.

I had always admired my grandmother—as a fading beauty, grande dame, ideal playmate, force of nature. I had never noticed that she lived alone, and I don't mean her living arrangements. Grandma H. had a solitary life. My other grandparents, the Schultzes, were always tripping over family members and friends to get from the kitchen to the bathroom. I knew they loved me, but they didn't exactly orbit around my sun. Grandma H., despite her more elevated social status, did. She had the time to put me at the center of her world, as well as the inclination, because the rest of her life had been emptied out. She had alienated herself from her own siblings, and rarely sought out intimacy with those who were willing to offer it: like my mother or my other grandparents, with whom she exchanged cool pleasantries on a good day and ignored on a bad day. While I was younger, I loved being her reason to wake up in the morning—because she was mine. But like all passionate love affairs, at some point that intensity burns itself out. That's when you fall back on friendship, on respect. With Grandma H. that would become a problem.

That fall, I signed up for acting classes at the local youth theater program. I thought I might have some aptitude at this particular hobby, since unlike my previous endeavors, motor skills were less mandatory. There was also the possibility, though I barely acknowledged it to myself, that it might give me a way to impress my dad.

Classes were terrible. At first, the teachers insisted we do warm-ups, stretching and jumping like in gym class, of all things. Then we had to mirror the physical movements of some other person, who always wanted to stick up his middle finger or pick his nose, making you do it even though that was what annoying boys did. The scenes themselves were awful, not at all like the amazing plays my dad performed in at the theater. Nothing about pain and sex and screaming and death. No, our scenes were from *Fun Acting Class Dialogues, Ages 6–11.* Which ensured they would be about Molly and Parker deciding who should serve breakfast in bed to Mom and Dad. Or Pedro and Yuki quarreling over whether they should take the bus or the train to visit old Mrs. Johnson.

My dad knew Mike, the teacher, from costarring in various plays. Apparently, they had even played boyfriend and boyfriend in one—which Dad said "was par for the course for Mike." Dad thought Mike was a wonderful actor, and seemed unusually happy that I was taking the classes. "How was it?" he'd ask, smiling, having picked me up in the car.

"Good. The scenes are lame-o, and I'm hungry. Mike danced with a scarf on his head."

"That sounds like Mike," my dad said, obviously making an effort. "I'm glad you like the classes."

"Yeah," I said, feeling suspicious whenever we had a normal conversation. "But there aren't any villains in any of the scenes. You always said the best characters are the mean ones, but everyone is good in this book."

"That will change once you start auditioning for plays," he promised. "Plays always have villains. I should know."

"I guess." I sighed. "I like acting. I wish I could do it all the time."

My father laughed, and looked at me warmly. "I like it, too. I guess we have something in common," he whispered, as though he were telling me a secret.

Once I started rehearsals for Indian #3 in *Peter Pan*, later for the Evil Imp in *Princess & the Pea*, and finally graduating to one of the Wicked Stepsisters in *Cinderella*, I had less time for playing with Mindy. But it was just as well; Mindy's interest in Boy-Girl had been waning lately, as I discovered one afternoon when she refused to take her clothes off.

"I want to make a popularity plan instead," she insisted, sitting cross-legged on my bedroom floor. "I read about one in my romance book. These girls made a calendar with plans for how to get popular by their prom, and they did it. We could try to do it by Christmas."

I was already in my bed, sheets pulled up over my naked body. "But we were going to play Boy-Girl," I whined. "You promised."

Mindy started pulling on my carpeting. She shoved her braid in her mouth.

"Come on," I urged. "My parents'll be home in an hour. We don't have much time. If you want, I won't tie you up this time." It was an addiction: the sickly-sweet scent of her mom's cocoa butter lotion and my sweat and her Tinkerbell perfume; the way her blue eyes widened in slight surprise every time I told her to do something; the golden image I conjured of myself when I closed my eyes and leaned down toward Mindy's face. It was a dream: the way, in a moment, I could become a domineering sex goddess, a naughty child, a boy—all at once. It was more frightening than anything else: how I relished that power when I stared coldly down at Mindy's bony frame; how I touched her with a barely repressed anger, ripping fabric and gnashing my teeth, the way I had seen in snippets of so many movies; how I imagined this was healthy, this is what everyone's parents did behind those perpetually closed doors.

"It's not like I want to play the boy," Mindy said, "but I don't get why you have to be so mean when you do it." She said our parents were going to figure out what we were doing, anyway, and then we'd really get it. "How many kids our age say they're going to take naps together in a locked bedroom once a week?" she asked. "Don't they think that's weird?"

"I guess so," I nodded blankly.

"Look," Mindy said, rising to her feet, "you might as well know. You're a lesbian."

I looked at her quizzically. What on earth was she talking about?

"At Kristen's birthday party, they were saying that a lesbian is a girl who kisses other girls. Who likes other girls *that* way."

"Eew," I said, wrinkling my nose. "That's gross. I'm going to marry John Travolta."

Mindy looked at me as though I was the dimmest person in the world.

"What?" I demanded.

"You want to kiss me all the time. That makes you a lesbian." She looked completely satisfied. I felt like I wanted to rip her face off, calling me names and acting like I was suddenly a pathetic child. Mindy was several months younger than me at another school and in no gifted & talented classes at all. And why hadn't I been invited to Kristen's birthday party? I had been to her house twice.

"So what are you, then?" I asked, wrapping my sheet around me like a toga.

"Shut up!" Mindy cried, her face turning blotchy, the way it did that time she had an allergic reaction to strawberries. "You better not tell anyone," she said. "You keep saying now that you want to be this big movie star? Lesbians aren't famous."

I hadn't even thought about that. My heart started to pound. I had never considered the possibility of anyone finding out about Mindy and me except my parents, but now I realized that having this get out would be even worse than when Phoebe Kimball and Tess Johnson smeared Chap Stick on each other's nipples to make their boobs grow faster. "I'm not a—whatever that is," I retorted. I dug my thumbnail into my index finger, hard, like I did when I got a shot. "You're right," I assured Mindy, with a sudden, visceral desire to see her gone forever. "No one will ever know."

That same year, we learned that something was wrong with my mother's father. He had become a capitalist. We learned he had been buying hundreds of dollars' worth of appliances. Food processors, electric can openers, Betamax recorders.

My mother was frantic. Not only were he and Grandma Schultz on a none-too-generous pension, but he had been a Communist. He might have fallen away from the party over the years, but it seemed unlikely that he would remove himself so far from his ideology as to become a Kmart frequent shopper.

The diagnosis was cancer of the pancreas. The prognosis was one year, possibly two. My mother told me, with tears streaming down her face, while Grandma Schultz sat in the next chair quietly with an expression of utter exhaustion. I hugged both of them tightly as I always did. But I felt far away, distant. He was still my grandfather, not yet Bill. He was not a person; he was a symbol, a role from central casting, the shadow of a man on a tractor who drank a lot of coffee and played a lot of tennis. He had skin that hung from his body like wet dough, mottled with age spots, and soft to the touch. I loved him, but I did not know him. I feared that when he did die, I would disappoint my parents by not mourning well enough.

The next thing I knew, Grandma H. asked me to be her maid of honor. I asked what for. Apparently, within what seemed like a handful of months, while I was being dumped by Mindy, my grandmother had been wooed and won by the most boring man on the planet. They made a striking duo: Miss America and Lawrence Welk; Beauty and the Tax Attorney. Rusk Haverfield, Esquire, age 112, had loved my grandmother from afar since she was just a young divorcée, struggling with raising my father and entering the corporate world. While his marriage played out, he had never forgotten my grandmother. Now they were both alone—he was widowed—and could be together.

It was a fabulous story, but it remained impossible for me or my parents to see Rusk as a player in this passionate scenario. The man appeared to have one grey suit, which he wore on Saturdays; one expression, slightly amused; one hobby, smoking cigars; one favorite food, split pea soup from a department store cafeteria downtown. He would have faded beside most anyone, but he vanished next to my grandmother. Nonetheless, she was thrilled. He was rich. He professed to love her. At her wit's end with her ungrateful granddaughter who really didn't want to spend *every* Saturday night at her apartment anymore, she clearly needed a new focus. This manna had dropped into her lap. Just when she had thought she would never fully achieve the socialite image she had tried to cultivate for so long, she would actually be a bona fide member of the club—albeit the senior set.

"I'm going to be Mrs. Rusk Haverfield," she announced, with utter glee. Looking past her pallid fiancé, she immediately began planning dinner parties with other rich men's wives. She would tell them her favorite story: the romantic fable of how she and her darling husband had courted. At night, she would read, or go to sleep with Rusk beside her—yet still, and always, alone.

It was fine by me. I really didn't have time for her or my parents, who appeared to be still plodding along in misery. I was too busy collecting my thoughts, parsing my sins and good deeds with tenacity and absolutism as if I were Catholic. It was hard to do because I had never been more confused about good and bad, right and wrong.

I had bad dreams about rape at night; fantasies about sex during the day. That was bad. I still got As. That was good. Someone had called me a lesbian. That was bad. I still cleaned out the litter box. That was good. Really thought about the bad things I did. Good. Did them anyway. Bad. All that back and forth made me unsure whether I was a bad girl who dressed up like a good girl, or a good girl who hid her bad-girl identity. Perhaps I should have thrown up my hands and called it a draw, but I couldn't.

"Are you a prude or a slut?" was the new question everyone had been asking this year, on the playground.

"I'm both," I defiantly announced to a friend.

"No way, José," she said. "You have to pick one."

I was living at a different velocity—child speed, in which major change happens in months, or even minutes. I couldn't keep track of my own thoughts or feelings. I didn't know if I was growing up or going nuts. Everytime a relative saw me, they'd say, "You've grown so fast!" and I'd think, Jesus H. Christ, you have no idea. Anyway, my parents started to seem simple to me. They seemed finished. They ate what they ate, they watched what they watched. Their problems—my mother being hurt by my father, his perpetual unhappiness and excessive drinking—were equally unchangeable. "You have to take the good with the bad," someone was always saying, and it was true. I would never like my father, but I had come to expect him to be there. Once I managed not to let it hurt, I'd be free and clear.

EIGHT

Checklists

To Do, March 15, 1958: 1) Get fitted for hearing aid, 2) Wrap up casserole for office party, 3) Divorce papers back to attny., 4) Rummy (or something!) with Dick, 5) Cx. subscription to Life.

Within a year of her separation from Jack, Ella Mae had become the Vice President of Public and Media Concerns and Manager of Marketing Affairs for a gigantic fiberglass and insulation manufacturer. It was a long title, taking up nearly four full lines on her office door plaque. Her secretary suggested Ella Mae abbreviate it, to something like VP of Public Affairs, and was frostily informed that her opinion would be solicited when and if it was required.

Ella Mae did not rise to this position. Family legend has it that she—a divorcée with only a high-school diploma and a stash of press releases written for hearing-aid companies—marched into the headquarters of that major corporation and literally willed the position from a handful of bedfuddled men in suits. Regardless of how it happened, she became one of the highest-ranked women at a major corporation without even a day's grunt work, making her the idol and scourge of the steno pool.

She loved the nine to five or, in actuality, the eight to eight. Each morning, after coffee and before the department meeting, she neatly stacked her yellow legal pads in the left corner of her desk; ordered her pens from red to blue to black; and positioned all of her While You Were Out . . .'s in front of the telephone. *Ahhhh*, she thought, basking in her primitive form of feng shui. She wasn't included in the boys' club field trips to nudie joints, but one or two of the guys usually made the effort to stop by in the morning to say hi and inquire about something altogether inappropriate.

"Hey, E.M., when are we going out? I've got a two-for-one at the steakhouse."

"When are we going to meet those kids of yours, Ella Mae? Got a photo or something?" The former Shaw High School homecoming princess smiled tightly and folded her arms to obscure his view of her breasts.

"Now there, Al." Or Tom, or Marv. "I don't want my boys to be exposed to your bad influence," she replied sweetly.

The last thing Ella Mae wanted was any reminder of her home life—such as it was. Bill had been shipped off to military school for some real discipline, one of the only things Ella Mae and Jack could still agree on. And then there was Dick.

She was the one still struggling with her hearing, testing new aids every few weeks and studying sign language late at night in case it all went downhill fast. Yet he was the one who seemed lost.

"You're in your own world these days, Dick."

Sitting cross-legged on the floor in front of a rerun of one of his favorite TV shows, *I Led Three Lives*, Dick made railroad tracks between the powdered mashed potatoes and the Salisbury steak station. We're waiting for the gravy train, he thought. Ha-ha. He carefully wrapped his entire hand around his cup of milk before raising it to his mouth. It had been not-so-gently pointed out to Dick by several boys at school that he tended to crook his pinkie when he picked up glasses. Dick didn't say a word when they ran away with his lunch bag; it was a small price to pay.

"And you're more than a little old to be playing with your food."

Dick wished he could stay with his father. His dad had a white Buick convertible with leather seats that still smelled new, and a big house right on Lake Erie, which was about seven shades of grey right now but would be green and perfect for swimming at summertime. Bill wasn't even there anymore, which meant Dick could lie out to tan without anyone calling him a 'nobody—get it? You're a nobody with *no body!*'

"You know, I just have no idea what to do with you. Since when don't you like rummy?"

Jack had a new girlfriend, Alice, a bank teller, whom he was planning to marry as soon as the divorce was settled. Alice's silverware was already in the kitchen drawers, and her nighties hung beside Jack's suits in the closet. Alice's daughters—two cute teen brunettes named Sharon and Terry, or Sherry and Lynn, or Monica or something—were moving in as well. Dick had seen the big cardboard boxes torn open and piles of unfolded sweaters, brassieres, and wool skirts inside. They smelled of Ivory soap. Dick had glimpsed a petite stack of red plaid cotton and blue jean shorts, clean and waiting for summer. He ran his hands over each pair, then quickly put them back in the box. For the next few days, he felt like he was holding his breath, waiting for someone to notice that he didn't fold the shorts back exactly the same way.

"Well, how do you like Old Maid?"

Last weekend at Dad's, they had all dined on chateaubriand and baked Alaska, and when Ella Mae picked him up that day, Dick had made sure to mention it. Even before fastening the seat belt, he had also managed to comment twice on how *huge* the house was and how people in the store had told Dick that people would pay a *mint* for that spiffy convertible. Ella Mae said that was very nice for Jack, but some of us would rather live on a budget than take handouts from our mothers. She'd added that she hadn't asked for any money from Jack in their divorce settlement because she didn't want anything from him. "And what if I want something from him?" Dick had snarled.

"I've been thinking, since the divorce is going to be final, you need a strong male influence in your life. Your daily life, I mean."

Dick hadn't spoken to his mother since last weekend, and he was planning on keeping that up until June. He had tried to call his father a few times, just to make her even madder. But Alice said he was out at the bar, and wouldn't be home until late. That must've been the case, because he hadn't called Dick back.

"Now, I've been trying to figure something out. You're not going to like this, but try not to get all testy until you hear me out. I've been thinking about having you attend an all-boys' school."

Whoa. Dick swerved to look at the TV. Advertising exec–cum–secret agent Herbert Philbrick had caught the Communist spy "red-handed" and managed to make it home in time for supper. When the wife asked how his day at the ad agency was, Riley smiled mysteriously. "It was fine," he said.

"University is a very good school for smart, talented boys. It might be easier to make friends. You'll meet lots of other boys like you."

Dick looked at his mother for the first time all evening. "Wait, um, Mom," he gasped, "did you say something?"

To Do, August 24, 1958: 1) Sched. press conference on asbestos-reinforced insulation, 2) Ask Jack re. tuition money, 3) Send Bill brownies and new underwear at military school, 4) YSL dress to consignment

The University School for boys, or US as it was called, boasted a top-notch staff of Ivy League–educated teachers and a course curriculum that rivaled local colleges. Unfortunately, it was peopled by boys who got ponies for Christmas, and enjoyed nothing more than a bloody game of lacrosse followed by stolen beer and a good pantsing.

Dick begged Ella Mae not to leave him there. She wept right along with him, just before pulling the car away from the curb. "I'll see you next Friday," she had told him. "Believe it or not, this is more painful for me than it is for you." Dick had serious doubts about that.

US was a strange place. Most of the boys Dick had known back in elementary school had one-syllable names that could easily be mistaken for grunts, like Bob, Jim, Joe. If their parents had had the audacity to name them something more melodic, they found a suitably terse nickname, such as Butch or Biff. The meanest boys had been the poor ones who showed up on the first day with Buster Browns when everyone else was wearing Thom McAn. Here, in a parallel universe, Dick noticed that some of the biggest bullies were the wealthiest, and they had names like Ashley, Lauren, and Leslie. Of course, if you even implied they had *girls' names,* these future Skull and Boners might tie you to a tree and attempt to asphyxiate you with a cummerbund, hissing, "Could a girl do *this?*"

If there was an overt homoerotic aura to this particular boys' school—cinematic scenes of delicate, Walt Whitman–quoting boys groping each other under scratchy institutional linens—it went unnoticed by Dick. From his first day, the resident tormentors sniffed around him like a dog near a pound of fresh sirloin.

"Hey, Dick, do you miss your dollies?"

"Hey, Dick, got any thin mints left?"

"Hey, Dick, are you growing tits yet?"

He was so preoccupied his first semester that he didn't realize his second period class was called "Myths and Legends," not "Miss Ann Legens," until he received the F at the end of the semester. Like a paraplegic in physical therapy, Dick's entire attention was focused on relearning how to move—his first line of defense against the testosterone masses that threatened to bend his hand back until he cried Uncle. There was a lot to remember, and he tested himself constantly.

Sitting: Curve back, and slump head. Don't sit ramrod straight like a nelly. Keep elbows away from body. You look too neat when they're tucked in. Whatever you do, don't cross your legs. Sit with legs stretched apart as though penis needs its own chair. Watch Ken Simon. He's a football player.

Reaching: Do it with full hand, never a few fingers. Stay away from draping or curving your arm, like some ballet dancer.

Walking: Arms should swing quickly—maintain right angles from body if possible. Butt must never move.

Watching: Glaring is good. If eyes water, even accidentally, rub a full sleeve quickly over them. Don't dab.

Touching: Shouldn't happen much. If boy-boy contact is made, look disgusted and make gross remark. If a hug must happen with anyone male, make sure to slap him on back the whole time. Afterward, a punch on the arm is in order.

Dick's assiduous studies in Masculine Movement 101 led to his being quickly supplanted by a modern dance aficionado as the target du jour. Nonetheless, the other students still kept a comfortable distance from such an unpopular new boy. And Dick, who knew he could not relax for even a second, chose to fail in school. There were not enough hours in the day.

Distraught that her formerly gifted son was becoming an academic disaster, Ella Mae herded Dick off to a psychiatrist the weekend after she received his first quarterly report card.

"You should talk to someone—since you won't speak to me," she said in the car, sullenly. "You're really letting me down, hon."

From that point on, every Friday evening Ella Mae would take Dick to the doctor, and afterward Dick would sob off and on until Sunday afternoon, when he would be redeposited on the front stoop of the school. "I never knew one boy could cry so much," Ella Mae muttered to Dick from time to time. Neither did Dick; often enough, he forced himself to cry against his will. It was simply pragmatic: a down payment on the indignities of the next five days, when he'd hunker down and bear it.

In their first session, the psychiatrist—a Freudian of un-determined European origin unaware he was a burlesque stock character—told Dick to play with "zee" toys. Dick was thirteen years old. If he still played with toys, he should be locked up. It was a trick question. He let his eyes linger a moment on the Bo Peep doll, with its ruffled pinafore and crook, before turning to face the psychiatrist, who was furiously writing down God-knows-what on his notepad. Dick lay back on the couch and counted the dots in the ceiling tile until his remaining forty-three minutes were up.

"This was very illuminating, Richard," the good doctor said, and flashed a gold-capped incisor. "You think you're clever, but we'll make progress yet." He held the door open for Dick, who strode out with arms carefully folded and hips that didn't dare to swish.

"Would you ever want to be a boy?" Koula asked, as the girls all walked home from junior high.

"Blech! No way." Karen shook her head ferociously.

"Yeah, boys are disgusting. I wouldn't either," Koula said, answering her own question.

"I guess not," Dinah said, pensively. "But I'm not sure what difference it would make."

Koula, who liked to explain things, looked sternly at Dinah. "No," she said. "Boys have terrible lives. They spit, and they have awful clothes, and they make stupid noises—" She paused. "And they have no friends."

Dinah thought a second. That did seem true. Boys thought being close friends meant you walked home from school to-gether—that's why that boy from history acted like he and Dinah were tight, even though she only told him what the homework was sometimes. Girls had unbreakable, forever kinds of bonds. Like how Dinah would be best friends with Koula and Karen for eternity, still gossiping on the phone late at night when they all had their own husbands and children. Boys were barely even sociable. The nice ones sat quietly and didn't say much, and the ones who did speak didn't usually have anything pleasant to say. Dinah couldn't imagine having to live in such a solitary world. Her parents and relatives always praised her for being such a sweet, kind, lovely, polite, considerate girl. If she had been a boy, what would she have been good at?

"You're right." Dinah sighed. "Being a boy would be terrible."

It was bad to be one of the class nerds.

But worse, Dick soon learned, to be one of the *stupid* class nerds.

At just about any other school in Cleveland, Dick would have gained a few status points for flunking the seventh grade. Not here. The smacks across the head or in the gut as he walked down the hall came with greater frequency since he'd been labeled a moron, so as a result, he spent more time than ever avoiding the dorm and mess halls in favor of holing up in the library.

Soon after school started up again, in a halfhearted effort to befriend two other geeks, Dick tagged along with them to the anemic sexuality section of the local public library (technically it was called something like "hygiene"). The other boys paged through well-worn, dubiously stained copies of *Psychopathia Sexualis* by Krafft-Ebing, among others, guffawing at descriptions of intercourse and masturbation, while Dick shifted his weight and made halfhearted allusions to checking out the comic book section. But the next day, Dick returned alone to check out a few sections of those books that didn't appear to hold as much interest for his acquaintances.

Dominance. Role-playing. And something called transvestitism, or cross-dressing, wherein otherwise apparently normal men got erections by modeling their wives' satin panties. Standing there in the deserted aisle, the soft, metronomic pulse of Dick's wristwatch had never seemed so distractingly loud. He took it off and shoved it in his pocket. He cracked one book open, just wide enough to read, his index finger carefully lodged in "Oral Stimulation (Male)" for a quick flip—in case anyone surprised him from behind. He read and reread the same few, brief passages, occasionally blowing on his fingers so they wouldn't leave a sweaty imprint on the pages.

Perhaps any other thirteen-year-old boy would have been terrified to learn that he had an unusual sexual proclivity, but Dick was thrilled that his yearning had a name. That it existed in enough other people to be written about in a book. That these people still, apparently, functioned in polite society most of the time. Occasionally, they simply needed to sit in the corner with a dunce cap on and be rapped on the knuckles while wearing a Merry Widow. Okay, a little strange, but then again, this "fellatio" concept that had recently been explained to Dick didn't sound any less unlikely. He placed the books back on the shelf with a private sense of validation.

Reading had never been so useful. Finally, Dick could touch himself under the sheet or while hunched in the toilet stall and have something to picture. He finally knew how to fantasize. All the images he had seen heretofore—mostly the macho man taking the maiden in his arms—hadn't worked for him. Thus, his masturbatory experiments had seemed wholly clinical, a physical release unaccompanied by any emotional involvement. That was over. Now he could close his eyes and go to the dungeon where full-breasted women would force him to wear short shorts, like his stepsisters, and spin wool, like Hercules in the Omphale myth. They would place a cap on his head and a ruby red kiss on his soft hairless cheek. And he would feel a warm rush over his body—*this body,* which finally responded to his internal commands. This body, which was finally almost his.

Rock Hudson was *it.*

"He is just the most gorgeous man ever," Koula sighed, foisting her empty Cracker Jack box into the trash bin at the movie theater.

"Yeah, he melts me," Karen added.

"He's a total doll," nodded Dinah happily.

"When I'm eighteen, I'm going to marry someone *exactly* like him," Koula stated.

"Me too," Karen echoed.

"Me three," Dinah cried. But in all honesty, she had someone else much closer to home in mind.

For their recent wedding anniversary, Dinah's father had given her mother a single red rose and a poem, which Glenn was too embarrassed to read aloud at the dinner table. Dinah, rummaging through her mother's drawers for lack of anything more interesting to do, had found the poem under a sweater. It was written in elegant script—her dad had such nice handwriting—and was the most strongly felt expression of love that Dinah had ever read. In later years she remembered the images were a little clichéd, and that the rhyme scheme was singsongy, but that didn't matter. I want someone who cares about me enough to write—to even attempt to write!—such beautiful words, she'd thought at the time. Someone like my father.

A few weeks later, still beaming about the poem (even reciting lines from it in bed in order to subdue nightmarish images of the Knocker) she decided to look through her father's dresser for more impressive expressions of love. But lining all the drawers was something else altogether: *Playboy, My Escort, Sheik.*

Dinah sat down, slightly dumbfounded, on their bed. How could her romantic father—who sang along with Nat King Cole in the car, and pontificated for hours about bringing power to the poor—be so fascinated with such sordid stuff? Did the FBI know about this? Did her mother? As she gingerly brought the topic up with her friends at subsequent slumber parties, and watched them nod knowingly in response, she began to realize that what she had found was by no means unusual. Her father's peccadillos had nothing to do with her mother. He was a guy, and weird longings for freaky sex were part of the deal.

"*Rock Hudson* probably even looks at naked ladies," Koula admitted. "That's why he doesn't make Doris Day do it."

"So it's normal?" Dinah asked, hopefully.

"Duh," Koula replied.

In later years, Dinah would come to believe that her dad was looking for a bit of manual satisfaction from his stash of soft-core, as well as a new cause. As he had been learning the hard way, nothing was more frustrating than a radical without a revolution. Yes, the anti-Commie rhetoric was still out there, even at company baseball games when the guys who went scab during the strikes would mumble "red" when William was supposedly out of earshot. But McCarthyism was basically over.

He hadn't expected to miss the tension. "This has to stop—eventually," people at the CIO and the Communist Party meetings both said. They were right, and William was miserable about it. He missed the adrenaline rush of crisis: that sick, sad, empowering, exhilarating feeling that you were under surveillance. And that you were important enough—threatening enough—to be watched.

William missed it. His wife did not. She had been happier, baking biscuits on Tuesday as well as Sunday. They had spent more time together, talking, dancing, taking a walk around the block. William still had meetings, but now that the height of the fear was passing, the members were relaxing into pettiness. Union members argued over who should be steward, Communists quibbled over whether it was hypocritical to serve Coca-Cola at meetings.

Glenn must have seen the brown paper bags William brought in and shoved into his bedroom drawers. She didn't ask any questions, yet another way to protect herself. Glenn was married to a certain version of William Schultz. She didn't think it was necessary to know everything about him. Perhaps, to her mind, full disclosure was incompatible with love.

In coming months, as William grew more fascinated with the sexual revolution, purchasing ever-more bondage books and magazines, Glenn did not see them. When William began asking Dinah what kids today thought about sex, Glenn did not hear him.

"Well, Dinah, that's just married people," Koula told her.

"I guess you're right," Dinah agreed.

To Do, July 8, 1960: 1) sched. hearing aid checkup, 2) settle up with University School, 3) finish unpacking boxes, 4) make meat loaf for Nixon welcoming committee

Jack was bailing on his father-and-son weekend with Dick: He and Alice were expected at a funeral in Pennsylvania. Jack told Dick that he would make it up to him; maybe they could toss around a ball the way they used to? he suggested.

"Uh-huh," Dick said. He had relied on that snappy rejoinder to carry on "conversations" with his parents all summer. It was intended to disabuse them of any notion that sending him to his fancy-pants boarding school, or prison (as he generously referred to it) had made him more articulate or intelligent. "I'll go see the *Riot in Cellblock 11* revival like I wanted to anyway. It's the story of my life."

"We're in a mood. Okay. I have to go anyhow," Jack said.

"Uh-huh."

"Have fun with your mother," Jack retorted.

Ouch, Dick thought.

Dick had said virtually nothing to his mother, and she had spoken all of four sentences herself since retrieving him from University School at the end of the spring semester.

"These bags all yours?" That was one.

"I can't believe you would do this—to yourself!" Two.

Three: "Won't you please tell me how you're feeling?"

"The new house is very nice, so I don't want to hear a word about it." Four.

For a month, they unpacked glassware, dishware, and boxes marked "Nostalgia." They hung fiberglass curtains on every window.

"I'm going to the Elect Dick Nixon meeting."

"Uh-huh."

"Won't you please tell me how you're feeling?"

Once she was gone, Dick would slouch against the sofa to watch TV game shows—*You Bet Your Life, Queen for a Day.* Alone, he allowed his legs to curl to the side, and sipped his soda with a bendy straw.

He had felt an incomparable surge of relief in that June 15 parent-teacher meeting, during which the headmaster informed Ella Mae that this "wasn't working out" and that Dick "while full of potential, didn't have the drive" to excel at US. He suggested that Ella Mae save her tuition money and spend it on "something with a tangible benefit." Dick's mission to be so downright mediocre that he would be forced out of school had finally succeeded. He immediately began to fantasize about going to public school with girls: talking to them in hallways, hanging out with them after football games, being one of the gang. Brecksville High School was 55 percent female. It might not even seem weird if all of Dick's friends were female; there were more of them!

But once that euphoria had passed, he was faced with getting through two more months of summer. He could only watch TV and eat for about ten hours a day. After that point, a serious thought or two was bound to start creeping in. That's when Dick got into trouble, because all his thoughts were of his mother's closet.

During the day, he did whatever he could not to think about it. He made sure the door to her room was closed. He exclusively used the downstairs bathroom. At night, it was worse. Ella Mae worked late and went straight to Republican Party functions. She didn't get home until eleven. Dick sneaked beer to get drunk so that he'd go to sleep early. He made absurd bets with himself: Dick, if you don't go in her closet for the next week, you'll live to be a hundred! And then one day, his attempts to preoccupy himself stopped working.

He walked straight into his mother's closet, yanked a scarf off a hanger, and tied it around his head like a babushka. He didn't breathe. He wasn't thinking. He sat at her vanity and applied thick coats of eye shadow in robin's-egg blue and orange lipstick. No mascara: too hard to take off. He puckered and blotted his lips against a tissue as though he had done this a hundred times before, although the wildly painted face in the mirror proved he hadn't. He walked around the house, swerving his hips before a hallway mirror, running his tongue over his lips, letting his arms rest gracefully at his side.

It was a moment Dick would never forget. It wasn't the exhilarating rush of orgasm, or the thrill of anticipation. It wasn't like anything he had imagined—because this was one fantasy that he had always aborted, right after it began.

He looked at himself in the mirror, and he saw who he was. It couldn't have been worse.

He ran from the mirror, and bumping from railing to wall, put everything away except the scarf. He shoved that under his pillow against his better judgment, hoping his mom wouldn't notice it was gone. In the bathroom, he scrubbed his face with cold cream, and then soap, until he was ruddy, raw, and clean.

Dick's first day at Brecksville High had been an immediate downer. The guidance counselor with the clammy handshake had seemed very impressed with Dick at first, eyeing his well-ironed sports jacket and immaculate fingernails. "So, a US boy?" he chortled. "Well, you'll find Brecksville to be no slouch in the academic department, either." Then the counselor peered at Dick's transcript.

"Yes, well, you need to take shop. I don't suppose they teach you the industrial arts over there, and you may benefit from that type of *manual* education."

Dick sighed, unloosened his tie, and stuffed it in his pocket.

By third period, Dick had been tripped. Although he was making his typical assiduous efforts to walk as ramrod straight as ever, he had been dubbed the "new girl" by fifth period. By seventh, Dick had found one way in which private school was better than public: With proper planning, it was possible to change for gym in the privacy of your own dorm room. Here, you were expected to shower *entirely naked*, while a chorus of boys remarked on the size of your penis. Horrified, Dick spent the entire period crouching in the locker room toilet stall and took a detention for cutting class.

Just to make the day that much better, Dick topped it off with a visit to the psychiatrist. "Every month for two years and I get nothing out of you," the doctor clucked, furiously scribbling on his pad. "You want to seem like a mystery. But really, you are like so many other teenage boys."

"I'll bet," Dick muttered, his only sentence for the session.

"How was your day, Dick?" Ella Mae chirped at the end of the day. "Did you make any new friends? How was the doctor? How are you feeling about yourself?" She was halfway through her second reading of *The Power of Positive Thinking*. "I really want you to think about asking out the daughter of Mr. Allen, from work. She's very pretty and she has a country club membership so you could go there together." She stuck her finger in her ear to adjust the volume level of her new hearing aid. "Sorry, did you say something?"

"Fine, Mom," Dick said, mindlessly, already halfway up the stairs to his room. "That's great. Everything's fine." That night, curled in his bed, he began his countdown on a sheet of looseleaf. Only 502 days left until graduation, he thought wistfully, nuzzling his stubbly cheek against the pillow.

Dinah couldn't believe that her school could do this to her. She was student council president, captain of the gym aides. She was dating Michael O'Connell, for goodness sakes, and he was a place-kicker.

"I'm sorry, Dinah," her dad had said. "I tried. I even wrote them a letter."

She was going to have to transfer to a new high school. Her homeroom teacher—the one Dinah had taken attendance for!—had turned her in after learning that the new house the Schultzes had recently moved into was outside of the school district. "You don't belong here," she had told Dinah, as though she was a foreigner. "Go where your parents pay taxes."

Dinah was stricken with the sudden realization that she would become a Transfer Student. Everyone knew that the Transfer Students never got to be club officers.

"This will ruin my life!" Dinah cried. She had tirelessly made herself a fixture at her high school's social scene, and that—being the daughter of athiest Commies in a Catholic, conservative community—hadn't been the easiest feat. She'd have to go to that ritzy school in their new suburb, where they would have all new rules. At Brecksville, they asked what your father did for a living and what kind of car you drove. William was a truck driver, and Dinah took the bus. This wasn't a good sign at all.

The only good thing that Dinah had even gotten out of this ill-conceived move was sleep. Now that she was away from her dreaded window, her nightmares had largely faded as well. Certainly that was a relief, but not worth giving up her whole life for.

It figures, Dinah thought resentfully. Just when I start to get it all together, my parents shake everything up again.

To Do, August 18, 1962: 1) b-day dinner for Dick's 16th (Duncan Hines Devil's Food Cake), 2) hearing aid checkup, 3) pay off psych. and cancel Dick's future session/s 4) write thk-you note to Norman Vincent Peale, 5) be better abt. getting everything done on to do list

Dick sat diagonally from the new girl in French class. She already knew all the passive verbs, and so spent most of the class period writing notes to friends, which she would fold carefully and intricately as though she was making origami. All girls seemed to know innately how to do that, and although Dick had tried it in his room with the door closed, he had never quite mastered the art.

This girl, Dinah, had more friends than Dick had acquired in his whole life, even though she had been in school for one month. On the first day, she bounded into class, wearing a pink angora sweater, costume pearls, and rhinestone-studded glasses. Other girls rolled their eyes at Dick when they passed back papers, or accidentally brushed against him. Dinah smiled. Somehow, for no reason in particular, she knew he existed.

He was trying to get better at being a teenage boy. After five years of practice, he had almost nailed sitting and walking. He was by no means average, but had found a niche of sorts by becoming the weird guy who says those crazy things.

"Does anyone have any more questions about tonight's homework?" the French teacher asked.

"I do," Dick would say. "Can we do it in English?"

Most of the class would groan. Dick wasn't the anointed class clown, who could garner an ovation with a simple burp. He knew he was an irritant, or freak, as at least one girl had called him.

That was okay with Dick. Hell, being a freak was at least two steps up the social ladder from being a fag. Besides, no matter what he said, at least Dinah would giggle. She really seemed to love his good material, and she even ate up the throwaway stuff. Before long, Dick had a mad crush.

If he could win her over, he would belong somewhere. He could play the boyfriend to her girlfriend, and they'd have a normal teenage relationship.

He promised himself then and there that he would ask her out if it killed him. Eventually, after about seventeen attempts—which transformed unexpectedly into requests for paper, an eraser, or the time of day—he did.

Dinah edged into the front seat of Dick's car. "Um, can I move this?" she asked, holding up a green silk scarf that was sitting on the passenger seat.

"Oh . . . oh, jeez." Dick blanched. He looked frantic. "Stick it in the glove compartment. It must be my mother's. Sorry."

"No problem." Dinah shrugged. Boy, this guy was nervous.

She hadn't been sure it would be the right move to go out with Dick Howey, class weirdo. He seemed nice enough, and he was funny (she thought so, anyway) but as her new friends at school told her, he wasn't likely to raise her social capital. Nonetheless, it was the best current option: she had broken it off with her boyfriend Michael, and the first infatuation she'd developed at Brecksville was unfortunately dating some skinny blond cheerleader.

What cinched her interest in Dick was the time he came over to the house to study French. After dinner, her dad had asked him over Dinah's protests—about his interest in politics, at which point Dick assured the family that he and his entire family were Republicans and were concerned that Kennedy would spend a lot of time playing footsie with the Russkies. Watching her father's face redden, Dinah kept trying to change the subject to, well, anything other than current events. Much to her relief, her nervous attempts to rejigger the conversation were unnecessary.

"I like him," William had said, after Dick had left later that evening.

"He's conservative," Dinah said, cautiously.

"Eh, not for long," William replied.

"What did you think of JFK's speech the other night?" Dick asked, backing the car over Glenn's rhododendrons.

"Um, I didn't really watch it," Dinah said. "Careful . . ."

"I was bowling," Dick said. "In my regular league. And I just thought, 'Wow, we're dead. We're all going to die.' I was so depressed that I went home and slept until two P.M. the next day."

"Yeah, it's scary," Dinah said.

"You know, we could still get bombed at any time," Dick said. "Even tonight."

"You sound like my dad." Dinah sighed. William had been ranting about the Cuban missile showdown all day, until he sank into a deep, silent funk and refused to leave his bedroom.

"Cool," Dick replied.

At a local diner, they ordered two cheeseburgers, a root beer, and a Cherry Coke.

"It's weird about Cherry Coke," Dick said, thoughtfully.

"What is?" Dinah asked.

"I mean, if you're going to go to the trouble of making Coke taste like fruit, or at least kids' cough medicine, why don't they go all the way? Where's the Banana Coke? The Broccoli Coke? The Brussel Sprouts Coke?"

Dinah laughed. "I suppose," she said, "but can you imagine the, you know, burping on the car ride home after drinking a glass of that?"

Dick's eyes shone. This girl, he though, was *something*. The pair ended up talking in the car until curfew.

"You know," Dick said, clearing his throat, "I feel like I can really talk to you. Like you're my friend."

"Of course I'm your friend." Dinah smiled back, casually.

Dick clenched his mouth to keep from tearing up. He had been doing so well, he couldn't screw up now. He leaned in for a kiss. His first.

"Um, thanks," Dinah said, pulling back from the embrace. "That was nice, but I should probably get home."

"Okay," Dick said, barely controlling his glee.

I have a friend, he thought. No, a *girlfriend.* The word was unfamiliar, and sweet.

At his next gym class, Dick stripped down to his bare ass in the locker room, feeling more nervous than the first night he thought the world was going to end. He stepped into the shower, right between two other naked boys. His heart pounded. He kept waiting for someone to call him a name.

"Howey?"

Dick turned, with a start.

"Gimme the soap."

"Uh, yeah," Dick muttered, feigning irritation.

His entire being slowly started to untense under the hot water. He had finally passed. His body wasn't going to betray him anymore. He was, in every sense of the phrase, a new man.

NINE

Coming Out, 1962

It was official: Dick and Dinah had become DicknDinah.

They went to football games. They talked. They held hands. They talked. They parked. They . . . talked.

"Boys like sex, right?" Dinah asked her new best friend, Margie.

"Of course they do," Margie replied, having climbed out the window more than once to rendezvous with her boyfriend, a Navy recruit.

"Well," Dinah hedged, "when Dick and I are in the car alone, he talks about life and stuff. And that's cool, you know? I like talking. But doesn't he want to—you know?"

Margie took a hit off her cigarette. "Oh my God, Dinah. You are so lucky to have this nice, smart guy who doesn't want to pressure you. Obviously he's waiting until you're ready. You should be flattered. It's totally *sexy*."

"Yeah, sure," Dinah demurred.

Dinah didn't know if "sexy" would have been the word she'd use to describe Dick, but he certainly did seem interested in her. On their third date, he had brought her one single red rose, and on their fourth, he had brought the supplies for a candlelit picnic in the park. (It was thirty-five degrees, so they had to eat in the backseat, but it was a nice thought.)

Most startlingly—or dreamy-like, as Margie put it—he had recently begun writing poems and stories for her and shoving them into her locker between periods. Some were really strange, like the one about the baby-sitter who sat on the baby, but others were bona fide love paeans, only without the word "love" in them. Dinah savored each belabored metaphor and heavy-handed description. She wasn't enamored of literature, generally speaking, and God knows she hated writing compositions. She was heartened, however, by his ability to express himself so well—perhaps misunderstanding that having a way with words isn't the same thing as being able to communicate. She trusted those poems, believing the torrid emotions expressed in them, even though Dick was hardly an ardent lover. She went on faith, and she did so in part because she had a more immediate goal in mind.

She wanted to go to the prom, and to have a boyfriend—to hit all the major milestones on the rites of passage checklist. It mattered more to her that she have those moments, than, truly, with whom she experienced them. She was going to go off to college, become a speech pathologist, and marry some nice man. She had a plan.

Dick's truce with his body was short-lived. War broke out every Saturday night around 10:30 P.M.: after dinner, after the movie, after driving to the park. Dinah was an innocent bystander. She craned toward him, breathing moist on his cheek. She was there, with her breasts and butt and tight angoras that left sweater pills on his jacket and adorable pearl chokers and rhinestone-encrusted glasses and her smile and at least fifteen other attributes he found totally arousing—at least intellectually.

Suddenly, he began to fumble awkwardly and reverted to nervous tics, like playing with his cowlick. What the hell am I doing? he wondered—just like a million panicked teenage boys before and after him, except that Dick wasn't paranoid that he wouldn't French right, or that he'd be awkward unfastening Dinah's bra.

(He was fairly certain he'd nail all three back hooks on the first try.) Plainly, he didn't want sex, not the boy-on-top, girl-underneath kind. He had something else in mind.

He began counting to fifty elephants. Dinah was just reaching down for his zipper by the time he reached forty-three. He didn't want her going there; he couldn't bear to have her know how *not* excited he was.

"Hey," he said, gently, straightening up and leaning against the car door. "Why don't we go watch TV at your house?"

Dinah pulled a pack of Lucky Strikes out of her purse. Margie had taught her how to inhale like Simone Signoret, all blasé-like. "Okay. But is anything wrong?"

Dick shook his head. "Everything's cool. I remembered that something good was supposed to be on tonight."

"Well, whatever you want," Dinah said. "Um—can I just ask you one thing?"

"Shoot."

Dinah rolled her eyes. "I'm being dumb, really stupid. But tell me—you know—it's not me, is it? It's not, right?"

Dick smiled tightly. She had noticed something was wrong. He had hoped that his painstaking efforts at courtship—the poems, the flowers, the upstanding boyfriend litany of fun date itineraries—would distract her from the lack of hanky-panky. He had failed.

"Of course not," he snapped at her. "What do you mean?"

Dinah looked aghast. "I'm sorry," she said, looking down and sucking on her cigarette. "You seemed upset."

"Yeah," he said, narrowing his eyes at her. "But it's not about *you.*"

"Okay, if you say so," she said, in a little-girl voice. "But you know you can always talk to me," she said, and placed a hand on his arm.

"Thanks," he replied.

✺　　✺　　✺

After a month and a half of dating, the lack of nooky was turning Dinah jealous. That's how Margie had put it, although she was clearly overstating the point. Dinah would have called herself only slightly annoyed.

"Do you have to be so obvious?" she finally asked Dick, as they stood one November afternoon in front of her fifth period class. "Anyway, I was asking you whether you wanted to go to Margie's party next week?"

"What? I'm sorry, what?" Dick's eyes trailed after Kimmi Johnson as she rounded the corner and disappeared down the next hallway.

"Fine, she's attractive, in that kind of way, but could you be a little more subtle?" Dinah hissed, and stormed into her next class.

Kimmi. That was a stripper's name. She was a total idiot. First of all, she was a cheerleader and wore her silly little uniform everywhere even on nongame days. Secondly, she was always flipping her eight feet of blond hair around like she was Miss America. If you walked too close to her in the hall, the overpowering smell of shampoo was likely to make you sneeze. On top of it, either she played stupid, or that question Dinah had heard her ask Dick about who wore grey during the war—the North or the South—was a frightening sign of how slow you could be without flunking out.

Dinah didn't care for her, and Dinah made a point of liking everyone—even if it killed her. Then at polka band practice one day, Margie said it was jealousy. "Pleeeeease." Dinah sighed.

"What would you think, if it were your boyfriend?" she snapped, as she ran a scale on her accordion. "Maybe he thinks she's cuter than me. He stares at her like he's trying to . . ." Dinah stared dispassionately at a poster of a giant purple treble clef.

"Picture her naked?" Margie laughed.

"No," Dinah pouted. "Like he's trying to memorize everything about her." She scowled at her reflection in the glass of the band door. "These uniforms make everyone look fat."

"Dinah, I thought you weren't in love with Dick anyhow," Margie scolded.

"I'm not," she said. "Look, I've told myself a hundred times that he's not all that sexual. Now I'm thinking maybe that's not it. Maybe I'm just not what he wants."

"Come on, so you're not Barbie. Since when did you ever want to be like that, anyway?"

"Never," Dinah answered, latching her accordion and putting it away in its case. "Never before, anyway."

That fall, Dick cowrote the class play with his English teacher, a former Borscht Belt comedian whose complicity in helping Dick put on the play was allegedly responsible for denying him a tenure track position. The production was called *This Is My Country or 1620 or Bust!*—a broadside against Thanksgiving, very irreverent and funny, in a circa '62, high school sort of way (i.e. some of the scenes took place in the Firewater Room of the Powhatan Hilton). Dick escorted Dinah to the opening. She bought a special powder-blue dress for the occasion and teased her hair up into a true bouffant. Dick wore an ill-fitting white tux and a button-down oxford shirt. He didn't feel comfortable in the one from the rental shop with the blue ruffles.

Upon getting into the car, she beamed at Dick and said how proud she was to be the date of the student who cowrote the play.

"You look really pretty," he shyly replied. "I'd have to say I'm the lucky one."

Dinah watched him blush, and try to press his cheeks to make the color go away. It was the crystallizing moment—should, for simplicity's sake, she have to pick just one—that she realized there was something to this guy. Something more than awkward pauses, mediocre kisses, and good political conversation. He was raw, she decided, but he had potential.

✤   ✤   ✤

Dick had no love for Sundays: the one day that Ella Mae still insisted on playing housewife. Every week, she'd stick some tough cut of meat in her pressure cooker around noon, extract it around six, melt Velveeta on top, and serve it on the bone china. She'd suggest they discuss the proliferation of reason over emotion; or the meaning of death in the Judeo-Christian tradition versus the Eastern schools of thought. (She had recently upgraded her self-help reading from Norman Vincent to John Locke and the Tao Te Ching.) "Okay," Dick would invariably say, shoveling his food in as fast as possible. "I'm chewing. You go first."

Once Dick and Dinah had been an item for a while, this dreaded ritual finally looked like it might come to a stop. Dick had somewhere else to be.

At last, one Sunday evening around Thanksgiving, amidst his mother's exaggerated sighs and "Now don't worry about me's," he bolted for the Schultz house, armed with a store-bought white cake for Glenn and a wrench of some kind for Bill. Be a nice boy, he reminded himself, pacing back and forth on their front porch. Don't piss them off.

He didn't need to worry.

"So, Dick, not still a virgin are you? How do you feel about polygamy?" Bill asked, ten minutes into supper.

"Dad," Dinah groaned.

"Mrs. Schultz, this chicken is really great," Dick said, trying to avoid eye contact with Dinah's dad. "And um, I'm sorry—you asked a question, sir?"

"Dick, you should look at some of my books after dinner," Bill chortled. "I'd like to hear your opinion on the sexual revolution."

"Dad!" Dinah scolded.

Dick wasn't shocked, exactly. Dinah had said her father was "a little different," so he had expected something—although not something this cool.

After dinner, Dinah and Dick sipped hot cocoa in the kitchen while Glenn and Bill retired to the living room to watch Walter Cronkite.

"Sorry about that, but that's vintage 'my dad.' You should see his stash. He's got every *Playboy* since Marilyn Monroe," she listed. "And that's only the half of it. There's a ton of—oh gosh, I can't believe I'm telling you this—but he has all this weird stuff, like this one on tying people up, and this other one by a famous guy. His name is like the cheese."

"Krafft-Ebing?"

"Yes, that's it. That one is really strange," Dinah said, nuzzling her head into the crook of Dick's neck.

"You know, I really like your dad," Dick said brightly.

"You do? Yeah, he's an oddball, but I love that about him," Dinah said, and smiled up at Dick. In return, he impulsively took her head in his hands and kissed her with all the passion he could muster.

The next night, Dick called Dinah around 9 P.M.

"Hey there, you," Dinah intoned deeply. "Anything new since eighth period?" She and Margie had practiced husky phone voices all afternoon. "The more you sound like a boy, the hotter it is," Margie had instructed, before erupting in peals of laughter. "Like Lauren Bacall."

"That was a great kiss last night," Dinah said. "You should do that more often."

"Um, yeah," Dick said, not hearing her.

"Did you know Mr. Grunewald has a hairpiece? He does, really. Someone told me today and then it started to make sense how his part sometimes looks like it's sideways."

"Dinah, there's something I want to tell you."

"Oh. Okay," Dinah said, suddenly serious. She would have another month to get another date for the Christmas formal, but the timing wasn't ideal.

"I like something that, well, maybe, I'm not supposed to."

Kimmi is such a bitch, Dinah thought.

"I thought you might understand."

"Um, what?" Dinah asked, exasperated. She fumbled in her bedroom dresser for a cigarette and matches.

"This isn't easy for me to say. I guess I feel like I can talk to you so I wanted to tell you."

"Tell me what?" Dinah snapped, and then winced. He was dumping her. It was *sooo* ironic. "I'm sorry. Go ahead. You can tell me anything. People have told me I'm a great listener."

"Okay. The story is, I like soft things. Like girls' things," Dick blurted. "Sweaters, or scarves. I wear them—sometimes. When I'm alone." He paused. He could hear her breathing on the other end. "Hello? Are you there?"

"Yeah," Dinah said, slowly. She had seen something about this in one of her dad's books—one of the strange ones. She tried to sound unfazed. "You like to wear dresses."

"Wow, no, nothing like that," Dick gasped. Scarves were one thing. Even sweaters. Ella Mae would scour the house if she lost a dress.

"So just sweaters," Dinah said, slowly.

"Yeah, pretty much," Dick said. "I mean, there are guys— they're not faggots at all—who like girls' clothes. It's not a big deal. I like girls. I love girls! I mean, I like you."

Dinah smiled. He had written about his undying feelings for her, but rarely voiced anything more intense than "you're nice."

"I like you, too," Dinah replied, relieved that the dance was safe. "I don't know. Doesn't everyone have some sort of weird thing they're into?"

"Do you?" Dick asked.

"No," Dinah quickly answered. "I meant, you know, men. Men are different than women when it comes to sex stuff."

"Yeah," Dick said. "I guess this is part of being a guy."

"Besides," Dinah said, slipping into her comfortable teacher voice, "it's not like you're some evil person. Soft sweaters—even, you know, if they're for—even if they're not for guys—who's that going to hurt?"

TEN

Coming Out, 1983

From time to time, like every other kid, I lied to my parents. Then, in a chain of events that I assume is not a universal childhood experience, I subsequently tortured myself for the next two years—gnashing my teeth, collapsing into weeping jags, and suffering stomachaches of undetermined origin at random intervals—before summoning my mother to my bedroom for a bawling, guilt-wracked confession worthy of a capital case.

The first time this happened was back in fifth grade, when I admitted to my mother that I was the bad influence who—back in third grade—had convinced my friend Jessica to take the glass pane off her dresser, prop it against her bed, and use it as a slide. "Glass what?" she had asked, giving me a far less dramatic reaction that I had expected, and perhaps hoped for. "Oh yes, that. Pane, dresser. Something broke. Right, I remember. Okey-dokey."

It had taken until the end of sixth grade before I had been ready to confess to my mother about the games that I'd played with Mindy. It was unnecessary, of course. Mindy was gone; she had moved out of town a year earlier. Her little predeparture allusion to the *National Enquirer* had stayed with me though, even precipitating occasional nightmares that Mindy would someday write an article about what we did—and thereby destroy my life. In my more rational moments, I understood that we were, well, *not famous*, and that we were children. Frankly, it wasn't Mindy's ability to keep quiet that was the problem—it was mine.

I couldn't get over the fact that I had lied to my mother. I was terrible at keeping secrets, especially my own, all because of my rigid belief that a lie—even by omission—always compounded the initial sin. I hated thinking of myself as bad.

So one arbitrarily chosen night, I perched on the edge of my bed in the dark and waited for my mother to bring me a cup of water as she always did. I sat up very straight when she came in and shot her a serious look.

"What's wrong, baby?" she asked, handing me a Dixie cup with little sheep on it. With dramatic flair, I propped a pillow up between us, cleared my throat, and launched into a litany of self-flagellation. It was the closest I could get to approximating the somber, ritualistic scenes of confessional booths that I'd seen in movies. (Unitarians like us usually talked about their feelings in broad daylight, with little ceremony and less penance. I hated that.)

"Please don't hate me," I begged. "Don't think I'm bad. Or evil. Don't throw me out of the house."

"Go ahead, sweetie." My mother sighed.

"Okay," I gulped.

And then I told her. About the nakedness and the rolling around and the fingers and the kisses and how good it felt and how sorry I was and how I didn't want to be in the *Enquirer*. It all came out in a tumbled rush.

My mother asked me to put down the pillow. "Let me tell you something," she said, pulling me close to her breast. "When I was little, I did the same things. Well, not the same. My little girl-friends and I pretty much held hands and practiced kissing and that sort of thing."

I looked at my mother. "How do you practice kissing?" I asked. "Isn't that just—kissing?"

She smiled. "Well, maybe, yeah. Anyway, I practiced with a little girl on my street. Just a few times, but enough that I worried I was doing something wrong, too."

I corrected my mother. "It *is* wrong. They tell us in school that you shouldn't have sex until you're old, like sixteen, or married or something. I did all this stuff when I was nine. I'm worse than anyone. I'm like one of those girls in the ninth grade who are already pregnant."

"It's experimentation," my mother said. "Everyone does it."

I nodded, even though I didn't believe her for a minute. "Then everyone's bad," I said.

"Probably, on some level, everyone is," my mother said. "You have to realize, Little Pooh, that the world isn't that black-and-white all the time. No one is all good or all bad."

"I want to be all good," I whispered.

"Then you're going to have a really rough time of it," my mother said, pulling me onto her lap. "By the by," she added, "you didn't need to tell me this. I appreciate your honesty, but you don't *have* to tell me everything. You're allowed to have some privacy."

"I lied to you," I said.

"The sad thing is that sometimes keeping a secret is necessary. Eventually, as you get older, you may need to learn that."

A few minutes later, my mother tucked me into bed and closed the door except for a crack, the way I liked it. If my father ever came in late at night, he'd always shut the door all the way.

ELEVEN

Typecasting

Of course, Jack *was coming to graduation. He wouldn't miss it for the world.*

During Dick's senior year, he and Alice had moved to her hometown in upstate New York. As far as Alice was concerned, Jack's mother had become a little parsimonious with the monthly allowances. Fortunately, her dad, the VP of a hardware company in Ithaca, was looking for a new salesman. Lots of money in tools.

Jack hated to say, but he just couldn't make it there. Someday, when Dick got out into the real world, then he'd understand. Work was a bitch.

It was April 1964. Dick told his father they would have to reserve the tickets for graduation by May 1, so Jack should definitely let him know one way or the other. Dick mentioned, feigning an afterthought, that he missed his dad. Jack said awww, and added that he missed Dick, too.

Absolutely, he would be there, though he couldn't speak for Alice. Jack wanted to check out that girl Dick liked so much.

After getting off the phone, Dick opened the boxes of his father's art that were still stored in the basement. (Alice hadn't wanted the clutter; anyway, she favored white porcelain statues of lions.) He placed Jack's wood block handcarving of an African warrior with a nose ring and grass skirt on the bedside table.

To be completely honest, Jack wasn't sure the timing would

work out, what with the hardware convention coming up in Roch-
ester. Jeez Louise, you wouldn't believe. Alice's father was a god-
damn slave driver.

Finally, two weeks before graduation, Dick got a final answer.
Jack and Alice would be driving in the day before graduation.
He couldn't wait to meet that girl. Diane, was it?

Dick unfurled the battered poster of Herb Score that had been
rolled in rubber bands and tucked away behind the winter clothes
in the closet. He taped it to his wall. Score had been hammered
with a ball in the eye only a season or two after being a rookie,
and had never pitched that well ever again, and Dick didn't even
like baseball anymore, but Jack wouldn't know that. He had never
seen Dick's bedroom in the new house.

Each senior at Brecksville High was allotted a handful of seats for
the graduation ceremony. Dick asked his homeroom teacher
whether those seats all had to be together. She was hunched behind her desk, clipping her nails over the wastebasket. She didn't
look up. "Policy's this: Everyone's parents sit together. Will that
be a problem?" This same teacher had mailed flyers home to Mr.
Jack, and asked Mrs. Jack to bake for the PTA sale—even though
Ella Mae had gently reminded her that Mrs. Jack wasn't the one
who voted for the school levies.

"I guess so," Dick said, almost under his breath, so that the
rest of his homeroom class wouldn't hear. "I have three parents,
including my stepmom."

"Oh," the teacher said, twitching her nostrils like she'd smelled
something bad. "Well, I'm sorry, but we can't make accommo-
dations for special families."

Dick didn't tell his dad. All Jack needed was another excuse.

"Now don't worry about your father," Ella Mae said, coming
down sharply on *father*. "This is *your* day. Nothing's going to spoil
it. We'll do something special after, the two of them and the two
of us." Dick said okay, although the amiable tableau his mother

had painted seemed more nerve-wracking than reassuring.

After keeping a countdown for two and a half years (and on some level, since kindergarten orientation), the actual event of graduation loomed unusually large for Dick. In deference to tradition, he even agreed to garb himself in the traditional nylon gown. He never wore anything even vaguely dresslike in public as a rule, not even on Halloween when it was *de rigueur* for red-blooded American boys to don a girlfriend's old prom dress to play Marilyn Monroe (or Jack Lemmon). He imagined that, in order to pull off such a costume, he'd have to act almost supernaturally macho—adjusting his peter through the tulle, for instance—to preclude any possibility of accidentally looking comfortable.

From a shaded podium in the middle of the football field, the graduation speaker—some guy who was successful in an anonymous sort of way—was barely audible over the cackle and squeal of the sound system. When the microphone functioned, he could be heard urging the graduating class to soar to new heights, find the silver lining, or shoot for impossible dreams. Dick, sitting a few rows ahead of Dinah, sometimes twisted around during the speech to smile at her, to mimic and mock the litany of clichés. She didn't seem to see him most of the time.

The caps flew. Dick missed catching his on the way down and let it stay in the mud. "Pomp and Circumstance" abruptly ended, without resolving the melodic line, as the senior brass section was bum-rushed by their parents. Ella Mae, too, in her hot pink Chanel knockoff and pillbox hat for special occasions, rushed out of the bleachers to see her son. He was standing with Dinah under the home team goalpost.

"Congratulations, Richard!" she shouted. "You, too, of course, Dinah," she politely added. "You know, Dick"—Ella Mae sighed—"I'm going to have to speak to my hearing doctor. I couldn't hear *a thing* that speaker said."

"Mom, no one could hear anything," Dick grumbled, looking past her. "So where's Dad?"

Ella Mae held out a small box. "I got this in the mail yesterday from your father's wife. They said they had—a thing to go to? I don't know. Now don't look at me like that. I didn't want to tell you last night. You were in such a good mood."

The box contained a manicure kit, with a tiny pair of pink clippers, an ounce of candy-pink nail polish, a minifile, and a type-written card for Miss Diane Schwartz.

"That's really sweet," Dinah cooed. "I never get my nails all nice, and now I have something to do that with. You know," she added, squeezing Dick's shoulder, "I'm sure I'll get to meet your father some other time. By the way, your suit's very pretty, Mrs. Howey."

Dick gave Dinah a dry peck on the cheek, before she rushed off, relieved, in the direction of her waiting family. Ella Mae took Dick's elbow and steered him through the crowd. "So, was this day everything you thought it would be? Don't worry about your father. Between you and me, I'm sure Alice has something to do with all this.

"I have a whole dinner waiting to be defrosted at home," she enthused. "All your favorite foods, just the two of us. What do you say?"

After prom and all the senior festivities, Dick saw Dinah less and less. By summer, they only occasionally spent time together. Once a week, tops, they'd hit a movie, or talk politics over onion rings and Cokes. Dick constantly wanted to interject the topic of "dressing" again, but he didn't want it to sound like an obsession. He only dared to venture there once, when he told her that he'd been sleeping with a woman's scarf under his pillow; he didn't mention it belonged to his mother, thinking that might sound kind of weird. When their evenings together drew to a close, they hugged good night with little romantic pretense.

When they parted in August before going off to their respective colleges, Ohio State University in Columbus for Dinah and Ohio University in Athens for Dick, it was far from a wrenching scene.

"Okay, I'll give you a call," Dinah said, as she stood on the curb and jangled her keys.

"You better," Dick said, wagging his finger playfully. They left the burger joint, each in their own cars.

They never had an official talk signifying the end of the relationship, which made it easier for Dick to think they hadn't really broken up. To his mind, Dinah was a keeper. He never would have confided about his desire to wear fuzzy sweaters back in tenth grade—a conversation etched into his memory, although barely noted in hers—unless he was in it for the duration. He assumed they were taking a break for individual soul-searching and personal growth, so their relationship could become that much stronger. As he drove back to his house that night, he was already mulling what they'd do over Thanksgiving weekend and winter vacation. How Dinah would be impressed with the maturity he had every intention of gaining.

For her part, Dinah didn't need a tearful farewell. She planned to see Dick at the five-year reunion. *Breakups are sad, but we all move on,* she reminisced for a day or two after their farewell before turning her impatient, giddy thoughts to the scores of randy college men she was about to encounter. Nostalgic sentiment about her strange, funny high-school sweetheart couldn't compete with unleashed estrogen.

Upon arrival at Ohio State ("good speech therapy program"), Dinah was assigned to what was known as the Jewish dorm. "Schultz," Bill had shrugged, as he dropped her bags off. "They assume." Dinah quickly bonded with her roommates, a cadre of girls from New York City who were dumbfounded that she had never seen a bagel. By the end of the first month, Dinah was dating a junior named Chuck whose goal in life, to her delight, was to convince her to drop her pedal pushers. When all the girls on her floor got together to kvetch on Sunday mornings, Dinah, too, could flick her ashes and tsk-tsk about lascivious boys who only wanted one thing.

While Dinah was easing into her new identity as a jaded coed, Dick was uncharacteristically becoming peppy at Ohio University ("good journalism program"). At first he had been a little wary of college; the generic school name and mint green cinder-block walls brought back some cringing memories of boys' school. On the bright side, he wasn't at home. His mother had been driving him crazy all summer with her latest round of reading material on "futurism" (not the radical artistic movement, but rather "the belief that good things will happen in the future!"). He had spoken twice to his father in four months. The first time Jack had claimed—in a raspy voice that sounded as though he'd been screaming or vomiting—that he had been "under the weather" during graduation. Translation: "under the table." Dick had come to understand why his older brother had run off to join the Navy.

Once he hit campus, Dick immediately loaded up on school spirit supplies, including a logo sweatshirt, OU three-ring binders in team colors, and a plastic beer stein. A few days later, he attended the freshman orientation assembly, where administrator after administrator extolled the virtues of "the latter-day" Athens. "This is a town," one declaimed, "which mirrors its ancient Greek predecessor not only in name, but in the pursuit of intellectual rigor and excellence. You, future class of 1968, are the latest additions to a collection of fine young minds thirsting for knowledge, following a lineage of learning that extends back to the pupils of Socrates."

"Except without the fudgepacking," laughed the long-haired hippie sitting next to Dick.

Dick barely heard him. He was ready to be swayed by motivational speakers. That very week, he commenced his crusade to make the Dean's List. He read the optional assignments; wrote in his assigned journal day by day, rather than scribbling the whole thing in alternating pen colors the night before it was due; practiced his throw for handball class well enough to defeat at least one guy, a linguistics major with peripheral-vision problems.

He wasn't only nailing his schoolwork; he was acing college, from being included in drinking games in the lounge to being able to use the bathroom urinal without worrying that he was going to be accused of doing it wrong. He looked like a college boy, having grown a goatee and no longer tucking his OU jerseys into his jeans. Sure, he kept a pair of women's panties in his dresser (he had ironed a label onto the elastic band that read "Elizabeth," just to back up his prepared story that they were a "souvenir"). But he wore them only at night, every now and then. He felt great! As he wrote in letters to Dinah that he kept in his sock drawer, at this rate he might become well-adjusted.

Two weeks before Thanksgiving, Dick was studying when someone knocked on his door. It was some guy who said he was a resident assistant and had gotten a phone call for Dick in the main office, and Dick said it must be my mom or maybe my girlfriend, I mean, *ex*-girlfriend, and this guy said no, it was a man, a friend of the family, and Dick should sit down, to which Dick said excuse me?, and the RA, looking like he hadn't slept in days, said, "I guess I'll just say it, the guy who called said your dad had a heart attack a few hours ago and he died, and God, I'm so sorry."

Dick nodded and asked the RA if he could use the office phone to call for a bus ticket back to Cleveland. "I'm so sorry," the guy kept saying. "I'm so sorry, man."

Dinah's phone rang on the evening of November 20. Chuck called her every evening to whisper that he wouldn't have to bother her if she'd sleep over at his house instead. She never said no. Instead she giggled. "I don't think so," she would say, or "I'm not sure." Qualifiers went over better.

It wasn't Chuck calling.

"Dinah, please. I need to see you." It was Dick. His voice had a catch.

"Of course," she said, without even thinking. Already, she could see his face mottled red; her face, round and open and silent. Him talking, her listening, all over again.

They got back together. My mother recalls that she felt sorry for my dad, and that besides, she liked spending time with him and their friendship was meaningful enough to compensate for the dearth of physical contact. She gave their reunion some serious thought. He did not. He clung to her; she was shelter, mother, life-support system. He believed that he was in love with her, though he did not tell her that. (It didn't bother him that, for him, "being in love" was a state of mind divorced from desire.)

Years later, my mother would adopt the language of twelve-step programs to refer to her relationship with my father: enabler, passive-aggressive, codependent. Perhaps she grew to pathologize their connection in the hopes of finding a reason for why she said, "Of course," on the phone that evening. And said, "I'll take the bus to see you," one week after that. Why she—who wanted so desperately to be *wanted*—started ditching lusty Chuck to pick up with her ex, nowhere near where they left off. Unless she wanted to be wanted as a friend, therapist, or nursemaid even more than as a lover.

Dick couldn't help becoming the center of attention; he was in mourning. His father's death shouldn't have been a surprise—there was the history of heart failure, and everyone knew he had been drinking heavily. Dick believed that only booze would keep Jack away from his graduation, and Ella Mae hadn't argued with that assessment. His death was still a shock.

Dorm mates, trying to sympathize as Dick moped down the halls over the next few weeks, asked, "Wow. Was it sudden?" Dick said yes. Some of them said, "Hopefully he had a good life," their voices trailing into question marks.

Dick said yes again absently, his mind turning over and over his father's story now written and finished at age fifty-two: an unhappy first marriage, a failed business, drinking buddies in two states, an unhappy second marriage, an empty trust fund, an un-acknowledged addiction, hidden artwork in cardboard boxes, two sons both adoring and estranged. Dick was not sure his father's life had been well lived at all.

"I'm afraid I'm exactly like him," he confided to Dinah on the phone, several months after Jack's passing. "I've got no follow-through." He had gotten a D in handball. He would not make the Dean's List, and in frustration, resolutely committed himself to mediocrity for the rest of his college career.

"Your dad was an alcoholic."

"Maybe I'll die young." He had been drinking more, just at parties, though, and only twice to the point of puking.

"Dick, why are you doing this to yourself?"

"Let me make a comparison, okay? My mother has all her shit together."

"Um, yeah, well, your mom is a piece—let's not talk about your mom."

"My dad was supposed to be this upstanding young go-getter, inheriting the furniture store and whatnot. But that wasn't him. He was actually a mess. He could never be what anyone expected of him, you know?"

"Please don't tell me it's because he was a tortured artist."

"He was different."

"You were pretty mad at him for a while there."

"He's *dead*, Dinah. I'm not going to carry a grudge."

"I still have that manicure kit he gave me. I brought it to school and everything."

"I forgot about that. He must have been thinking a lot about personal grooming right there at the end. Do you know, for my eighteenth birthday last August, he sent me a bottle of aftershave and an electric razor?"

"That's nice. You'll shave again someday."

"He never knew I stopped."

That March, Dick and Dinah made a commitment: disliking each other's respective schools, they both planned to transfer to Kent State, where they downgraded their expectations to a bachelor's degree (for her), a draft deferment (for him), a couple cases of homebrew, and maybe a good time.

Curiously, in contrast to what one might expect of a young couple deciding to uproot their lives in order to reunite, neither suggested they spend the summer prior to sophomore year *together*. It was two years before the Summer of Love; they were ahead of their time. On some subterranean level of consciousness, they each knew that they were about to enter into a celibate relationship as surely as if she was taking the veil or he was joining a monastery. Dick secretly mapped out a tour of the dirty bookstores of America via Greyhound, and Dinah decided to give it up.

After pleading off sex with Chuck—her Monday through Friday suitor—for the entirety of freshman year, and having decided to commit to Dick, Dinah lost her virginity on a pile of coats at a kegger with a male of undetermined name and physical appearance. She never even knew his major. She then leapt into another hot and heavy tryst with a beautiful, smooth, olive-skinned French hunk named Claude whom she picked up, implausibly enough, by cruising the parking lot of a Big Boy.

Poor, unfortunate Chuck! What a difference a few months made. Dinah knew Claude was out for notches, but so was she, now that her recent purchase of a birth-control six-month pack had eliminated that pesky ovulation problem. All summer long she greedily assented to picnics and sex and candlelit dinners and sex—as if she could save those sense-memories for a rainy day, as if it worked like that.

Dick was on something of a pilgrimage as well. Jack's death had instilled a gather-ye-rosebuds mentality in him. He told Dinah and his mother that he wanted to see AAA-approved destinations: the Grand Canyon, Mount Rushmore, the Golden Gate Bridge. His actual itinerary was based on *Swank* magazine classifieds, where they listed the X-rated stores of New Orleans; the cross-dressing haunts of Denver; and Finocchio's, San Francisco's infamous drag club. Ella Mae, extolling the virtues of seeing the world, bought him a ninety-nine-dollar "stop anywhere" bus ticket. And stop everywhere he did, sheepishly ducking into porn stores across the Midwest to buy paperbacks by Anonymous and underground she-male magazines. He took them, wrapped in plain brown wrappers, back to his hotel room. He pulled the shades, hooked the DO NOT DISTURB sign on the outside knob, and spent the evening paging gently through each book, savoring every paragraph.

In Denver, he found a theater where *Glen or Glenda?*, the controversial film about a man with an angora fetish, was playing in revival. He had heard of it, of course, in punch-line form. But Ed Wood, at least, was still a guy—a guy who liked girls' things.

Although Dick managed to gain entry to any number of seedy over-twenty-one destinations on his trip, the place he most yearned to visit was the most elusive. How many times had he read about Finocchio's? The establishment was always advertised in *Swank*, next to mail-order brides and penis pumps.

However, Finocchio's, the leading national purveyor of girl-boy shows, was not a subversive destination. The Disneyland of drag, it warranted a stop on Gray Line's Bay Area bus tour. The men streaming in and out of the entrance appeared overwhelmingly guylike, as they belched and patted their bloated bellies and spat more than seemed possible. Their wives and girlfriends, looking quite embarrassed, exited muttering what they wouldn't give for legs like that! (Oddly, women's legs, of the shapely type idealized in writing utensils and novelty scissors, look better if they're actually men's.)

Dick had daydreamed of going to Finocchio's to see all the other "straight but" guys: corporate suits by day, blond bombshells by night, that sort of thing. They could share a few beers, talk about corsets and chicks, cars and high heels. Slap each other on the back and depart regular dudes, except for the thigh-highs underneath.

Once he was there, though, he was frightened. He stared at the hordes of tourists and their bored-looking bus drivers. Despite his normal-seeming veneer (trimmed beard, thinning hair, plaid madras short sleeves and chinos with a comb in the back pocket), he knew they would sense why he was there. They would think he was there to become one of the full-time queens: the guys you'd joke about during the day, and hear about on the ten o'clock news at night.

At 3 A.M., three hours after closing, Dick stopped pacing back and forth on the adjacent block, and began to stumble back to his motel through a nastier corner of Chinatown. He was so terrified by the prospect of entering a drag club that he had no energy left to worry about getting mugged.

The would-be lovers did not talk about the summer of '65. Dick knew Dinah had dated someone, but was unaware that Claude had gone so far as to propose marriage. Dinah was certainly keen on getting married someday. Yet she had been totally flabbergasted by the request, since she considered Claude, with his frivolous, cocky air, little more than a charming boy toy. She didn't have the slightest desire to live in France, as he desired, nor to become wife to a man who had admitted—in advance—that he planned to take a mistress well before the paper anniversary. She explained to Claude that a marriage couldn't be all about sex, in the absence of everything else. Settling back into a groove with Dick, she hoped against hope that a relationship could exist as just the opposite.

She had no complaints at first. Unlike high school, when Dinah had to coax Dick into her group of friends, Dick now made friends easily. He had learned how to seduce a crowd with his humor, leaving them doubled over and choking out compliments. "Dick is such a dude!" one pothead told Dinah. She was pleased.

Beyond social intercourse, they had even begun to have *sexual* intercourse. It was bimonthly at most, and awkward at best. Dick was more curious about Dinah's body than genuinely excited, and thus he approached the whole experiment with the tenderness and sensuality of a scientist peering at slides under a microscope. Dinah, while unimpressed by her lover's prowess, considered the development a major improvement nonetheless.

It should come as no surprise that Dick had more in mind than the missionary position. Several months into their "new relationship," as quid pro quo for their normal sex life, he asked her very politely, and pointedly, if he could dress for her.

"For me?" Dinah asked. "Don't you mean, for you?"

"No, no, no," Dick pleaded. "Come on, it's just a sex thing. We're experimenting! Play along."

Dinah was a little intimidated the first time, sitting in Dick's off-campus bedroom and waiting for him to unveil himself. He was changing in the closet. Maybe he would have a boa and an evening gown right out of *Gypsy*.

"Ready?" he hollered, from inside.

"I guess so. Whenever you are," Dinah called back.

If he was going for musical theater, Dinah thought with some mortification, he was *Bye Bye Birdie* all the way. Dick was wearing pink short shorts, white Keds, a button-down halter top tied above his belly button, and a headband. Thanks to the unholy combination of four-inch high-heeled sandals and an orange shag rug, he kept tripping in midsaunter, giving him the appearance of a drunken catwalk model. That is, if Gidget had been a catwalk model.

The whole thing lasted about ten minutes, start to finish, before Dick said he was done and went to change in the bathroom. I really feel sorry for men, Dinah had thought, still sitting on the bed and picking at her dead cuticles. The crap they want to do.

As the year progressed, Dinah was increasingly dissatisfied with their revised relationship. Despite his proliferation of casual acquaintances, Dick still leaned on her almost exclusively for the heavy stuff, especially his cross-dressing talk.

"Guys don't have close friends like girls do," Dick had rationalized, and maybe he was right, but between his father's death and the sex stuff, there was too much for one normal girl to shoulder.

Plus, ever since Dick starting dressing in front of her, he'd been acting a little snippy. "You know, you might want to stay away from red and heavy patterns," he advised her before they were about to leave for a Christmas party.

"She is gorgeous, don't you think?" he would mutter, loudly, while they watched some hot babe on TV. He seemed to have developed this thing for blondes. Dinah got the feeling that this might have something to do with the fact that she was a brunette.

Clearly, if she wasn't going to kick Dick to the curb, she needed some help. During Christmas vacation, she cornered her parents before the Sugar Bowl. Bill liked to watch football; Glenn tolerated it and read a *National Geographic* to pass the time. "You can always come to us," they had both said for as long as she could remember.

Dinah told them that she wanted help in dealing with Dick's problems. "He's lonely, and sad," she told them. "He depends on me. He likes to wear women's clothes."

Glenn and Bill sat silently in matching armchairs. Glenn rocked back and forth. Bill looked out the window; he had been in a funk all day. "Okay," Glenn said. "I see."

Dinah said that she wanted to figure out how to help him. She knew Dick had had a bad association with mental-health professionals, based on his bad childhood experience, so she was hoping that they would pay for *her* to see a psychiatrist.

Glenn nearly leapt out of her chair. "No kid of mine," she growled, "is going to see a shrink."

Dinah's cheeks burned. She felt as though she'd been slapped. Unbeknownst to her, Dinah's parents subscribed to every progressive school of thought, from atheism to socialism, except one: psychology. Dinah had had no idea—though in subsequent years, she wondered if her mother simply felt threatened by the intimation that a woman romantically entwined with a man prone to, say, extreme curiosity in kinky sex practices might want to get her head examined. Perhaps Dinah had hit too close to home. But as her mother continued her tirade against Dinah for her interest in seeking professional help, she mentioned not one word about Dick and his newly revealed proclivity for women's sportswear.

"You don't talk about these things," she told Dinah—in precisely those words. "Or at least don't talk about them to us."

Dinah looked over to her father, still sitting quietly. For once he had nothing to say, and Dinah stormed out of the room. Incapable of staying mad, over time she convinced herself that her parents had too much faith in her abilities. They think I can do anything, she told herself, rationalizing time and again why she wrote the names and numbers of psychiatrists down only to toss them out a day later. Hell, she thought, maybe I can.

On Valentine's Day of sophomore year, Dick gave his girlfriend a rose. On Valentine's Day of junior year, he gave her a poem about a rose.

"A rose by any other name would have been eaten, crammed into the tooth of the mind," he read.

"See, it's about love and how it eats you alive," he added, in the way of explanation. Dinah smiled, and excused herself to the bathroom where she cried for ten minutes.

Dick had published poetry in the Kent State literary magazine the year before. Suddenly he wanted to see foreign films, with subtitles. He bought scuffed paperbacks by obscure philosophers at used bookstores and read them in a state of agitation, sipping black coffee and bumming Dinah's cigarettes. He traded in his chinos for denims, his madras for a turtleneck.

This makes him sound like a stereotype, an oversimplification, which is exactly what he was after. Becoming a caricature allowed him to live by a certain set of undeviating rules, not allowing for individual quirk. Finding the niche to slip into, courtesy of his burgeoning reputation as a poet so inscrutable that he must have talent, was a godsend. He assumed the role of Richard Burton–cum–Jack Kerouac, the disdainful outsider, with unparalleled relief.

The role brought casualties with it, of course. Dinah was not Elizabeth Taylor, some tempestuous, haughty bitch able to match world-weary insult with witty rejoinder. At first, she was mystified at where this guy she liked had disappeared to. Later she was wistful that maybe, somehow, he'd return. The signs were not good.

Dick felt a surge of something—maybe that hormone that had always eluded him, the mythical, terrifying testosterone—every time Dinah winced, or shuddered; every time she cried. She was soft, and female, and easily hurt. Changing colleges had meant she was a transfer student once again, and not quite as known and adored by the general student population as she might have liked. Lately, too, she had been cut off from her parents and her insipid teaching classes had caused her to doubt whether speech pathology was really an efficient means of saving the world. Therefore, she was vulnerable; Dick could push her away and reel her back in.

Perhaps he was punishing her for having seen him as a weepy, dependent naif in lipstick and foundation garments, forgetting he had forced her to watch. Or he was jealous. Here Dinah was, lucky enough to have been born female, and she didn't even bother to make the most of it. She didn't iron her hair, barely wore makeup, stayed away from sex kitten lingerie. She was spoiled, unappreciative of the bounty she had been given.

None of that occurred to Dinah. As far as she could tell, her dear, bitter, bitchy boyfriend didn't seem to have a problem with his masculine side. On the contrary, for someone having a hard time being a guy, as she would say for decades to come, *He was awfully damn good at it.*

He criticized her body, an easy target. At best she had a tenuous confidence in her attractiveness. Although buoyed briefly by her encounters with other men, such faith was hard to sustain over several years, especially in the face of frequent rejection. Dick suggested Dinah could lose a few pounds. He informed her, one night, as she stroked his thigh suggestively, that maybe, if she did something with herself, maybe he could get a hard-on for a change. She wept, while he changed the channel on the TV.

For the first time, he started in on her intellect. He mocked her inability to decipher his wretched poetry, to locate his inapt or sometimes fictional allusions. He corrected her pronunciation. "In-*comp*-ar-a-ble," he said, and sighed in an exaggerated fashion. "Not in-com-*par*-a-ble." Again, she was bait. She believed Dick to be a bad poet, but otherwise brilliant, while deeming her own intelligence merely adequate. He pushed her away and reeled her in.

He let each admonishment settle in, long enough to lacerate, and then offered up a truce: an ice-cream cone, a beer, a hug, a kiss, a walk around the block. It wasn't much, but for my mother, the eternal optimist (and frequent self-deprecator), it was enough to give her hope.

It's so hard to know why self-protection kicks in at one point and not another, in absence of a climactic fight or crowning insult. No such moment happened, not that either Dinah or Dick could later remember. At some point, Dinah ceased to hear his insults, or they stopped hitting their mark. She started to see the absurdity of feeling put down by a man who couldn't put out.

"Good-bye," she told him, on some day during the spring of junior year. "I've had it. I'm gone." Instead of merely feeling alone, Dick truly was.

TWELVE

Makeovers

What is Dick thinking? First he gives me this really pretty blouse, except that it's three sizes too small. He does have great taste, but he never ever remembers my actual size, and then he wants me to try it on, which gets embarrassing. I got out of it by saying I didn't want to ruin it when I needed to cook the turkey later.

—Dinah, 1982

Sometime in '83, my father held a family meeting much like the Bradfords and Bradys— except there were only three of us standing in the kitchen, and no imminent Hawaiian vacation in the offing. Unceremoniously, Dad announced that he would no longer be acting at the theater. I stared fiercely down at his big leather shoes while he explained how he'd "lost interest" in performing— or, more to the point, as far as I was concerned, in being out of the house three to five blessed evenings a week.

My mother clearly knew it was coming, but she seemed as dismayed as I was. She had her own reasons for wanting my dad safely ensconced in costume. There was one I knew: that, for her—immersed to a far lesser extent as box office manager and later as producer—the whole exhausting practice of running from work to home to the theater to home was only worth the trouble if she got occasional quality time with her husband out of it. He was more likely to be sober and pleasant in the presence of cast-mates. There was another reason I didn't know: that the only definitive barrier standing between her husband and a gingham frock, as far as she knew, was his acting hobby.

After my father made his blunt announcement and headed off to the living room, cocktail in hand, my mother consoled me.

"I know you like going to the theater, Noelle," Mom chirped, and squeezed my hand. "But, look on the bright side. Dad's just going to be around more, and so maybe we can all do more things together. Vacations, or board games or something. That sounds fun, doesn't it?"

She was smiling without the slightest bit of conviction. I was sure he had finally driven her completely mad.

Dick doesn't want to act anymore, and I don't even want to think about what that means. I hope to heck he finds something else to keep him preoccupied or it's going to be like off-season year-round, what with the dressing up all the time.

—Dinah, 1983

Years later, when I was in college, my father confessed that he decided to stop acting on the opening night of the last play he performed—*Good*, by J. P. Taylor, a portrait of a morally con-flicted Nazi officer. Dad had a seven-minute monologue in act two, and on that night, he went up on the lines. He ended up kneeling at center stage for no fewer than two deadly quiet minutes, while his mind frantically scanned for the words. My father thought this lapse was the beginning of the break*down* which would lead to the inevitable break*through* to his new life, which sounded too much like a discussion of *King Lear* I'd heard in English class to be plausible in real life. I thought he'd probably had a few too many Bloody Marys and not enough celery sticks. Regardless of the cause, that moment of silence changed every-thing.

"Being onstage," he told me, "with nothing in your head is like being inside a soap bubble. Shiny and slippery with no point of reference." He got no assist from the audience, who fidgeted in their seats, rifled through their purses, picked at the gum on the seat backs, and generally looked anywhere but at him. For the first time, they were not frightened by his onstage mien. They pitied him.

Despite his elaborately constructed costume, from the greased moustache to the starched, unyielding Nazi uniform, he was na-ked in front of everyone.

After my father made his announcement, I went upstairs in order to stop thinking about my parents. It wasn't so hard. I shut the door, and threw myself on the bed where I nibbled the glued-on felt toes of Bernie, my filthy stuffed panda, until I grew disgusted with myself, thereby changing the subject in my mind from my selfish dad and clueless mom to my own unmistakable grossness.

In what was becoming a nightly ritual, I yanked out my stash of *Seventeen* magazines. I had subscribed to it since my single-digit years, courtesy of my mother, who didn't seem quite com-fortable with her decision although I swore that it was the best thing she had ever done for me. Recently I had begun to regard those hallowed 220 pages, including dozens of astringent ads and classifieds for John Casablancas modeling school, as a Bible.

This is not an exaggerated metaphor. I read and reread and reread *Seventeen* every day, sometimes repeating axioms from self-help articles in my mind ("thou shalt not tweeze above the brow line") as I walked to school. I worshiped cover girls Whitney Houston and Terry Farrell, and tore their images out to stickum over my bed right next to the male teen idols already there. I would have absorbed the magazine intravenously had that been a medical option. As the next best thing, I followed every instruc-tion, no matter how bizarre, to the letter.

Seventeen told me to cut up a plastic six-pack holder and wear all six pop tops as "fun, original" bracelets. I did. They told me to scissor geometric shapes into my stirrup pants. I did. They told me to "be myself," although I wasn't sure how to do that while wearing bracelets that chafed my wrists and stirrup pants with trapezoids cut out of the butt.

The magazine had substantive articles, too, which told me that other teen girls (I was not quite a member of that demographic yet) were mostly afraid of nuclear war, rape, a parent's death, sex, divorce, breakups and the freshman fifteen, although not necessarily in that order. I embraced all these fears as my own, as a means of jump-starting my incipient teenagehood. I couldn't make myself age faster, but I *could* go on a diet—even though I weighed in at a mere eighty-two pounds. I couldn't get a boyfriend, but I *could* role-play breakups in my mind, so that I'd be better at them once I was old enough to date. However, I could not be persuaded to be frightened of divorce; it was a good thing, and no one could make me think otherwise.

My dad mocked my attempts to follow *Seventeen*'s prescriptions. Obviously, he was so miserable with his own life that he had to ruin whatever slim chance I had of being a normal teenage girl. "If *Seventeen* told you to jump off a bridge, would you?" he asked me on the day I walked around with a raw egg massaged into my hair for two hours, adding much-needed protein to my follicles and an odd pungency to the air.

"You're so funny, I forgot to laugh," I retorted, as albumen congealed on my forehead. "*Seventeen* would never tell me to do that. You wouldn't know that because you're a boy." I quickly ran out of the room before he could yell at me for talking to him in that tone of voice, but he stayed quiet.

After my father abandoned the theater, Mom and I saw him around the house a lot more—for about a month. Then, with no warning, he embarked on a new obsession. He decided on an activity less revealing than acting, and far more guyish, if not truly

masculine. He picked up a sport, one of the only athletic endeavors in which beer supplants Gatorade as the drink of cham-
pions. He became a bowler. Overnight, he began heading to the
alley as many as five times a week—a different league for each
day. After a very short time, he was carting three balls in different
surfaces to the alley; adorning himself in shirts with embroidered
tenpins on the back and Dick in cursive over the left-front pocket,
special gloves, and specially ordered bowling shoes.

He might have looked like he was channeling Jackie Gleason
had he not recently upgraded his overall wardrobe. He had in-
vested in mirrored Ray-Bans, which made him look like an extra
from *CHiPs*. He sported his leather jacket all the time, even in
the summer. He had also purchased a very cool red convertible,
yet another accessory of his new image.

He could afford all this pretty easily. He had quit teaching
nearly to the day that troops pulled out of Saigon, and hightailed
it into a professional arena more befitting his lack of idealism. By
the early eighties, Dad's ad copywriting had really taken off, and
made him one of the best-paid local guys in the field. He was
becoming well-to-do, by Cleveland standards anyway, and somewhat acclaimed. There was a Cleveland advertising award ceremony at which he won a grocery bag full of awards—gigantic
gold-colored pushpins encased in Lucite blocks. My mom said
they were a great honor, but ugly, so they were kept in a linen
closet.

My dad never mentioned the writing trophies (nor the bowling
ones that later streamed into the house, thanks to his Rottweil-
eresque tenacity); he always professed that awards and honors
were meaningless, with the possible exception of bowling a 300
game, and would once again bring up how Woody Allen was so
cool because he never went to the Academy Awards. His ridicule
was chastening. I stopped trying to impress Dad with my own
meager academic certificates, minimedals, and report cards as I
had in younger days. Instead, I stored mine in the closet, adjacent

to his bag. He might change his mind someday and want to look at them.

That same autumn, my mother's father died. We got a call late at night from my mom, who was with him in the hospital when they let him fall asleep. He was sick and old. No one was surprised. Over the phone in a sniffly voice, Mom told me she was going to keep Grandma company for the night in case she got too depressed. She told me to get a big hug from Dad. As soon as I hung up the phone, my father frantically phoned Grandma H. to ask her if she'd come over and sit with me for a while. I heard him say he was sad and needed to be alone. I couldn't figure that out; it wasn't *his* father who died.

I had no problem with Grandma H. coming over to assuage my sorrow, except that I felt okay. The awful, terrible truth is that my first thought on hearing of his passing was how interesting it was that I knew a dead person. Knowing someone on the mysterious "other side" made me feel smarter.

Grandma H. and I sat side by side on the living-room sofa. "Oh, honey, you can let it out," she said, softly, urgently, tugging me down to her breast. "I know how much you'll miss him. We all will."

"I can't cry right now." I sighed. "And," I added, frowning, "I didn't even think you liked Grandpa Schultz."

Grandma H. pulled a travel-size pack of minitissues from her pocketbook. Her eyes were welling up. "We didn't know each other very well, but of course, I'm sad he's gone. It's a horrible thing. You're hurting right now, and I don't want you to keep all that pain inside. That's how you get sick."

"Sick like cancer sick?" I asked, and curled my knees to my chest. "You're saying Grandpa got sick from being sad too much?"

Grandma shook her head. "These things happen. It's life. I only want to be here for you, honey." She rolled me over onto her lap.

I didn't move. "Now go ahead, and cry," she said, in a commanding voice. I complied, all over her velour pants.

"That's it, there you go," she whispered. "Grandma's going to make it all better."

My father walked in the room; his eyes were rimmed red, darker than after drinking. "Thanks, Mom," he said to Grandma H. "I appreciate your coming by to help Noelle out. It's a hard time for all of us."

"Doing what I can during a tough time is what family is for," Grandma H. said, smoothing my hair out. "I am here for both of you."

Going into junior high, my biggest fear was that as I walked down the hall, older boys would grab my bare arm and stick me with a syringe, or haul me into the bathroom, hold my head over the toilet, and threaten me to take a hit off their crack pipe or else drown in the bowl. Then I would be an addict. I would steal things and hang out with unkempt people who burned things over bonfires in tin drums before dying tragically early like the girl in *Go Ask Alice*. This is actually what I expected.

To my surprise, once I got to Wilcy Junior High—a brick-and-concrete behemoth just across from the Burger King—I realized my fear was completely misplaced. I should have worried that as I walked down the hall, older boys would *not* grab my butt, or my chest, or say they wanted to stick me with something even more taboo than a needle.

Courtesy of an early menstruation, Debbie, a friend I had met in BASIC computer class at nerd summer camp, had very precociously large breasts and bones recognizably hiplike. So did our other good friend, Nancy, whom Debbie and I had met in seventh-grade orientation. When we all convened in the cafeteria during lunch, Nancy often sighed in a tone of world-weary exhaustion that she had been "goosed" or "pinched" half a dozen times since homeroom. Debbie nodded solemnly in agreement. "Me too," she echoed. "Like what else is new though. Boys are breast-obsessed."

"Wow, that's rough," I said, trying to sound supportive, subtly inching my chest toward the lunch table and slumping until my nonboobs were under the sight line.

"Look, you are so lucky that you don't have to deal with that," Nancy said to me.

"Totally," Debbie added. "Nancy, do you have any Midol? I've got cramps bad." They exchanged sympathy glances, apparently withering with despair about the fact that *they owned the universe.* On some level, sure, I knew that being grabbed was unpleasant and embarrassing and so on. However, I didn't care. Rape still gave me nightmares, and maybe I should have made the mental connection between assault and clothes-on public harassment. But like all the other girls I knew, I didn't make that leap at all.

Since grade school, we had been indoctrinated with the notion from parents, teachers, and each other that boys pulled your pigtails if they liked you. Any self-respecting girl yearned for the yank of a hand on her hair. Which was the worse fate: to be touched in a bad way by some random guy, or not to be liked by any boys at all?

Unable to make my breasts grow, I did everything else possible to become "gooseworthy." First, I got braces, a set of upper and lower hardware with multiple rubber bands the orthodontist was recommending anyway, since my retainer had only done a so-so job getting my big horsey teeth to stay together in a straight line. This may seem like an unorthodox and counterproductive choice, but I believed braces would make me appear older than about ten-years-old—a fact that wasn't immediately clear from my body and baby face—and so it was a necessary step toward attracting sexual interest.

As soon as I went off soft foods, I scheduled an "electric" perm from the hairdresser who was always joking with my mom that they should run away together to make mad passionate love, while she laughed nervously and looked a little nauseous. The hairdresser proclaimed, as he choked me with Final Net, that the new style would make me look "alive." I looked like I had glued my fingers to the static ball at the science museum. I was very pleased.

Once I was done with the major stuff, it was time for attending to details. I examined my trusted *Seventeen* for makeover options. The beauty editors always featured before and after photos. Before, the girl always wore a plain white T-shirt and grimaced in no makeup and unwashed hair under bad lights. After, she smiled brightly—as well she should have—in a vibrant sweater, insanely colorful cosmetics, and an elaborate don't-try-this-at-home hairstyle. She looked better, she felt better. Her life was about to change, in part because she was so pretty now and also maybe because she got to be in *Seventeen*.

Magazine in hand, I paid a trip to the mall, where I got fancy-name socks to match all my shirts; a rainbow palette of department store counter eye shadows (rather than choosing just one, I streaked all three up to my brow in chunky stripes like Neapolitan ice cream), and bought shirts made of netting, rhinestone crucifix earrings, and a bra in size AAA. My mother seemed to think I didn't need one yet since my nipples were not droopy enough to warrant underwire support. I knew she was wrong. I needed a bra for snapping. God forbid I got caught in an undershirt; I'd never hear the end of it.

My carefully orchestrated image redux was complete just after Halloween, and I walked into Wiley with a newfound sense of sex appeal. I burned hot—*red-hot*—in my stretch pants with carved geometric shapes and bra with the little pink rose in the middle and fishnet blouse with a turtleneck underneath. And as I had hoped, someone tapped me on the shoulder as I maneuvered through the throng to first period. I halted in my tracks, just waiting to be made uncomfortable.

It was the principal. "Young lady," he said, from way up where his head was. He looked about seventeen feet tall. "Pants with holes are against school policy. Did you know that?"

"Nooo," I whispered.

"I'm going to have to send you home to change," the principal said. "Try to dress more appropriately for school in the future."

"I'm sorry, sir," I said forlornly. "I thought that's what I was doing."

Both of my parents had to sign the note that said I had been sent home on account of "unfortunate attire" and bring it back in the next morning. Mom left work a little early, after enduring fifteen calls with me hyperventilating on the phone about being really, really bad and getting kicked out of school. She normally covered for me with Dad, like the time that I bought the hundred-dollar jeans jacket on her credit card when my limit was supposed to be $40. She was cognizant, in the way he wasn't, that my tendency to inflict distress on myself was usually far more extreme than any punishment they could mete out. "They let kids wear chain mail to that school, and they can't wear pants with holes." She sighed. "What about the poorer kids? Although really, Noelle, is there some reason you feel the need to destroy your clothing?"

I shrugged. As Dad's car sped up the driveway and screeched to a halt in front of the garage, my stomach started to tense. I told my mother I was going to be sick. I propped myself against the wall and waited for the screaming.

He stomped in the house in his uniform of shades, denim, and leather.

"What?" he grumbled, his version of hello. "Can I get a drink?"

I moved away from him across the room.

"What the hell are you wearing?" he asked, and folded up his glasses.

"Dick," Mom said, cautiously, with her hand on his shoulder to steady him, "the school told Noelle that she might want to choose other pants."

"No kidding," he replied, prying three ice cubes from the tray and plunking them in his glass. "She looks like a . . ." his voice trailed off. "You can see half her leg."

My mother kissed me on the forehead and told me to go to my room. "Am I in trouble?" I whispered. "Have I been bad?"

"Shhh, not now," she said, fixing her eyes on my dad's back.

"I'm sorry," I said, clinging to her, wrapping my arms around her.

"You're fine. Everything's fine. Now shoo," she said, and forcibly detached me from her body. She was still watching Dad.

I climbed up to my room, careful to step heavily on the surefire creaks in the hardwood floor, then took my shoes off and darted back in tiptoed stocking feet to the head of the stairs.

My mother chastised my father for nearly calling me something. Loud sigh. She said that if he made me feel any worse about myself, she would kill him. And that his problems shouldn't be taken out on me. Like being a teenager, almost a teenager, wasn't hard enough. Swear swear. She was talking a lot. He pointed that out. He kept asking her if she was finished, and she kept saying that she wasn't even close. Slam. Tumbler on the counter. I knew that sound anywhere.

A few minutes later, Mom called me down to dinner and said we'd be eating alone. Dad had gone bowling, but that I shouldn't worry. He had had a rough day at work and wasn't mad, at least not at me.

I hadn't been fooled; over the course of seventh grade, my father had become stranger. A *Sports Illustrated* swimsuit issue came one day in the mail. That was weird. A week later, an *Esquire: Magazine for Men* was rolled in the mailbox alongside my Rick Springfield Official Fan Club newsletter. That was more unusual still. A bottle of Brut cologne sat on the kitchen counter, still in its bag from the drugstore. A tape of *Rocky* was left in the VCR. Messages from work for "Duke," his new nickname, were on the answering machine. The signs had been building for some time, and they were no longer subtle. I had watched enough television to know that Dad was having a midlife crisis.

Unbeknownst to me, my father was intentionally stockpiling masculine accoutrements. He meandered like a zombie through the aisles of the drugstore, tossing Mennen aftershave and Xtra large condoms into a red plastic basket. When the weather permitted, he lay in the sun as much as possible in an attempt to fricassee himself into George Hamilton. The one thing he couldn't do in his quest to become a better man—if not actually a better person—was have an affair. The ultimate guy accessory wasn't working at all anymore.

It's been six, seven months since the last time. Dick says he didn't know I was keeping count, as though that was the actual issue. I've tried not to press it; he's been under a lot of pressure lately, but I told him that the drinking could have something to do with his lack of interest. He didn't want to talk about it, no shock there, so I got some pamphlets on drinking problems from AA. I want him to see someone, a doctor, but he won't. He asks me to stop bringing it up, saying I do it all the time, which is not quite true. Every few months at most. I would stop bringing it up if he could act regular.

—Dinah, 1984

The Bar Mitzvah season started in the spring, when the oldest kids in my grade started hitting the big 1–3 and cracking jokes like "I'm a man now. Can I make a woman out of you?" Befitting my status on the periphery of the wanna-bes, I got some invitations to some of the least spectacular of the coming-of-age parties. About once a month, then, I played tic-tac-toe with Debbie through a long, boring Hebraic service, before swapping a gift-wrapped Duran Duran album for good cold cuts, flat pop, a bad mix tape, and a choice of three games—spin the bottle, spin the bottle with Frenching, or truth or dare—while the adults were busying themselves in the adjacent bar. It was totally miserable, and unfortunately necessary. I told myself that kissing games were a rite of passage, part of becoming a teenage girl (at least as Judy Blume had conceived it). As puberty rituals went, at least it was a step up from the girls in Africa who had to put weights on their earlobes until they hung to their shoulders.

I liked kissing. That really wasn't the problem. No one wanted to kiss me. I saw it on their faces as the empty liter stopped whirling on its axis and came to a sputtering halt in front of me. The boy was vaguely queasy, flushed. None of the other boys whooped or did high fives. He kissed me real fast on the lips; or just next to my lips; or if he was really nasty, as one boy was, he puckered up, came in for a long slow one, while everyone stared with bated breath, before ducking so I passionately smooched the air in front of most of the gifted & talented pre-algebra class.

That was Alex. He had the beginnings of a gut, chronic dandruff, and smelled like cat. The minute he blew me off, my estimation of him rose about 2000 percent. My pigtail had been pulled.

While I was being tentatively kissed and resoundingly rejected in basement rec rooms across Cleveland, my parents were locked up in their own bedroom talking.

My father no longer dressed up in women's clothes in front of my mother without an invitation. But there was a catch: He had started ordering her to extend the invitation. She didn't think that was exactly fair, seeing as she didn't actually enjoy seeing him cross-dress, not to mention the fact that he wasn't exactly jumping at the opportunity to realize her sexual fantasies in reciprocity. Forever the supportive mate, she gave it a go anyway.

Once or twice, they climbed up the stairs to the attic, where amidst a blizzard of dust motes, she instructed him to wear a pretty dress or an elegant negligee. The whole scenario made her squirm, and although he seemed to like it, she soon refused to participate. "I'm out of this," she told him. "You can do this all by yourself," she spat, before running down the stairs to the second-floor bathroom. "You want to be alone all the time anyway."

I saw Dr. Lowenthal yesterday. I picked him because I guess he helped Kay after her husband died. I told Dick I was going, and he wasn't happy, but he didn't try to stop me. Anyway, the doctor was very nice. He told me that I was fine and healthy and that Dick's problems—both the dressing and the way he's been with Noelle—were his alone. He said Dick needed help, serious help, but that I was just fine. He told me to go home. I went back to work. I can't afford to miss work, since I'm so new there. But I started feeling really down. My mom called about Noelle's school play, and I slipped and mentioned seeing the doctor. I said that my bad ankle was acting up because I really didn't want to get into all that again with her. Later, Noelle had this whole big dance concert she wanted to perform for me. I swear it was two hours long, and I fell asleep halfway through. I really tried to stay awake. She can be so exhausting! It's hard to be a single parent. Joke.

—Dinah, 1985

Against all odds, by eighth grade I had managed to nab Alex's friendship—if not his undying love—through the systematic torture of someone even less cool than me. The victim was a foreigner (a transplant from New Jersey) with a funny name (Lula), a habit of eating rotten bananas at lunch, and a startling gullibility. Having been on the receiving end of bullying made me feel slightly sorry for Lula, but that twinge of humanity was easily squashed by my intemperate lust for potbellied, mean-spirited Alex.

The plot began by accident. Debbie and Nancy were popping Midols at lunch, with the usual moaning and groaning about how *terrible* it was to have cramps and how *totally completely lucky* I was not to have my period, while I ate my pizza and fumed. Lula sat down beside us, uninvited, and gazed with awe at Nancy taking one of her little white pills.

"Oh my God, is that birth control?" Lula asked, with wide-eyed astonishment.

Nancy rolled her eyes. "Yeah, I'm on the pill." We all burst into the laughter of the superior, and the subject was dropped. I later mentioned to Alex, while balancing a petri dish of frog intestines atop a Bunsen burner, how deeply stupid Lula was. Actually, I called her a "loser dorkus." Alex looked at me anew, as though he had finally seen something in me to respect, and I felt bathed in a warm glow of happiness.

For the next few months, Alex and I—with the able help of our friends—convinced Lula that every eighth-grade girl at Wiley was on the pill. That, in fact, we all had sex regularly. With each other. And orgies every Friday night! At Nancy's house! With rope! Once we convened at Nancy's and called Lula at home, each of us on a different phone, shrieking simultaneously into the phone that we . . . were . . . oh my God . . . having . . . an . . . org . . . as . . . m while Lula sat mutely on the other line. We probably sounded like we were being stabbed. Then we hung up, and grabbed a slice of the pizza that Nancy's parents had ordered before going to the movies. After ripping all the pepperoni off, Alex and his boys said something like, "This sucks. Let's go have some real fun," and left without saying good-bye.

Dad blacked out one too many times, and Mom called the doctor to make an appointment. "How many times do I have to tell you I'm not going to see a psychiatrist?" he snarled at her.

My mother shook her head, with some measure of disgust. "Forget psychiatrist," she said. "You're seeing the real doctor."

"I don't need to do that. I'm fine."

"You are not fine," she retorted. "You are killing yourself."

"Don't say it," he said, holding up his hand like a shield.

"I'm going to say it. I'm going to say it because I care about you. You are going to kill yourself if you keep this up, just like your father." She walked out of the room and went upstairs to read a library book she had hidden under the bed on the travails of living with an alcoholic.

Dad kept the appointment, more to appease a pissed-off wife than to take care of himself. It was a good thing he did. The doctor informed him that he might very well die of a heart attack unless he ate better, exercised, found ways to reduce family and job stress, and most vitally of all, curbed his drinking.

"Do you think I'm an alcoholic?" my father asked.

"You're working on it," the doctor replied.

For the moment, my father decided not to commit suicide. When he arrived home from the doctor's office, he poured himself a tall glass of Clamato on the rocks. To his amazement, and ours, my father was only an aspiring alcoholic. He stopped drinking, but suffered no withdrawal. As it turned out, his addiction was not to the actual drug, but rather to the sensation of being out-of-body. He had to stop drinking in order to keep breathing; yet ironically, without acting or alcohol to escape into, he feared he might stop wanting to live.

Five months into our grand master plan to destroy Lula, she was as clueless as ever. "So do you tie each other up?" she asked over lunch. "And are there whips?"

I nodded. "You bet," I said. "You should see it."

Despite the fact that Lula was still game, Alex was losing interest in our little hoax, and in me. He had moved on to mocking a seventh-grader with bad acne who everyone said gave blow jobs in the first-floor bathroom. That terrified me, since there was no way I was going to be putting one of those things anywhere near my mouth, which essentially meant I would have to concede (the girl who went farther *always* won). He was so busy taunting this scrawny little girl that he barely had time to notice the new me, which I had recently revamped—in both senses of the word.

The Madonna look hadn't worked, so I had decided to reinvent my image as a cutesy thing. I started, naturally, by reconceptualizing my penmanship, modeling it after that of several girls more popular than I was. Now my letters were superpuffy, like overblown balloons, so big that only five or six words could fit on a line of notebook paper. I dotted "i's" with big circles and shaped my lowercase "e's" into fat little Pac-Mans. I schooled myself in Valley Girl as a second language, reciting "gag me with a spoon" and "totally bodacious" into a tape recorder at home in increasingly higher registers. I also started wearing my hair (extra blond from all the Sun-In) in a mammoth ponytail atop my head, ensuring that I would be impossible to take seriously.

I didn't give up on Alex easily. I let my bra strap show while he was talking to me. I said something was "bitchin'," and immediately wanted to sink into the linoleum. He didn't hear a word I said; the whole time I talked, he barely looked at me. He was immersed in writing hate notes to put in the blow job girl's locker. I tried to get revenge on him by telling the forever dim-witted Lula that we all weren't really doing it, but that made her cry and threaten to tell the principal that we had lied to her. Scared of getting in trouble (I imagined detention, where I had never been, as something out of the old movie *Blackboard Jungle*) for pretending not to be virgins, I told Lula that I was just joking, and that of course, I'd had sex so many times I couldn't count.

Toward the end of eighth grade, my parents decided that they wanted to move. Mom said Dad was making too much money to stay in our house; a $200-per-month mortgage wasn't enough of a write-off. Dad wasn't there (he was bowling), and it was just as well, for he couldn't have given a whit about the taxes. Money had been Mom's area. All he told me was that he wanted a house where "I'm not on top of the neighbors. Where there's some privacy." A place where the curtains didn't have to be taped to the walls; where the windows didn't need to be sealed shut, just in case you were doing something you didn't want anyone else to see.

I asked Dad why he needed so much privacy. He explained he didn't like to have an audience while he was sunbathing. I nodded. *What a nutso*, I thought.

I was not ecstatic about the move. It was a half hour away from Debbie and Nancy. It was a huge house, out where they still call it a suburb but only because the residents are too yuppie to admit they live in the country. The only good thing about moving that I could see was at least I would have the opportunity to have another makeover, and this one—unhindered by schoolmates' memories of me grading during recess back in elementary school—could really catapult me into the ever-elusive in crowd.

Nonetheless, I wasn't sure how I could get over the main indignity inherent in this whole move: that Dad was finally leaving— and *we were going with him*.

That summer, I turned fourteen, and two important things happened: I saw hope for my father, and I told my first big lie.

First, the lie. I hit fourteen. There was cake. There were jeans and records. And still no period. One week later, livid that I was still a nonmenstruating teenager—like a champion gymnast or something—I marched up to the upstairs bathroom, wiggled out of my panties, and proceeded to color in the entire crotch with a red Magic Marker.

"There we go," I sighed.

I pulled my jean shorts right back over my bare butt and ran downstairs to my mom, who was folding laundry and watching

Hill Street Blues. "Look!" I announced, thrusting my ketchup red undies in her face.

I expected her to take them from my hands and scrutinize them under bright light. But because she was trusting, or sane, or simply trying not to laugh, she averted her gaze from my neon wad. "Well, how about that?" she said, in all seriousness. "Guess we'd better get the stuff."

I smiled triumphantly. She pulled out an enormous pile of pads, each as thick as an air mattress, off the top shelf of her closet. "I've been saving these," she said. "I thought you might not want to start with a tampon." She handed me the box. "Go to it," she said. "Unless you need help."

"Please," I scoffed. "Like, everyone knows how to do this."

"Well, okay, then," my mom demurred. "I've been through all this, though, so remember I can help you out."

I looked at my mom, back to folding socks contentedly and, with a sudden sense of horror, realized that she was a woman. Even though I dressed up in her lingerie and read her sex books and saw her naked, I somehow usually managed to see her as a wholly asexual entity. And frankly, I liked her that way. I shook off the creeps and went back upstairs.

Back in the bathroom, I ripped off the adhesive backing on the first pad with a flourish and proceeded to stick it directly onto my butt, before running to call Debbie and give her the big news. I was disheartened later, when I pulled out about fifty-seven hairs in the course of removing my pad, but I figured this was why so many of my friends used tampons.

I'll have to remind myself of that next time I get the curse, I thought happily, almost forgetting that I had made the whole story up.

One month later, on a hot and humid August day, my father turned forty.

He had spent all morning out of the house staring at pot

holders at Kmart. He had gone into the store ostensibly to buy a new drill-bit set for his ever-growing, never-touched tool kit. The hardware aisle had been hard to find, and he had meandered through large tins of cheese and caramel popcorn for about fifteen minutes before ending up in kitchenwares.

There were some pot holders with illustrations of brick hearths, oven mitts in the shape of cow or frog heads. But mostly, perhaps because they had recently gotten a new shipment, there were multiple pot holders of flowers, of every hue and genus. Of course, my father no longer could distinguish one flower from another as he could back when he perused botany manuals. He did not accompany my mother when she bought wagonfuls of marigold and petunia flats to plant at the side of the driveway. He rarely sent flowers either, preferring to give chocolate for card holidays. Now, suddenly, he couldn't take his eyes off of them. Fifteen minutes later, he left Kmart empty-handed.

That afternoon, he said there was somewhere we needed to go. I said I needed to do homework, and he said I needed to go with him. He ushered me into the convertible and took me to a graveyard. He drove all the way in, to a place that seemed about five miles from the main road, and asked me to get out. "Don't kill me," I joked.

He didn't seem to notice. "I want to show you something," he said.

He walked me back to a plain marble stone near a fence over-looking the cobblestoned Little Italy section of town. "This was Jack's," he said, squatting in front of the stone. "My dad. Your grandfather."

My dad barely ever had mentioned his father. All I knew was that he had been a whittler (according to my mother), a jerk (according to Grandma H.), and an alcoholic (according to every-one). I knew he had died a long time ago, when my father was 10, 15, or maybe 30. I dropped to my knees.

"He was a very good man," my father murmured. Dad was pooling sweat, probably because it was eighty degrees, and his leather jacket was on. "He wasn't very happy, though, and he didn't do a lot of things he wanted to do."

Dad looked over at me when he spoke, but I preferred to glance down at my hands. I didn't like seeing myself in his sunglasses.

"Jesus, he was a real stickler for manners. I guess that's why I can be—well, so hard on you. He was a fine dad, though, in a lot of ways while he was capable."

Apparently, Dad's dad—I couldn't really think of this anonymous dead person as my grandpa—was "disabled," too, in the way Mom referred to Dad lacking "capabilities."

"I wonder, you know, if he'd approve of the way I'm living my life," Dad whispered. In a gasp, a low rumble emitted from his throat. He began to rock back and forth, pulling his knees to his chest, and wailing as though his father had died all over again.

Tears were pouring out from under his sunglasses, and I wanted to hold him, to reach out in some way with a hand or a tissue or something, because he was hurting, really hurting, in a way I had never experienced, but I was paralyzed. My arms and hands felt frozen in place, as though they had been stapled to my sides. I was too scared of him.

"I'm sorry, Dad," I said, starting to cry myself. "I'm really sorry."

THIRTEEN

Something Old, Something New

As the sixties progressed, my mother hewed to her childhood promise never to put herself in the line of pepper spray. She voted Democratic and sent small checks to senators who were "for" education. She stayed away from anything smacking of overt demonstration—no placards or buttons or bumper stickers on the VW bug for her. My dad, who was able to thwart terror-induced paralysis about the draft through frequent inebriation, imagined military enlistment as akin to boys' school—except suffering gunshot wounds instead of Indian burns.

But Vietnam did determine the course of his life in one significant way: It forced him to teach English to about five hundred seventh-graders in inner-city Cleveland. It was either that or flee to Ontario, which intimidated him a little because he'd never been out of the country and it sounded cold. (It never occurred to him to admit his penchant for feminine garments. During senior year of college, he swore to friends that he'd commit *hara-kiri* if his number ever came up, but he would have suited up in fatigues in a split second before coming clean about cross-dressing.)

He had no hidden, idealistic agenda. His new job did, however, introduce him to a new group of drinking buddies, a small crew of English and history teachers with whom he would get sloshed nightly at the Pepper Pot and grouse about hangover pains over weak Sanka the next morning in the faculty lounge. It was a life, or a way to escape one. Happily, he found that inhabiting the new role of Mr. Howey, English Teacher, required so much of his energy and attention that he could go days at a time without aching to wear the "special" clothes in his lower right-hand dresser drawer.

When he had heard—to his own befuddlement, since he had all but flunked out of college—that he'd gotten the teaching gig, he immediately stored his Beatnikware (they might be good some-day if he wanted to paint something), and adopted a new Silent Majority mode of dress. He purchased a brown suit, an orange tie, and a gold watch that was so big and heavy that he had to massage his sore wrist at night. Although most of the male teach-ers seemed to wear the same short-sleeved button-down with yel-lowed sweat spots, Dick had made it a personal policy not to take off his sports jacket at school. The boxy built-in shoulders made him look bigger, and he never knew what might intimidate his seventh-graders—several of whom were juvies working their way up to felonhood.

His new straitlaced look, accompanied by a newly minted zero tolerance attitude, was a defensive weapon that protected him from encroachment of all kinds, whether they were posturing would-be gang members or anyone else he deemed unwelcome. For example, if Mr. Howey ran into a student with his mom or dad at a nearby store, the parent would usually smile deferentially, and ask how little so-and-so was doing in school. Mr. Howey would remain stone-faced, and keep his eyes suspiciously nar-rowed, as though he fully expected the parent might drop his or her pants and shit right there in the aisle. The parent then would appear properly cowed, maybe even angry, shake Mr. Howey's hand, and drag his or her offspring toward the exit. That type of exchange, unpleasant as it was, seemed unlikely to result in the parent walking away murmuring that Mr. Howey was a big wuss and calling the school board on his gay ass. Instead, he or she would call Mr. Howey an asshole, which was no problem at all.

After all, Mr. Howey wasn't Dick; he was Dick's beard.

These out-of-body feelings were not unusual; they had become routine, and even comfortable. The discomfiting moments were those spent in his secret silk sheath, sauntering around his bedroom, feeling ashamed, prurient, dubious, criminal, insane, peculiar, eccentric, and completely at one with himself.

My mother was in a strange transitional period herself. After a year or two of hapless dating, she swore that she'd rather abstain entirely than suffer through another blind date with a shell-shocked vet whose idea of fun was smoking hash and catching up on years of missed intercourse. Instead, she threw herself into her work, easy enough to do since she'd been waiting to be a speech therapist all of her life.

Easy until she realized that speech impediments were the least of the problems of the children from Cleveland's poorest neighborhoods. The kids, sent to her to reverse the damage of cleft palates and lisps, walked into her classroom in shoes without soles. They had no books, no pencils, and, sometimes, no parents. It seemed almost insulting to teach "Sally sells seashells by the seashore" to children whose houses didn't have running water. Dinah would buy them pens and socks and folders and books with her own small salary, persuading the kids (and their guardians who didn't take handouts) that the gifts came from the school. During their one-on-one sessions, instead of completing vitally important diagnostic tests to be placed in a file somewhere, she held each child, silently. Words seemed a whole lot less important.

Close to two years had passed since Dinah had seen Dick when she heard, in passing from an old acquaintance, that he was teaching in the same school system, at Patrick Henry Junior High. Her curiosity was instantly piqued. Was he dating? Was he still wearing halter tops in his bedroom? Was he still the funniest guy in the world? Had he found a new confidante? Since their breakup years before, she professed not to think about him at all—and mostly that was true. But then, she'd be walking down the street when curiosity seized her. She would stare at the nearest pay phone, as her heart rate crept slowly upward, and convince herself not to call the son of a bitch. Besides, with the war and all, she told herself, he was probably drinking a cold beer somewhere in Canada already.

A few weeks later, though, she'd wonder again. Was he happy? Did he think about her? Was he apologetic about what a jerk he'd been? Had he learned his lesson? Now that she knew he was definitely right in town, she didn't hesitate. She looked up his phone number and, barely even noticing it was one in the morning on a school night, made the call.

"Hello, Dick? It's Dinah . . . Schultz."

"Holy shit," he blurted, before stuttering a more polite hello.

"I'm so glad you called," he said, trying to sound pleasant but cool.

Dinah twisted the phone cord around her index finger, watching the tip deepen into a purplish red. He was talking about how he'd graduated, barely; what he thought of teaching, which wasn't much.

"What have you been up to, Dinah?"

"Hmm? Besides cutting off my circulation?" She laughed too loudly, and unwound the cord from her finger. She told him how she had dated another teacher, and that it hadn't worked out. She mentioned that her dad had been glum about the war and the slow disintegration of the party (a number of comrades had squeezed him for money).

"Some Communists they turned out to be, huh? Dad's been in such a funk. He's been playing a lot of tennis at the rec center and reading his *Playboys*."

"And Glenn?"

"I don't think *she* knows how she is."

Dick told Dinah about dating women (only two; but he said

there were five, and implied that he'd had sex with at least one of them). He mentioned each of his new friends from work one by one, so she could be impressed by the sheer volume of proper names. He thought he sounded happy. Of course, he was talking to her.

"You know, you sound really good, Dick. I'm glad."

"Yeah, well, we all grow up eventually. Those of us with arrested development included. I have to say, I never thought I'd hear from you again."

"I never thought you'd hear from me again either."

Dinah lay back on her bed, staring at the ceiling fixture as Dick bitched about the student who, when asked to diagram a sentence, drew a switchblade instead. Dick had thrown him against a wall and held him down until security got there. He really had his stuff together, she thought. He had friends. He had had sex. He had stopped writing bad poetry. He said he wore suits, like a grown-up guy. She was dumbfounded. She blushed in a manner befitting a smitten teenage girl—although she had never actually been one.

They spoke until four in the morning. Right before they hung up, Dick whispered, "You've made my day." It was the first of many understatements to come.

One year later, Dick was pronounced a man, and Dinah became a wife. Their roles now cleanly demarcated, typed on official-looking paper, they confidently strode into their reception and into the future.

Given the on-again, off-again nature of their relationship, this event would seem fated had it been a tad more romantic. Their journey from "hello again" to "I do" was brief because Glenn didn't approve of Dinah sleeping over at Dick's apartment without legal sanction. (Not that the lengthy estrangement had breathed some sort of excitement into their love life; Dinah was simply too lazy to trek back to her parents' house at the end of a long evening. It was easier to keep her toiletries in one location.) Although Glenn wouldn't contradict her husband's rhetorical theories on the subject of free love, when it came to the very unabstract concept of her daughter living in sin, Glenn was willing to make her opinions known. William, like a college boy upset when his favorite underground band scores a top ten hit and becomes all the rage, was himself growing detached from his various movements since revolutionary thought had hit the cover of *Newsweek*. Now he rarely contradicted Glenn's more conservative views, voiced by her to a degree she never would have dared back in the less-enlightened fifties.

Fortunately, Dinah was ready for twelve sets of Corning Ware. She knew a marriage with Dick wouldn't be based on a passionate, searing love, the kind written about by ancient bards and latter-day coffeehouse folk singers, and she considered that a plus. How many girlfriends had she watched get married to their so-called soul mates, only to have their passion burn out shortly after the paper anniversary? At twenty-one, those girls had subscribed to *Bride's*, they had spent a ton of their parents' money on princess-bodiced wedding gowns and three-tiered fondant cakes. And by twenty-three, they had traded their bridal magazine subscriptions for the ones that told them how to keep romance alive. Dick and Dinah were good friends, and lovers often enough. That is to say, he proffered occasional sex; she agreed to watch him cross-dress. It was a fair transaction, and not Dinah's main concern, anyway. She wanted him to be nice.

Dinah brought up the subject of marriage with Dick while they were watching TV. They discussed it during the commercial breaks, and agreed by the closing credits.

The honeymoon was short. The honeymoon period was just slightly longer.

Within weeks of the wedding, Dick became totally inarticulate. Dinah had learned that muteness tended to come right before some mention of dressing like a girl. Sure enough, Dick started saying he wanted to go to "this place."

"Give me more, hon," Dinah pleaded.

"A kind of place where, you know, people do that thing I do . . ." Dick looked helpless to finish his sentence.

Dinah, still feeling her way through this wife thing, didn't want to be unsupportive. She occasionally picked up one of her students' phrases to make them feel more comfortable with her, and so now she compassionately echoed Dick's stutter-stop speech.

"Well, sure, no problem," she said, cautiously. "Let's go to the next whatever—thing."

It took her five minutes before she got nervous, wondering what she had agreed to do.

The cross-dressing organization, a P.O. Box type of endeavor, met in random hotel suites across the city. The first meeting Dick and Dinah planned to attend was in a fourth-floor suite at a motel near the airport. The motel was big enough that anyone striding in and heading for the elevator with a duffel bag in one hand and his wife's clammy fist in the other was unlikely to be questioned by the reception desk as to whether they needed any assistance. It was perfect.

Waiting in the mirrored elevator, examining the sign for the complimentary breakfast buffet, Dick and Dinah looked as flushed and bewildered as two teenagers about to sneak a rendezvous. But as they were about to learn, clandestine is not the same as risqué—or even interesting.

The suite had been only slightly modified. In addition to the sofa and armchair set upholstered, apparently, in hair shirt, several club members had brought in extra lawn chairs. There were several trays of brick cheese and crackers, a lump of brownish grapes, and a few bottles of Coke. The men, mostly in dresses, were sitting in silence, stabbing their cheese cubes with toothpicks and looking at each other blankly. The women, mostly in slacks, stood in the kitchenette chopping celery sticks, spooning peanut butter into a glass bowl, and discussing the weather. Dinah thought she would bust a gut. Never, in her mildest dreams, had she imagined that the perverted, sexually deviant world of men in dresses would turn out to be more milquetoast than a Kentucky church social. There you at least had booze.

Trembling with anticipation, Dick darted into the rest room and began to dress from the bottom up. Panties, then stockings, then support bra, then socks, then that gorgeous paisley satin wrap dress he had ordered for Dinah but—oops!—was about four sizes too small. There was a sign tacked up just next to the mirror that read in capital letters: "Girls: NO FOUNDATION OR LIPSTICK ON THE TOWELS. WE PAY FOR THESE!!! USE THE PA-PER TOWEL ROLL ON THE SINK. THAT'S WHAT IT'S THERE FOR! ALSO PUT THE SEAT DOWN. IT UPSETS THE OTHER LADIES."

When Dick came out of the bathroom, the other men stared, astonished. He was gorgeous, model-slender and taut, with ele-gant cheekbones and real eyelashes longer than most of the fakes. Except for the beard, which he had chosen to cake over with foundation, he looked pretty foxy. Even Dinah had to think so— suddenly feeling a little dumpy herself in her old pantsuit and sneakers—although she didn't know how she felt about having a husband who made such a beautiful female. He looked more poised and comfortable in heels and hose than she ever felt, to be sure. Was that because it was a fun, occasional thing—like dressing up on Halloween—or because he belonged in that get-up? She brushed the thought away, and tried to appreciate the awestruck compliments from the other wives. "Your husband looks stunning," one said. "I'd love to know where he shops."

Not long into the meeting, one of the the most famous cross-dressers in America happened by. Virginia Prince was one of the pioneers on the talk-show circuit, in town to talk about her life as a gal on the *Alan Douglas Show*. Although she lived as a woman, she did little to hide the fact that she still had all her original plumbing in place. She came in the room without knocking, grabbed herself a napkin's worth of hors d'oeuvres, and flopped into a chair, legs fanned in a perfectly unladylike "**V**."

"Gals," she barked, "what's wrong with you? Your better halves are in the kitchen fixing the food while you all are in here sitting around doing nothing? *What kinda women are you?*" There was a long, uncomfortable pause. And then, as though catapulted from industrial springs, all the men—Dick included—shot across the room, nearly colliding at the entrance of the kitchen, and proceeded to elbow and cut in front of each other for the opportunity to carry a tray or utensil into the main room.

One wife tugged on Dinah's sleeve. "I could use Virginia back at home," she whispered. "Michael never sets the table. He hates to be domestic." She smirked. "Well, he likes the aprons." Dinah watched Dick—no better at maneuvering for a tray to carry than he had been at any sport requiring eye-hand coordination—aimlessly circle the furniture in the next room. He was carrying one chip.

They left two hours later, and Dinah could barely restrain herself until they got back in the car. "I'm sorry, I'm sorry," she choked, grasping the dashboard for balance. Her apologies were unnecessary; her husband, too, was in hysterics.

"My dear wife! Welcome to my sick, seamy underworld." Dick laughed. "Although I have to say, that was some serious spinach dip."

Ella Mae was thrilled about her son's new marriage. *It's so exciting! What a wonderful life the two young lovebirds will have together!* She wrote that on their wedding card. She was supportive. No one could deny it.

At Dick and Dinah's first anniversary party, held with friends and family in their one-bedroom apartment, Ella Mae made a gesture toward her daughter-in-law. She pulled her away from the fondue pot in the dining room to suggest they spend some quality "girl time" together.

"Well, okay," Dinah said, as she blew on a cube of bread lacquered in hot cheese. "Would you like to go see a movie or something?"

Ella Mae shook her head, and sipped her Canadian Club and water. "No, no, nothing like that. You know I prefer the theater. I was thinking we could go on a diet together."

"A diet?" Dinah repeated. She subtly sucked in her tummy.

"To wear the latest fashions, you pretty much have to eat like a bird, don't you?" Ella Mae laughed. She let her eyes graze on Dinah's middle. "I thought it would be fun. Men love that lean look." Ella Mae shot a dazzling smile across the room at her new beau, a consultant of some sort she had met through her new marketing job at Stouffer's Frozen Foods. He was stuffing his face with a hunk of Dinah's apple pie. "What do you say?"

Dinah put down her cocktail napkin and skewer. It was safer that way. "Um, Ella Mae, actually, I'd been meaning to ask you for some time now. How's your hearing aid? Is it working okay? I hope your hearing's not getting worse. The doctors are watching it, right?"

"Oh my goodness!" Ella Mae squealed. "I forgot! Dick, Dick, come over here." Her son warily walked to the other side of the dining room and cast a quizzical glance at his wife. "The doctor told me last week that it looks very unlikely that I will lose my hearing completely at any point now. He said if it was going to happen, it probably would have already. So I'll just have to wear this old thing." She stuck her finger in her ear. "Dinah," she smiled, "thanks so much for asking."

At the end of the evening, after proposing another toast to the "couple of the hour," Ella Mae leaned over, and said, "So the Weight Watchers group meets Monday nights at seven sharp. I'll call with details. Next time I'll bring the cottage cheese!"

Dick hugged his mother good-bye and turned to Dinah. "She wants you to go on a diet?"

Dinah pulled a cigarette out from the pocket of her sweater vest. "I need a light," she muttered. "Yeah, a diet. I'm going to eat a lot of cottage cheese. It's going to turn you on."

Dick shifted his weight back and forth. "You look fine," he growled, no doubt attempting to be warmly supportive.

Dinah lit her cigarette and exhaled. "Don't worry about it, hon," she said. "I can handle Ella Mae." Besides, she was beginning to think that maybe losing a few pounds *would* make a difference.

Over the next year, Dick dragged Dinah to another cross-dressing meeting or two, with the vague hope that being around other crossdressers would make him drop the whole damn obsession for a while. However, except for the clothes, most of these guys were not like him in the slightest. Some were old; others were boring; a few claimed to hate reading; another few disparaged "real" women. And only a few of them looked half as womanly as Dick. He was unlikely to pick up beauty tips from Thomasina (Thomas), the accountant with halitosis who streaked lipstick all the way to her earlobes on both sides in a style more befitting Maori tribal markings; or big-and-tall women's retail suggestions from Esmeralda (Vince), a former college quarterback who never remembered to zip up her dresses (you could always see the tattoo of Betty Boop on her back, which ruined the illusion of timeless elegance).

Dinah didn't want to go back to the club, but it got the interest out of his system for a while. For a few weeks afterward, he'd let her snuggle up and kiss him for a while without clearing his throat and breaking the mood by saying, "Now I don't want to break the mood, but would you mind if I . . . ?"

Fixing a person is like fixing a car, she thought. You learn everything about the car; everything about where it's been driven, the manufacturer, the previous repair history, and, of course, whether other cars have this problem. Then you get under the hood and work and work and work until it's all right.

After six months, Dinah was a size ten, the smallest she had been since ninth grade. Dick hadn't noticed, even when she pointedly called his attention to it by swirling around the living room in tight-fitting dresses and asking how she looked. He always nodded, and said fine, in a detached way as though she was asking him what he thought of a new set of place mats. She tossed her cartons of cottage cheese, and started sautéeing with lard again. No one should have to see her mother-in-law once a week anyway, she reasoned.

As for Dick, his mind was elsewhere—Coventry Road in Cleveland Heights, to be exact, the location of the theater he had joined. It was a new kind of liberation to be immersed in a hobby he could discuss in polite company.

Dick had only been involved for a short time with Dobama Theater when, to his and his wife's mutual astonishment, they had discovered that when he was in a play, he didn't need to cross-dress. They never discussed it, but both noticed the coincidence. He never dressed in his female apparel during the season; that desire only resurrected itself during the summer break. It was a relief to Dinah, who figured a fetish couldn't be all that big a deal if it could be relegated to only three months a year.

They didn't quite comprehend why being in plays worked so well when nothing else had. Was he addicted to being in costume? Dinah wondered. Or addicted to being someone else entirely? It occurred to her that just being *with* Dick could be tiring; therefore, maybe being Dick himself was so exhausting that, from time to time, he needed to get away.

In late October of 1971, Dinah missed her period. It seemed unlikely. There had been only one sexual interlude that she could recall in the recent past, and she was on the pill. Dinah had a day off from school, and was about to light up a cigarette when the doctor's office called.

"Congratulations, Mrs. Howey!" the doctor chortled. Dinah quickly snuffed her cigarette, and placed her hand to her stomach. "Unbelievable," she murmured.

Dinah spent the rest of the afternoon in a delirious daze, imagining small yellow booties, a hand-me-down crib from one of her cousins, and maybe a mural on the wall to trigger the baby's nascent creativity. William and Glenn would be so excited; Ella Mae would be pleased. Hopefully the baby would have Dick's vision; she herself couldn't make out the lamp on the bedside table without glasses. And his sense of humor. But he, she, it should have Dinah's laugh; hers was a little less labored than Dick's. And Dinah's dainty pug nose; God forbid any baby be burdened with Ella Mae's honker.

She wasn't sure how to tell Dick the news. He had been having a crappy week at work; rehearsals for his latest play were on hiatus; and he still hadn't kicked a bit of a hangover from a late night at the Pepper Pot with a few history teachers. So when he barreled in the door that night, sopping wet from a hailstorm, she simply blurted it.

"I'm pregnant," she said, barely containing the mirth that had been percolating inside her since the doctor's call.

Dick looked stricken. He dropped his briefcase on the kitchen floor.

"Whose is it?" he asked, with some apprehension, as though he really didn't know.

Dinah opened her mouth to respond, but her voice caught and she ran into the bedroom. She spent the evening in there, curled around a pillow and whispering to her stomach.

"Everything's going to be all right, baby," she said. "Mommy loves you. And Daddy—he will, too."

❖   ❖   ❖

Dick brought his wife a dozen roses the next evening after dinner. He apologized for his horrible, inappropriate question and swore he was preoccupied because the principal had yelled at him that afternoon for requesting new textbooks while there was some binding left on the old ones. It wasn't true, though. He couldn't believe that he had functional sperm.

However, after realizing that one of his millions had come through, undeterred by the dearth of opportunity and infrequency of Dinah's ovulation, he started to come around.

During breaks, he read up on pregnancy in the school library. He read about preeclampsia. Down's syndrome. Emergency C-sections. Mental retardation. He read about babies born without mental faculties or limbs, although, to his credit, he didn't share his macabre reading material with his wife, who was looking more and more like a satisfied Buddha every day. Besides having a natural inclination toward nihilism and morbidity, he couldn't believe that his genetic material wasn't corrupt on some level. Somehow, he was certain, the baby wouldn't turn out okay. But he didn't want Dinah to know that.

From her perspective, after his initial panic attack had subsided, he'd made every effort to be a part of the pregnancy. He bought a small stuffed Scottish terrier whom they dubbed Fitzgerald to speak to Dinah's growing abdomen. Fitzgerald, an erudite pup, hated Nixon and liked to recite Woody Allen. Dinah loved those lazy evenings, propped up on a pillow on the couch as Dick crouched on the floor speaking to her stomach through Fitzgerald. She was so mellow that Ella Mae saying that they'd have to get "back on the diet wagon after baby comes" didn't faze her. She patted her mother-in-law on the hand and smiled like she owned the world.

Dinah did become inflamed when the school administration informed her that they'd noticed she had put on a little weight— "a little baby weight!" they had chuckled—and told her to gather her things. But otherwise, times had never been better. Being the best wife she could be was an uphill challenge with a quirky and unpredictable husband. Being a supermother had to be easier.

I was born on July 6, 1972, after a difficult labor during which my mother was put to sleep and my father had his wildest dreams realized.

Groggy from the drugs she hadn't expected to need, my mother kissed me, said, "It's a girl!" and fell back asleep for several hours. My father did a quiet happy dance in the waiting room, having learned I was not only healthy but also *female*. He'd spent eight months of the pregnancy utterly terrified that he was going to have to suffer vicariously through boyhood again.

While my mother slept, my father sat with me in a rocker next to her hospital bed, and there made us both a solemn vow. "I'm going to be the best dad ever," he said. "Forget me—all my bull— stuff. You are going to be the be-all, end-all, okay? I'm going to take you to Girl Scouts, and buy you dolls and tea sets, and give your boyfriends dirty looks. I can do it. You wait and see."

PART TWO

Fabrications

FOURTEEN

Clothes Lines

What a strange power there is in clothing.
   —Isaac Bashevis Singer, "Yentl the Yeshiva Boy"

I had a conversation with a friend several years ago in which she, sipping her vanilla latté thoughtfully in a Brooklyn café, asked me why someone—meaning my father—would risk it all to wear a dress.

"I don't get that," she explained to me. "I'd give anything not to wear girly crap again."

She was wearing Birkenstock sandals, a toe ring, khaki drawstring pants, a ripped high-school-band T-shirt, long dangly earrings, and a temporary tattoo of a mermaid. She had just finished telling me how she had recently been a bridesmaid and forced to wear a drop-waisted sea-green monstrosity.

"I looked like a Life Saver," she spat. "The nylons were so disgusting. I haven't worn those since high school when I had Catholic school uniforms."

"I'm sure you looked fine." I laughed. "But yeah, it doesn't sound like your fashion sense."

My friend was dumbfounded. "*Fashion* sense," she repeated, disdainfully, as though the words singed her tongue. "I wear what's comfortable. I'm not into clothes at all. I hate shopping! I'm just—*me*."

❋   ❋   ❋

I, too, hate fashion.

By mere dint of working in the magazine industry, brand names have imprinted themselves in my consciousness—often against my will. I don't try to learn them, but they're everywhere. In captions: "Gwyneth Paltrow wears Pucci on the red carpet." In credits: "Shirt, Tommy Hilfiger, $75, Macy's West." In the hallways: "Darling, you look smashing in that Armani."

It's not easy to get away from fashion during after hours either. If I walk down Fifth Avenue after work, I'll pass dozens of stores that terrify me: barren white rooms, embarrassingly immense, housing twelve black dresses, three cashmere sweaters, and two angular saleswomen in dry-clean-only who seem pleased enough until they see you peering—at which point they try to freeze you cryogenically with a stare. They may clothe themselves at sample sales and charge their gym memberships to the parental units, but they would rather have zero commission than one that comes from you. (Tangentially, this is one of the only truisms of the movie *Pretty Woman* that is borne out in the real world.)

In an effort to shrug off their disdain, once I get home, my husband and I will mock the shallow insouciance of the *fashionistas* who still shop 'til they drop. We'll denounce fashion, and then plop down on the living-room sofa in our no-name sweatpants and T-shirts. We feel more comfortable in the slouchy clothes that we have chosen than in our own naked, imperfect bodies.

Stories are yarns, or tapestries. We weave them, thread them through, watch them unfold. Fictions are woven, fabricated, embroidered on the truth. Eventually, they unravel. Clothes make the man. When we feel vulnerable, we feel naked, stripped down, undressed. This isn't a random exercise in metaphor: This is how we see clothing—as part of our history, our identities.

＊   ＊   ＊

This is the analogy my father uses: Imagine that you have to wear a polka-dotted dress with a fluffy white cotton pinafore and a large Minnie Mouse bow in your hair. Pretend that it isn't Halloween, but that everyone seems to think you look fine in that getup. Even if everyone regarded you normally, would you feel okay in that outfit? Or would you be dying to get out of it—no matter what?

When I was eighteen, I tried to write an essay—the first of many efforts, later aborted—about my father's transgenderism. I wrote that "my father could have made a statement against the materialist culture that tells us we are what we wear. Instead of standing up against this tyranny, my father sat down." I was eighteen. Passionate, political, wrong.

Being a transsexual isn't just about clothes, any more than being a woman is. However, that doesn't mean clothes are meaningless either. Clothes are a representation of identity—for men, women, everyone in between.

And, for what it's worth, my father didn't go through "all that" to wear a dress. She prefers suede blazers with pleated slacks.

FIFTEEN

Phasing Out

In the late summer of 1986, we moved into a pea green split-level behemoth that my mother dubbed "The Big House." This nickname referred only to the fact that the house was indeed *big*, not as a commentary on our increasing insularity—although that double meaning would have been apt had we been smart enough to think of it.

The house was on a daintily named side street just east of the Strawberry Lane cul-de-sac, in the exurb Moreland Hills—best known as the birthplace of President James Garfield and home to the highest per capita concentration of trophy wife–owned novelty sock shops. Moreland Hills was new money, and although my father's salary was paltry by local standards, we did feel almost rich. Our new digs had it all: fourteen rooms, a wet bar, a hot tub, an acre-plus of wooded tranquillity, a downstairs bathroom with two sinks in case you wanted company while hand-washing. I hated and loved it.

In the negative column was the house's isolated location. Endless walls of windows overlooking a pitch-black woods, and gratuitous nature noises made the house seem like a template for a horror-movie set. I had not yet battled back my childhood paranoia enough to withstand such terrifying things as deer hooves and falling branches.

In the plus column, there were doorknob locks everywhere,

meaning the chance of getting caught with pants down (and pil-
fered panties on) was slim. The neighbors were far, far away,
meaning we could live without the threat of chitchat or incon-
venient ingredient requests. The house was a haven for those of
us seeking confinement: me in my bedroom, Dad in the den,
Mom shuttling between the two of us in her usual social-worker
capacity.

Like all teenagers, my room was a combination altar/refuge/
bordello. I decorated it in stark grey, red, and black since I had
recently decided that pink was too junior high, and had gotten
the notion that rooms should "mature" every year, much like a
cheese. In preparation for the impending best years of my life, I
tossed the stuffed animals (particularly the Garfield with that
menacing Ted Bundy smile), a quartet of gift shop–purchased
snow globes, my stickers, and everything else that smacked of
childhood. I replaced them with much more adult items, like
framed mirrors with beveled images of teen idols won at Guess
My Weight? amusement-park booths and a collection of colored
shoelaces which, to my mind, formed a gorgeous mosaic. It probably made for an excellent sociological portrait of the middle-class
teen girl in a transitional phase.

My mother had picked up the habit of using that word, "phase,"
to refer to my recent trend of doing things she didn't like: talking
back, wearing purple mascara, "forgetting" to clear out the dishwasher. In the past, she had always used "phase" to describe Dad's
habit of immersing himself in something, then dropping it altogether—like acting, drinking, bowling, being a snot. I was not
pleased at the comparison.

"You're a teenage girl," she helpfully explained. We were driving to Grandma Schultz's house to pick her up for a doctor's
appointment. More and more, all our important talks—about sex,
death, the fact that the cats were pooping in the kitchen because
the litter box was so full—were occurring in vehicles, where I was
a captive audience and therefore forced to pay at least minimal

attention. "It's really hard and confusing because you don't know who you are. You're going to keep changing all the time."

"I know who I am. You don't like it because I have my own mind now. And," I added, thrilled with my own brilliant insight, "you always said Dad goes through phases, and he's not a teenager, is he?" Satisfied, I kicked my shoes up on the dashboard.

"I wouldn't bet you money on that," she said. "And take your feet off the dashboard."

Regardless of what my mother thought, I knew I was finding myself, which is what teenagers did. I was perfectly on schedule. My father, on the other hand, was not supposed to be self-absorbed, not at his age.

Over the summer, painfully aware I wouldn't be locking lips with any real boys, I locked myself in my room with borrowed lingerie and dirty music as often as I could get away with it. I wouldn't masturbate, technically, but not for lack of trying. Always the dutiful pupil, I followed the diagrams in various books around the house. I didn't think this type of thing should be improvised. I moved my hands around down there, but it didn't feel half as good as back in fourth grade when we climbed the knotted ropes in gym class and I got so happy swinging back and forth that I thought I would pass out. Instead of masturbation—which was "healthy," "normal," and not at all related to vision impairment—I thought of my little stealthy dress-up games as pantomimed fantasy, in which costumes and an imagined audience were the best parts.

The normal activities of the day (breakfast, calling friends, reading) lacked profundity. I lived for the heightened drama of my time alone, when I could stare pensively out the window and gaze longingly while a power ballad throbbed in the background, as though I was in a music video. Although, tragically, I never marketed the idea, I liked to pretend I was being filmed for broadcast on a very special network dedicated to me. Boys who had rejected me, and girls who hadn't invited me to sit at their lunch tables would watch in awe, shocked at how horribly they had neglected to notice my obvious charisma and white-hot sensuality.

Now that my mother had exempted herself from being a spectator, Dad generally waited until he was alone to dress up. He'd wait for the telltale turn of the lock and the car backing out of the drive. He'd fidget for a few minutes until it was clear no one had forgotten a purse before scrambling up to the master bedroom. Nylons would be plucked from their plastic egg. He'd shimmy into a silk cocktail dress. A frilly apron. Whatever was clean.

If it was clear that Mom or I were on a short jaunt, he'd stay in the bedroom. If he was especially confident that we—but especially *I*—would be gone for a long time, he would walk around the house, feeling incredibly daring every time he walked past a window and then stupid and ridiculous when he dropped to the floor at the first sound of the mail carrier or a distant lawn mower.

He engaged in quiet activities: He read or washed the dishes. He longed to vacuum, but the whir of the motor would have drowned out important incoming warning noises. On some level, then, he was never really alone. He later told me that he was always conscious of my existence in the world, playing and replaying themes in his mind of What I Would Think of Him, and How He Would Warp Me. He was also aware of my mother, tolerant but frustrated, and reaching a limit. To a lesser extent, he knew that he was pushing himself further, as though to precipitate some sort of break.

He wasn't quite careful enough. A few times, my mom managed to walk in on him. Once he was meandering through the backyard in a wrap dress and pumps, admiring the rows of pink cabbage roses in the backyard, and had forgotten to tote an emergency change of clothes and a washcloth along with him. Another time she caught him lost in reverie, sipping a glass of Merlot at the wet bar in the basement, his stockinged legs seductively crossed beneath a chiffon gown and whispering to no one. Bacall trading luscious innuendos in her smoky, basso profundo with an imaginary Bogie.

"You can't do this, Dick," she said, each of the few times she encountered him dressed outside of the master bedroom. "What if I was Noelle, and I saw you? You'll traumatize her." My mother was frightened. Since moving into the big house, the spaciousness of the house and seemingly private woods had seemed to give Dad permission to act out more boldly than he had ever dared back in University Heights. "She can't find out like this," my mother said, in a tone approaching panic. "She'll never get over it."

My mother may have been right. When I was twenty-five, I met Jasmine, another daughter of a transsexual. Her father did not come out. He was found out. There's a big difference. Jasmine came home one day from school to find him trussed up like a strumpet in tip-to-toe lingerie, preening before a video camera right there in front of the living room. He didn't notice her until the screaming started. He apologized, but a few days later—now that the big secret was out—asked Jasmine if she wanted to hit the makeup counter at the mall. Her dad wanted to get a makeover to celebrate being out. She has spoken to him (or her) about five times since.

When I am complimented on my tolerance and boundless understanding by people, they forget that I was gently ushered into the truth. Jasmine was pushed.

I was in too-large patent leather pumps and a teddy, entertaining an invisible, dashingly handsome JV soccer player when Grandma H. called. I plopped down Indian-style on my bed, weirdly mortified that I was speaking while in bad-girl skivvies to my grandmother—as though she could catch my licentious broadcast on the Telepathic Network.

She requested I join her to see a performance of *Annie*. I refused. She cleared her throat and cheerfully tried to change the subject. I made it clear I wasn't feeling very pleasant. We hung up. It wasn't a unique conversation for us by that point in time.

In loyalty to my mother, I no longer wanted to associate with my grandmother. I refused her invitations to theater productions, her house, seafood restaurants. I was not very nice about it, and not sorry either. I thought feeling bad about mistreating Grandma H. would have negated the whole point of the exercise.

That said, this deference to Mom went only as far as shutting my grandma out of my life. It did not include, say, being nice to my mother, who I had recently discovered was quite stupid. I realize this is paradoxical, but I was fourteen, after all.

"Noelle, can you wash the dishes before I get home?"

"God! Does everything have to revolve around, like, cleaning things?"

"Noelle, can you answer any question without saying no?"

"Uh . . . yes. See, I just did!"

"Noelle, do I have to be wrong all the time?"

"Like what am I supposed to do, Mom? Like not tell you when you don't know what's going on? Like you're Mussolini the big fascist and I have no freedom of speech?"

After she threw her hands up in disgust, I would storm to my room, slam the door, write I HATE YOU in gigantic block letters over and over on a sheet of paper for fifteen minutes, exit my room, find my mother, burst into tears, throw my arms around her, apologize profusely for being such a bratty awful kid who didn't deserve such a wonderful parent when there were people starving in other places, and ask what we were having for dinner.

I had attained the dream I had cherished since I was a preteen: I had become adolescent.

☼   ☼   ☼

My parents' marriage turned seventeen that summer. Dad marked the occasion by extending an invitation to my mother for a night on the town and handing her a box full of long-stemmed red roses. As usual, he had planned his grand gesture down to the last flourish, and then made the mistake of ad libbing.

"Are you going to wear that?" he asked my mother, with roses cradled in her arms. She was dressed in a sparkly purple dress, bought off the rack that afternoon at Higbee's Department Store. She hated shopping, but had left early from work to try on several different dresses in the hopes of finding something a little more snazzy than the stuff she reserved for weddings and funerals.

"It's new," she said reflexively. "You don't like it?"

"No, no," he shrugged. "It just seemed a little fancy for the evening."

"You're wearing a sports coat," she pointed out.

He put the roses down on the counter. "Look," he said defensively, "if you don't want to go, we won't go."

They left in silence a few minutes later and talked only of work and Ronald Reagan's unfortunate foreign policy initiatives until dessert. Over chocolate mousse, she said, "You know, we really have to do something."

He said, "I know."

She said, "I really do love you."

"Same here," he replied.

That night, they slept in spoons for the first time in months—first, him with his body curled around hers, and then vice versa. In years past, my mother would have woken up the next morning with a renewed sense of optimism and perhaps would have made some pancakes for all of us. Dad, feeling blessedly normal, might have asked me to go on a rare bike ride (I can recall two), or a trip to the used record store.

Instead, at 9 A.M. the next morning, my father made an appointment with Danielle Smith, a psychologist. My mother went to work on the books for my father's freelance writing business, hoping to find as many tax loopholes as possible. They assumed I would be going to an expensive college in a few years, and you never knew what could happen between now and then.

I was intimidated by my new high school. It was right out of a John Hughes movie, all fancy-pants with lots of natural wood, carpeted hallways, and a Lite Rock radio station playing on the P.A. system in between periods. My old school was half-black and half-white, one-third well-to-do and one-third welfare. A handful would end up at Harvard, another smattering would become lifers in the state pen. On the other hand, this new institution of learning, Orange High School, boasted a 80–90 percent white, wealthy student body. The vast majority were destined to be overpaid paper pushers like their parents. The parking lot was packed with Alfa Romeos and BMWs that were once sixteenth-birthday presents. I didn't much look forward to driving age and parking the vehicle I inherited there; my mother drove a Toyota.

Fortunately, my latest makeover idea was not reliant on having a large disposable income, thanks to a summer filled with beauty disappointments. I had exfoliated my elbows and knees once a week since June, sloughing every dead epidermal cell I could locate, and I looked no better at all. My period had finally come, not a moment too soon, and my breasts had not swelled even as far as "Stage 2: Budding" in the encyclopedia's breast growth chart. Therefore, I had given up, for the time being at least, on the whole cosmetic aspect of transformation. The articles section of *Seventeen* magazine had been urging me for ages to be myself, and get involved, and show people who I was. Thus, I decided to achieve startling high-school success by *being good at everything*.

It had been done. I had read about Renaissance men: men of dark good looks (obviously, I had never seen portraits of Leonardo da Vinci), brilliance and wit, with extraordinary scientific and artistic and athletic skill. I would be a Renaissance girl, and impress everyone into liking me. This seemed like a good plan for a school where SATs determined the hierarchy of the cafeteria lunch tables, where kids in five Advanced Placement classes disdained those in only four.

In my quest to be well-rounded, my new ideal, I immediately signed up with the cross-country team. Within a few weeks, I had broken a long-standing athletic record by achieving the distinction of running the slowest time in a countywide girls' track meet since the advent of Title IX. I left the team about two days later, after they grudgingly handed me a team T-shirt that would at least make me appear athletic to strangers from other neighborhoods. Weeks later I joined the swim team, but quit almost immediately. I couldn't get over my fear of diving in headfirst, which the coach claimed was a nonoptional skill.

However, I hadn't yet given up my new goal of being all things to all people: Now that team practice was not taking up all my valuable 3–6 P.M. hours, I joined Amnesty International, the debate team, the science olympiad, the literary magazine, and the language club. Since each group only tended to meet once a month and do little but vote on officers and eat pizza, this seemed like the easiest possible way to meet my own personal diversity quota.

Danielle Smith, Ph.D., a highly recommended woman who was always being interviewed on some morning talk show, was the first therapist my father had spoken to since his days with Dr. Freudian Archetype. Dad was still highly skeptical about therapy, and entered the doctor's office, a room decorated in only the gentlest hues of the color wheel, with trepidation approaching full-on catatonia.

He recalls little of the first meeting except scenery: the pink clock on the end table, what seemed like a dozen mauve pillows on the sofa, Dr. Smith's mop of golden curls. And a few spare moments: pulling his wedding ring on and off, a nervous habit he'd acquired; telling the doctor that there was nothing wrong; using the term "fuckin' A" twice, like a street hood, except he wasn't talking about a souped-up Harley but rather the feeling of dressing like a girl.

My mother wasn't doing so well. Stress-induced eczema covered her hands like a thin pair of gloves. She was getting grey, here and there, enough to be almost noticeable to other people. She had the dark circles. Now that I had become terrible company, she spent most nights alone in her bedroom, reading about imaginary love affairs. She was growing old too early.

She decided to schedule her own therapy sessions with Dr. Smith, whom she distrusted on sight. In her royal blue suit and curly blond locks, the doctor embodied all the physical traits my father seemed to admire in women. My mother—although she professed not to be biased at all—tended to prefer neutral, earth-tone, Earth Goddess types of women.

Dr. Smith won her over nonetheless, simply by telling her that everything was exactly as bad as she feared it was.

"You've got a big problem," Dr. Smith said, with little ceremony. "And you can help solve it."

Mom abruptly stopped telling her life story, and wept. After being shooed home by no fewer than three mental-health experts over the course of seventeen years, a medical professional—an *-ologist*—had finally given her a diagnosis. Everything was broken, meaning everything could somehow be fixed.

In October, we decided to take a vacation over a long weekend to New York City. The timing was perfectly horrible, except for the fact that we had tickets to *Cats*, which was a pretty tough ticket to come by.

I'm sure we did about fifty other things first, but in my memory, we went directly to Bloomingdale's, which had gained an enormous mystique in my mind from its frequent mention in magazine fashion credits. Once inside, it looked like a department store, and not even a very exciting one, but I rushed undeterred toward the Juniors section to purchase as many things with the word "Bloomie's" on it as possible.

My mother slunk behind my father, looking a little haunted, as he urged her to go buy herself something. I didn't notice how she blanched each time he nudged her along, when he waved his hand upstairs toward the designer women's sections and said he'd love to see her try something on. I thought he was being nice for a change, making an effort. Mom didn't budge, though. She seemed frozen in the aisle, under the track lights, in front of a barrel of the pre-Christmas sale ornaments.

She started to shake, violently. "Mom," I cried, running over to her and forgetting entirely about the attitude problem I worked so hard to maintain. "Are you all right?"

"I've got to get out of here," she said, through clenched teeth.

"What on earth . . . ?" Dad scoffed.

"I'm, um, feeling claustrophobic," she whispered. She steadied herself on the ornaments. Her eyes couldn't focus on me, even though I stood right in front of her.

"We'll go," I said, slowly, like when I spoke to little kids. "Okay? Hold my hand."

My mother took my hand. Her small palm, the same size as mine, was cold as ice. I led her out of the door, with my father skulking behind in the men's section. He stopped to look at some ties, while I ushered her outside onto Lexington Avenue.

She leaned up against one of the windows in which a gaunt white mannequin was watering a pot of fake flowers with tinsel.

"Are you sure you're okay?" I asked.

"I'm fine." My mother smiled and wiped a few tears off her cheeks. She blew her nose into a spare tissue stuffed into her pocketbook. "Whew. Bet you think your mom is crazy now, huh?"

❈   ❈   ❈

When we returned from New York my mother told Dr. Smith that she had had a panic attack in the aisles of Bloomingdale's.

"Claustrophobia?" the doctor asked, quizzically, making a note on a yellow legal pad.

"I didn't want him to see me," my mother said. "I couldn't try on those clothes for him."

"Why not?"

"I'm a size sixteen. I shop in the Women's section—the one they usually stick in the basement. He wouldn't know that because we haven't shopped together since, oh gosh, I don't know when. I couldn't tell him that I'm not little enough for those designer clothes. He would have looked at me."

"Looked at you."

"In that *way,* you know, I couldn't do it. I couldn't stand to have him look at me."

"You were afraid he would call you a name, put you down."

"Not really. If he said something, I could respond. It's the saying nothing that kills me."

My mother told my father that she was going to tell me about him on a weekend mall trip. She expected him to put up a fight, balking that I was too young to be trusted with such sensitive information or that he should be there to explain more about the situation, but he said little. It was time, past time. They both knew it. There was never a question on his side, nor hers, who should be the teller of the Big Secret. He didn't know me well enough.

"Make sure she knows I love her," he said to my mother, before we left for the mall that Saturday.

"I'll try," she replied coldly.

We were gone at the mall for three hours and twenty-two minutes, according to the digital VCR clock. My father drank seven Clamatos, spent an hour trying to read one article, and paced. He didn't come to see me once I got home. He heard me run upstairs and breathed a sigh of relief from the fact that I had survived the news intact.

"How was it?" he anxiously asked my mother.

"Fine," she said, and poured herself a rum and Coke. "She'll be fine."

"Does she hate me?"

"Probably less than she did when we left here earlier." And with that, my mother put her head in her hands and wept. My father, feeling like he was the last person who should console her, backed out of the room and, seeking once again to numb himself, cocooned in the den. Just him and the recliner and the TV.

In my memory, I was told one afternoon about my father's cross-dressing, and he moved out the next day. According to the calendar and my parents' recollections, he actually packed his bags six months later. But I think my memory is on to something: Dad had left long ago.

After my mother and I returned from the mall, I purposely avoided the den, where my father was watching bowling tournaments as though this was any other day. I ran up to my bedroom and curled up in a fetal position on my bed. I recall staring at the objects in my room as though they had suddenly become foreign: the row of magazines ordered from prettiest cover model to ugliest, the box of pencil-slim tampons, piles of dirty laundry. I rocked back and forth on my bed, clutching my knees to my chest under the tent of my sweater, the way I used to do when I was little and didn't worry about stretching shirts out.

That night, I called Debbie, and we talked about our mutual crushes. I bragged about my new jeans. As I had promised my mother, I didn't say a word about my dad. I'm not sure what I would have said anyway. It's not like my father was wearing a Goldilocks costume in the living room. I had seen him walk by to go to the bathroom. He seemed exactly the same. Friends like Debbie already thought my father was a little weird—kind of sinister and creepy, the way he lurked by the television with that faraway look about him; I had no desire to make him, and myself by proximity, seem even stranger.

After a three-hour conversation, I plucked a book off my shelf that I hadn't looked at since sixth grade, when I was a big Culture Club fan. It was a paperback bio of Boy George, which seemed as close to a reference manual on this phenomenon as I was likely to find in my book collection. I read the whole thing that night, with a flashlight under the covers. I was allowed to read as late as I wanted, but I didn't want to be spotted with it in hand. It seemed like getting caught going through their underwear drawers.

Over the next few days, my mother and father both cornered me repeatedly to ask if I had any questions about cross-dressing. I said I didn't, and that was true. I wouldn't have known what to ask. The only thing I cared to know was whether they were getting divorced. My mother pretended the question was borne out of fear that my nuclear family was about to implode.

"No, no, honey, of course not. We're nowhere near that." She must have thought she was lying for my benefit, although it was really for her own. She was the only one left of the three of us who still believed—on any level—that we could be a family unit in any way other than by basic census definition.

She hugged me tightly and comforted me. Only she was the one crying.

My father approached me as well. I was sitting on my bed, painting my toenails chartreuse, when he knocked on the door in a syncopated rhythm that was supposed to make me feel like this wasn't a Heavy Talk.

"Come in," I yelled.

He sat down on the opposite end of the bed. He nervously readjusted his comb-over, and shifted in his seat. *Ha!* I thought. *Now you know what it's like to use silverware around you.*

"I thought you might want to know something about this," he said, staring at his lap. His face was cloudy white, like bad tap water. He proceeded to tell me how he had wanted to wear women's clothes since he was little, how it wasn't something he could control, how he never wanted me to know about it and so he probably pushed me away.

"Uh-huh," I said, and blew on my toes. "Well, thanks for telling me all that."

"You're sure you don't have any questions? Noelle, come on, look at me."

"Fine!" I grumbled. I looked at him. I tried to imagine him into robin's-egg blue eye shadow, rosy rouge cheeks, an evening gown. In my mind, he was the picture of what had happened to Baby Jane. He was Jack Lemmon without the wig, Ziggy Stardust with a gut, Gene Simmons without such a long tongue.

"What do you want to know? I'm open. I'm willing to talk. Anything you want to know."

Anything I wanted to know.

I wanted to know what he wore when he was alone, and whether he looked crazy, and whether he was crazy. I wanted to know what being mean had to do with wearing men's clothes. I wanted to know whether Grandma H. had done this to him by dressing him in Little Miss Muffet outfits. I wanted to know if I would wake up one day and want to wear a jockstrap. I wanted to know why he suddenly cared what I thought about things. I wanted to know why I should give a damn about him one way or another.

"I'll let you know if anything occurs to me," I said.

The secret may have been out, in a sense, but my father was no more likely to dress up with me in the house than before. It was one thing to be an aberrant abstraction. It was another thing to be freaky right there in the flesh. It was true that he engaged in dress-up more often now, sometimes two to three times a week, but only he and Dr. Smith knew that.

The only demonstrable change in my father's behavior was, predictably enough, a new phase. Seemingly overnight—or so it might appear to my mother and I, since we didn't really interact with him most evenings—he morphed into a health nut. Mueslix started appearing in the cabinet, yogurt in the fridge. A Jazzercise videotape was purchased, and it wasn't mine or my mother's.

I was not a morning person, and no matter how vain I could be when I was conscious, at 7:15 A.M. I would rather have had my perm puff like a giant laundry lint ball than miss three more minutes of post-REM. It took me a month or so before I realized that Dad, he of the grouchy hangovers of my childhood, was rising at six to aerobicize himself to "Car Wash."

He told my mother that the exercise regimen was intended as another means of protection against dying young like his father. He told the therapist that he wanted to look better in his clothes, that his legs were too lumpy, and he couldn't stand his abdominal tone. In a way, he was telling them each the same thing: He wanted to live. More often now, that sentiment was inextricably entwined with another thought, one he had suppressed since his grade-school days: He wanted to live as a girl.

One morning, standing in front of the shaving mirror in the bathroom, with an electric razor in one hand and a can of shaving cream in the other, my father thought, "Maybe I shouldn't even be a man at all. Maybe I'm really a woman." It took him a second to realize he had actually spoken.

The words should have been sucked back into his mouth, never been said or even pondered. They should have been framed. It was a perfect, and perfectly horrible moment. It was like the moment that he lost his voice onstage multiplied by ten million.

Mom ate pork chops and asparagus and mashed potatoes, slowly, leaving half her plate full. Dad ate asparagus—he was cutting back on meat and starches. They were having dinner, just the two of them, while I was stuck rehearsing *Once Upon a Mattress* at school, the latest activity added to my growing list.

They recall speaking in code, as though the room were bugged, and punctuating their speech with heavy pauses.

"I think I . . ." Dad said, "want to do this."

"Okay," Mom said. She chewed her food. "Really do it?"

"I think so. Maybe. I don't know."

"All the time? Everywhere? Work? With Noelle?"

"God, no!" Dad choked. "I can't even think . . . well, if she . . . no, it's not going to come to that. I just want to . . . more. More than I can here."

"All right, then," Mom said with a sigh. She lit a cigarette from the pack sitting next to her plate.

He screwed his nose up and made an effort to inhale from the opposite direction. "This is great asparagus, Dinah," he said. "I'll have an apartment in Solon. Ten minutes away. I'll see her on the weekends. If I . . . need to let Noelle know about any . . . developments . . . with the cross-dressing and doing it more, or more in public, I'll tell her then."

"I'm done," Mom announced, and pulled away from the table. "Would you mind getting the dishes?" she asked, and walked upstairs.

Later that evening, I was in my room doing nothing at all, staring up at the ceiling while blasting "I Want to Know What Love Is" and singing along solemnly when Dad knocked on my door. I liked to do that now when I was alone. Just stare and sing. It was as dramatic as dressing up used to be, but somehow more dignified. It wouldn't occur to me for years that I might have been dressing up in my father's—rather than my mother's—lingerie, but somehow the news of his behind-closed-doors activities had subtly squelched my own. Maybe it was some form of subconscious rebellion against being like *my parents*—like not eating sautéed onions because they did.

Dad told me he was moving out, and as he was wont to do lately, asked me if I had any questions. I did: one. I walked past him into the master bedroom, where my mother was stretched out on the bed reading.

"Are you okay?" I asked.

"This will be better for everyone," she said, putting on her brave face. "It's going to be you and me now. I'm not saying Dad and I are getting a divorce. This is temporary, so you don't need to worry."

"I'm fine, Mom," I said, and we lay there wrapped in each other's arms for hours. I heard Dad walk back downstairs. I swatted down a wayward impulse to hug him, too. I couldn't be sad about this. I had waited forever for this moment. I told myself that once he was gone, there wouldn't be anything to miss.

Mostly everything was the same. The bran flakes and all the vitamin bottles were gone. All the Don DeLillo books were off the shelves, along with a stack of my old fashion magazines. The office was empty, although his awards and mine were still in the closet. The *Sports Illustrated* swimsuit desk calendar was in the wastebasket. The trash had been taken out.

One of the closets in the master bedroom was cleared out. The teddies in Mom's underwear drawer were missing. The makeup had vanished. There was no aftershave on the bathroom counter, no razor in the toothbrush holder.

One of the photo albums was missing. An essay I wrote for English class had been taken off the freezer door. His chair was gone.

Mom was asleep on the couch. A bottle of Grand Marnier, cap off, and a shot glass were on the coffee table next to her. A dribble of liqueur had congealed at the bottom.

The recliner had been in one place for so long that it had formed grooves in the thick wall-to-wall carpet. I got down on my hands and knees and combed my fingers through the carpet fibers until you couldn't tell that a chair had ever been there.

SIXTEEN

Closet Cases

Pity ensued.

My father's side of the bed was barely cold by the time that relatives and friends of my mother started showing up with tuna-noodle casseroles and greeting cards for me. I was now "a child of divorce," and subject to all the rights and privileges thereto appertaining. Gentle voices whispered that I should get some sleep, chill out, kick back. Round owlish faces peered at me intently, urging me to weep like the dickens.

But I couldn't sit shivah for my broken home with them. Partly, I was defending my mother. I didn't want to be a martyr at her expense; she was so weepy and prone to headaches these days that I was more inclined to bring her chicken soup than antagonize her. I thought she had made the right decision by splitting with Dad, so it seemed the least I could do was not act as though she had single-handedly decimated my life.

I was far less noble when it came to my father, whom I publicly defended most of the time but privately excoriated for precipitating every bad thing that had ever happened to us. I wished heartache and unhappiness on him, in feverish purple prose, in the margins of my notebook. *He* was the one who had ushered us all into the realm of absurdity. Thanks to him, no matter how avidly I applied myself in the pursuit of All-American girldom, I was a freak, too: bizarre by association.

❊   ❊   ❊

Shortly after I learned that my father was a crossdresser, I met Todd Millsaps, the most normal boy ever: six feet tall, blond hair, blue eyes, just a tube of Clearasil away from being an Aryan poster child. He was third Gentleman and I was Other Lady in Scene 5 in *Once Upon a Mattress*, and I was smitten on sight. Like me, he was an amalgam of prepster, nerd, wholesome kid, outsider. He was one of the very first boys I had actually flirted with, maybe because, as he huddled, red-faced on a prop mattress backstage during a performance, he looked more terrified than me. We missed our cue and were scolded by the director, but that was of no matter: By the curtain call, I had nabbed an actual date.

On our first outing together he was afraid to kiss me. We were standing in an alcove just next to the entrance to the movie theater where we had not held hands or shared an armrest. We had even carefully taken turns grabbing fistfuls of popcorn in order to avoid the slightest chance of touching. Nonetheless, in an unusual display of chutzpah (or perhaps, the anxious certainty that I might not get the chance again to lord something over my friends) I decided there was no way I was going to let the afternoon end without kissing. As I saw my mom's car pulling into the parking lot to pick us up, I planted a tight pucker on his cheek, in a stealth move that made him jump as though I had poked him with scissors.

"Whoa," he shouted. "Um, hi! Wow."

I giggled, in a halfhearted attempt to be coy and mysterious, and called shotgun. He sat silently in the back and nearly bolted out of the car once we got to his driveway. I rode all the way home half-listening to my mom update me on Grandma Schultz's medical condition—she had recently been diagnosed with bone marrow cancer—before lapsing into my little world of glee. I felt very brazen and very old. The kissing games were over. Now I could do it for real.

Todd was an ideal first boyfriend. He yelled "scud" or "zoiks" if he stubbed his toe (he wouldn't swear if you paid him. I offered $50 on several occasions, and he turned me down flat). He decorated his room with all things Luke and Leia, and genuflected at the altar of Walt Disney—his family made a pilgrimage to Orlando once a year, with nary a fear that each year Tomorrowland might become just a little less thrilling. From the beginning, it was clear that Todd appreciated that I, too, exuded a certain Snow White goodness.

Although I continued to torment myself over whether I was a good girl or bad girl, prude or vixen, I was aware that I projected exclusively the former. My physical inventory, now that I had graduated from my awkward period, was thoroughly ingenue: blond hair, wavy and long; brown eyes, glasses-free; teeth, newly straightened; breasts, none; hips, none. The metaphysical inventory was equally unthreatening: schoolwork, safely above average; friends, B to C–level popularity; likelihood of being seen at a pot party, nil; potential for writing poetry about desperate loneliness in study hall, fully realized.

Nonetheless, I was not quite as sheltered as Todd might have thought, which alarmed me terribly. He treasured my nonswearing, nonsmoking, nonexperienced self more than any male ever had. In the beginning, thus, I labored to obscure the ways in which I was not a complete naif.

We first kissed, lip to lip, on the big white sofa in our basement rec room. I tried not to let on that I had done it before, since he clearly had not been a veteran of preadolescent sexual parlor games. We sat facing each other and tried to strategize the meeting of mouths. After fifteen minutes, my nose started to feel bruised and so I gently took over, explaining that I had practiced on a honeydew (an anecdote I stole from about a dozen different young adult novels).

I tilted my head right, but then he mirrored me exactly. "No, no!" I said, too sharply, and gently angled his head the other direction. I puckered, as he did a split second later, perfectly timed to make us both feel ridiculous. I pushed my lips directly at his lips, and tried to use my jaw muscle to force his open, since they were clenched tight as a vacuum seal, but that upset him. "Hey, cut it out," he grumbled.

It took us about an hour to get it right and to my relief, he was happy in the end that I had known what to do. "A melon, huh?" he said, all flirty and beaming.

One night on the cusp of summer, Todd and I spent the day at Geauga Lake amusement park. We stuffed ourselves on mega-cups of greasy fries, and plunked down some twenty quarters on skeeball. I shrieked on every roller coaster the way I'd seen girls do on commercials. It made my throat scratchy, but Todd protectively wrapped his arm around me after we exited each ride.

The evening was unseasonably humid for preseason, so we walked down by the faux dock, hoping to glimpse the lights from the SeaWorld show on the other side of the lake. Now and then, we stopped to kiss, as other kids our age made gagging motions as they walked by us. It was a beautiful clinch: his head in my neck, my arms draped over his Mickey Mouse sweatshirt, his hands encircling my waist. "My fingers meet," he marveled. "You're so tiny." I smiled, pleased my little girl looks were finally showing some demonstrable benefit.

My mother later picked us up in the parking lot, and this time I walked Todd to his front door to say good-bye. We pecked, cursorily, in case his mother was near a window, before he turned to me and blurted, in a panicky high register, "I love you!" I stood there, dumbly, as he slammed the door in my face. It was the most romantic moment *ever*.

My father moved out in the afternoon, and Todd came by that evening. By that time, we had been dating for a few months and so he was, naturally, the first friend I told about my parents' separation. We sat in what had become our usual place, on the basement sofa with our legs kicked up on a secondhand coffee table.

I was slumped so far down that my chin rested on my chest, while he carefully stroked my hair. He didn't understand exactly why I was so upset, since he had deduced that Dad and I were not "all that close." I told him I was afraid Mom and I would get murdered—two women alone in a house, and all that, plus I was worried about her getting lonely. Even as I spoke, I felt sharp guilt pangs about being coddled by my boyfriend while Mom was upstairs watching TV with the cat.

How could I tell Todd that I already missed my family? Despite the fact that I had grudgingly accepted that we were not "normal," I had already come to see that normal was really whatever you were used to. I was perfectly accustomed to despising my father, and actively wishing him gone. I was used to seeing my mother in a perpetual state of yearning, plastering on that same neighborly smile to get past the worst moments. I hadn't quite realized that ending our dysfunctional symbiosis would mean that we all, eventually, would have to change.

I told Todd how glad I was to have him there. I huddled against him, clutching his button-down shirt until he had to practically pry away my fingers to leave for home.

The next afternoon, I was at rehearsal for another play, *Our Town*—I played the gossipy Mrs. Soames—when I started crying, out of nowhere, in the middle of a completely unpoignant scene. Several of my friends in the production clamored around me, some proffering ibuprofen. Figuring this fact was going to become apparent if I had any sleepovers in the near future anyway, I admitted that my parents had separated. One of my closer friends, Libby, nodded knowingly.

"Were they fighting?" she asked.

"No," I murmured, and blew my nose.

"Was your dad having an affair?" asked another girl.

"Um, I don't think so," I muttered, with slight annoyance.

"I'll bet he was having an affair," the girl said triumphantly. "They all do."

It was an improbable moment. There I was, crouched on the stage, surrounded by girls asking questions more relevant to their parents' divorces than mine. The spotlight still lingered on me (the lighting crew had taken a five-minute break, thanks to my outburst), and feeling raw and sniffling and embarrassed, I lied. Just like in the soap operas when an ominous voice-over echoes in someone's head, my mother's gentle warning rang in mine: *Don't tell anyone about your dad. He could lose his job, we could lose the house, you could get teased at school.* When my mother had first given me the "keep it quiet" speech, I hadn't given it any thought. What was there to tell, anyway? Dad does something weird in their bedroom. Whose parents didn't? And who wanted to talk about such gross things, anyway? Before my parents separated, I was unlikely to bring up my father in conversation. Like most teens, I only brought up my parents in the context of their doing something absolutely unjust for my own good, or when they were screwing up my otherwise wonderful life. Until my father moved out, there had been no need to lie about his cross-dressing. The issue hadn't come up.

"It was probably sex," I said, inching as close to the truth as I could.

"Men suck," Libby said.

I forced a smile and got back into character as the know-it-all busybody who couldn't keep a secret if her life depended on it.

Shortly after Dad moved out, Grandma Schultz moved in so that we could help her recover from the chemotherapy she was undergoing to treat her cancer. We propped her up in an adjustable bed in Dad's empty office, where she proceeded to drive my mother crazy.

Since I had dispensed with being snide to my mother—I had come to readily acknowledge that era as a "phase" myself—my grandmother was there to take my place as resident tic. She was one of the few who knew Dad's cross-dressing secret, though all of us pretended she didn't, and still she blamed my mother for the failure of the marriage.

"Dick is such a wonderful man," she'd say, as my mother would roll her over to change the bedpan. "Whatever are you going to do without him?"

"I'll manage," my mother would reply, tightly.

"No marriage is perfect," Grandma would tut-tut, while my mother set a bowl of homemade chicken soup down on her TV tray.

"Mom, get some sleep," my mother would groan, and retire to the living room for another ice-cream sundae and a nap.

Grandma Schultz wasn't the only one who pointed the finger at my mother for the separation. Grandma H. called me to complain that if my mother had just kept herself up better ("as I believe I've mentioned to Dinah, nicely, a time or two") my family would still be together. She then told me how proud she was that I was handling this all so well. She sounded earnest and compassionate, and her voice made me feel like ripping my ears off. I did my best to get off the phone before I started screaming.

Quality time became a regularly scheduled event soon after Dad got settled in his new apartment. This is what it meant: Every Saturday we ate hamburgers somewhere. We drove to a café in awkward silence—I had spent my childhood avoiding the prospect of car rides alone with my father, where the lack of conversation was palpable, making me ever more aware of the bad radio-station selection. Once there, we eagerly perused the menus for the maximum allowable time; the waiter usually had to come back twice before we were willing to let them be pried from our claws. How's school, how's work, how are Todd and your other friends killed enough time—if I really incorporated maximum detail in my stories—to fill up airspace until the burgers showed up. I still got nervous using utensils in his presence, and didn't want to be accused of eating with my mouth open, so I gladly kept my mouth shut until the check came. That's when any important news might be imparted, such as, say, the news that my father wasn't just a cross-dresser but was something called a transsexual.

This tidbit came at a fifties-theme diner where I had gorged on a milk shake and a quarter-pound burger while Dad sipped a diet soda and a side salad with vinaigrette. The waitress was processing Dad's platinum card.

"So you're like the people on *Donahue?*" I asked, nonplussed.

My father frowned, and motioned for me to keep my voice down. "I guess, sort of," he whispered, looking around as though the place might be bugged.

He leaned toward me and explained that a transsexual was someone who felt that they were born into the wrong gender. It went a lot further than clothing, he said, but all the way to your inner essence—whatever that was. He said he was going to start dressing as a woman, sometimes, but not anywhere nearby where someone we knew might run into him. He'd drive down to Amish country or somewhere he could be incognito (I feared he was giving too much credence to the movie *Witness*). Speaking of driving, he was giving Mom the red convertible because it was too eye-catching. He planned to get a small sedan with tinted windows, like cars belonging to celebrities or criminals.

"So," he asked, *again*, "do you have any questions? This must all be overwhelming and a little confusing."

He was right on the money, but my perplexity had less to do with transsexualism or cross-dressing than a fundamental bewilderment that he was so damn interested in me. We had rarely lumbered past "How are you?" and thus, an in-depth discussion of gender confusion seemed a bit of a leap. Quickly, I changed the subject.

He didn't appear to notice my discomfort. Before I got out of the car, he kissed me on the cheek and told me how happy he was that we were "really talking."

✿   ✿   ✿

As my sophomore year commenced, Mom was working late more often, not getting home until I had already nuked a plastic tray of macaroni and cheese and relieved whichever home health aide we were stuck with—either the chain-smoker, or the Creole woman who refused to make anything bland for my poor grandmother, whose palate heretofore had never made contact with anything hotter than paprika. Mom told me she had a lot of stuff keeping her at the office. "You wouldn't believe the kind of crap I have to deal with," she told me, with a heavy sigh. I was sure she was right, although I figured the crap in question probably had more to do with Dad's latest revelation than agency paperwork.

I knew how she felt. On my parents' orders, Dr. Smith and I began spending forty-five minutes every week peeling away each family secret (I had recently learned that my grandfather was a sexual revolution acolyte and a Commie). I reeled the rest of the week, buzzing on constant sensory overload. My thoughts zigzagged this way and that as though a fabulous game of pinball was going on in my right lobe. I didn't need to try drugs; I felt thoroughly disoriented, inhabiting a surreal landscape of opposites where black was white, and of course, male was female.

It helped to be preoccupied with school, my bevy of extracurriculars, and later in the day, companionship. Grandma wasn't the best company: she was usually either snoring or screaming at Reagan on C-SPAN or watching the baseball game (ever since my grandfather had died, she had adopted all of his passions, from liberal politics to the Cleveland Indians). I had little to say about batting averages, and so I began spending a marked number of evenings with Todd's family, the kindest, gentlest folks who ever made me feel like a total weirdo.

Todd's family was so unrealistically good that I wouldn't have been surprised if they ran a secret porn ring out of their garage. His parents—a teacher and a calligrapher who worked summers at a day camp—were bake-sale people who drove a minivan before it was cool and chortled along with Garrison Keillor on the radio. It didn't seem possible that they could exist in the same world that made my family, and I was certain they could sniff the weirdness on me, the way a dog can suss out a tumor in its owner's body. They were perfectly kind, always offering me a slice of pizza, or a hug. Todd's mother, in particular, seemed very sympathetic that my parents had split, which had the inverse of the intended effect. I had come to despise sympathy, as it seemed like a gentler way of pointing out how crazy-different and unfortunate I was. In response to her kind queries, I imperiously recited my grade-point average, my latest accomplishments in drama or other club activities, and practically oozed with joy over my parents' mature, loving decision to lead independent lives.

I couldn't bear to have normal people feeling sorry for me, or acting derisive toward my parents. Mom and Dad never needed to worry that I would confess our secret; pride alone ensured my acquiescence to the closet way of life.

In some sort of mean-spirited desire to bring Todd down to my level, I launched a campaign to go all the way. I felt fairly confident in our relationship, and it had increasingly become more important to me to take him off of his pedestal than to keep myself atop one. Getting him to have sex was more difficult than one might imagine, since by the spring semester of sophomore year, we had already been dating for a year, and he was, after all, a teenage boy. But he was a very good teenage boy, and more obedient to his virtues than to his testosterone.

In the beginning of our relationship I'd practically forced Todd to feel me up by shoving the deadweight of his hand against my padded training bra. Horrified, he had drawn his hand back and run into the bathroom, choking back tears. I followed behind him. Pounding on the bathroom door, I had wept to Todd that I was really, really sorry.

I didn't know what on earth was wrong with me. Boys always

moved faster than girls and here I was, moving a teenage boy to tears by making him touch my flat chest. If anyone should have recoiled from bases one through three, and ended up hiding in a bathroom snuffling into a roll of toilet paper, it was supposed to be me. I was mortified that my sexual urges were so strong. I promised myself I would try to "let things happen," rather than force them. I would let him make the moves. If nothing happened, so be it. Better that than be labeled one of those hateful, frightening words scribbled in toilet stalls about girls who pushed and pushed until they got what they wanted: *Bitch. Cunt. Nympho. Slut.*

I tried to slow down. I wrote a letter to *Seventeen* asking what to do when girls wanted it worse than boys. I got a form letter back that advised me to speak with my guidance counselor. I didn't think Mrs. "There's Nothing Pre-About the PSAT" Tillson was up to the challenge, so I tried talking to my mother while she was grilling hamburgers outside on the barbecue. A bit startled, she told me to respect Todd's wishes and be patient. She burned two patties when she forgot to turn them over.

Soon enough, slowing down wasn't an option. Over a period of six months or so, Todd decided he could be a good boy *and* get some nooky on the side. Once I got the green light, I began to study how I could make him want me more: flashing a bra strap between class periods, showing up on the basement pool table in nothing but undergarments, growing my blond hair long and wavy and wearing ball gowns to formal dances because he got into that whole Disney heroine thing.

In my addled teenage mind, I had finally achieved a perfect middle ground between prude and slut. It all boiled down to public relations. Play prude in the light of day, and slut in the dark—it was the stuff of every male fantasy I had ever been privy to (the secretary who lets down her hair, the straitlaced nurse with a bod for sin). Best of all, it kept me in control of how I was being perceived by everyone, especially Todd.

I learned how to choreograph a seduction: this one like Kelly McGillis in *Top Gun*, that one like Rebecca DeMornay in *Risky Business*. (I was quite skilled at standing, leaning, and angling myself in the right way, having honed my abilities during the dress-up games of yore.) I had come to realize that, without actually pushing Todd's hand down my shorts or up my tank top, I could quietly make sexual activity—if not actual intercourse— happen. I could drop hints, mimic sexy scenarios, and once we actually fooled around, I made believe it was all his idea. This seemed completely normal to me. When I strutted in front of him in a teddy with a boom box playing "Hungry Eyes" in the background, I was showing my devotion to his needs. That "ha-ha . . . now I've got you" feeling that swelled in my stomach? True love, pure and simple. I was still a child playing boy-girl with Mindy, and adhering to the same rules: She who directs the scene wins the game.

In the summer after sophomore year, I began accompanying Todd and his parents to colonial-themed art fairs, where we would dress up in ruffled shirts, knickers, and bonnets in order to sell framed, calligraphied aphorisms from dawn until dusk. Todd and I spent the early evenings together, wandering hand in hand past hastily constructed booths of Ye Olde Lemonade and custom-made flag holders, and a seemingly unending line of RVs to house the craftspeople themselves.

"Isn't this romantic?" he murmured.

"Pretty," I responded, distractedly. I was in the middle of a rural Ohio field, surrounded by motorized trailers containing people dressed like pilgrims, and all I could think about was transsexualism. I started to cry.

"What's wrong?" Todd asked. "Here, sit."

I sat in the bale of hay and wept into his fluffy white shirt. "Nothing," I sniffled. "It's just my father."

"What about him?"

"It's this . . . thing," I cried, harder. "I can't tell you."

Todd looked straight at me and engulfed my shoulders in his enormous hands. "I love you. You can tell me anything, okay?"

I could hear myself saying it over and over in my head. *My father wants to be a girl.* It wasn't so many words. It couldn't be that hard to say. Todd wouldn't tell; he was too conscientious for that. So I spilled—sort of. "Um, there's this thing. It's about my dad, and it's really bad, and I can't tell because he would lose his job and we'd lose our house and everything."

"Jesus," Todd whispered.

"I can't tell you," I intoned, terrified that I had hinted too much. "I shouldn't have said anything because I could really get in trouble."

"Oh my God," Todd said. His face was the color of typing paper. "You're scaring me."

"I'm sorry," I said. "I can't help it. I promised it would be our secret. My family's and mine."

During that period of time, I managed to terrify my boyfriend and alienate my old friend, Nancy, all because I couldn't tell them the truth. Nancy had recently decided that one possible reason that my family had relocated to the hinterlands was—racism.

"White flight," she announced, somewhere in the middle of a two-hour phone marathon. "You guys moved out there to a lily-white suburb in the middle of nowhere in order to get away from black people."

"That's not true!" I hollered at her. My mother had confessed to me that the move was made, in no small part, because my father wanted more privacy for gallivanting in girly attire.

"So why did you move out there?"

"Because!" I shouted. "Just because! I don't have to explain anything to you." I slammed down the receiver. We made up a day or two later, and I fudged some explanation that we moved because my parents wanted more greenery in their lives, and apparently that, ha-ha, even Mother Nature could not keep them together. We moved on to other topics of far less import, and I slunk into sadness, certain no one would understand me again.

I continued to see my father once a week—or less, if I could finagle it. On each outing (no pun intended), he had morphed ever so slightly. No one except me seemed to notice. He wasn't becoming a woman as much as he was ceasing to be a man. He was disappearing, so slowly that it would be imperceptible if you weren't paying close attention. Waiters still addressed him as "sir" and "Mr. Howey," but little by little, "Duke" was being phased out.

The obvious manly markers, the ones I associated most strongly with my father, were the first to be traded in. He purchased hair, in the form of a muddy brown toupee that was almost legit-looking. His leather jacket was replaced by a beige windbreaker; the thick gold watch for a slim Timex. His musk of aftershave and Vitalis had been supplanted by the clean, bland smell of floral soap. His once-robust gut was now inverted to the same extent, and his penchant for roasting his flesh in the sun had abruptly stopped. Thanks to an exclusive diet of romaine, yogurt, and caffeine, he was as pale and gaunt as a girl just out of anorexia rehab—which, I suppose, was the image he was going for.

The disappearance of the accessories that, added together, formed the image I had long held of my father was indeed jarring. But the less obvious alterations, the ones only my mother and I were honed enough to notice, were the truly distressing ones. On one visit, I noticed that his fingernails were long enough to click against a tabletop. Another time he dropped his wallet on the diner floor and I glimpsed his panty line. The buttons on his oxford shirts had moved from right to left. ("It's raised my dry-clean bill about five dollars," he once joked, nervously, when I pointed it out.) Slowly his stubble was vanishing, courtesy of thousands of dollars of electrolysis, as was his moderately low voice, which vocal training was lifting into alto territory.

His physical appearance was changing, and at approximately the same rate his attitude was improving as well. He was swearing less, saying "thank you" more. He blushed once.

He found my life endlessly fascinating: "Tell me about your social studies class!" "How was the spring formal?" "Did you take pictures of yourself in the dress?" He impressed his interest and enthusiasm for my endeavors upon me as much as he could, but, far from being thrilled, I was offended. He is being sweet, I thought, because he thinks that's what women are like. Down deep, I had a more personal reason for not wanting him to be nice to me. It would have rendered those years of striving to be the ultimate daughter in order to please him, and the subsequent angry tirades alone in my room, all for naught. I had worked too hard to hate him to forgive him then—or perhaps ever.

It's one more irony that I was offended by my father's propensity at the time to see women and men in black-and-white archetypal terms, since I was as likely to fall into that trap myself. Although I loved Todd, I had grown concerned that he was not aggressive, arrogant, or snide. Sure, he was handsome, and had acquired a self-confident carriage that was quite attractive to all the ninth-grade girls. Unfortunately, he was *never* nasty to me, and rarely even sarcastic. He was a nice guy, which in my mind automatically translated into not guy enough.

It's now obvious that I was seeking out a disapproving male voice in my life since my father, who once so reliably filled that role, was neutering himself in more ways than one. I was no dummy; I made that very same observation to Dr. Smith at the precise moment that I developed a passionate crush on a boy at school who got his kicks from pointing out the fact that I had small breasts.

I was violently, pornographically attracted to this boy, who mocked and teased me in what seemed like a relentless on-slaught—though in reality, it was probably only a few barbed comments per week. Every time I took a shower, I would bring in my mondo plastic basket of shampoo, soap, loofah, exfoliant, body butter, and about twenty-seven superfluous beauty products, and I would prepare to fantasize. As I sudsed up in the shower (which I didn't do very often; it wasted a lot of expensive soap), I imagined him staring at me like I was an extra in *Porky's* and approaching me for sexual favors. Once consummated, the fantasy came to an abrupt conclusion. Once he had been had, he was useless to me until I could win him over once more.

In December of 1988, as I did every year, I clambered onto my mother's bed late at night and told her what I wanted for Christmas. The list was short: clothes, bedroom furniture, and the birth-control pill. The last one got her attention. She dog-eared her romance novel and put it down.

She quizzed me on my readiness, and even more carefully on Todd's. I assured her that we had discussed it—which we had, for about a year and a half, when I had started whining to him that we should please, *please* get on with it already.

"Well, then," she said, "I guess we'll make an appointment with the gynecologist."

"Thank you, Mom!" I shouted, and planted a wet kiss on her cheek.

"No," she said, "thank you for trusting me enough to talk about this and for being smart about it, using protection and all that. I'm proud of you. And amazed! I never could have spoken to *my* mother about this sort of thing." Reflexively, she swiveled her head to make sure the baby monitor—which Grandma Schultz could speak into if she needed a glass of water or help getting to the bathroom—was off on our end.

"You're my best friend," I told her. "Besides, you guys have made it really, really clear that you aren't exactly traditional parents. I don't see why I should have to pretend that I'm this little virgin girl. If Dad can be out to me, then it should go both ways."

"So you're telling your father about having sex?" my mother asked, with a bemused twitch of her lips.

"Holy sh . . . oot. Sorry," I giggled. "Can you imagine? He'd be like getting out the ten gauge to nail Todd in the back, don't you think?"

"Don't tell him." Mom laughed. "No matter what he's wearing, he's still your father."

When Todd and I lost our virginity on New Year's Eve, I screamed with glee. Sex itself felt a little strange, a general rubbing sensation no more inherently exciting than getting VapoRub smeared on my chest when I had a cold. But what it *meant* felt incredible. He loved me. He wanted me more than he wanted to be good.

On New Year's Day, Dad stopped by the house to catch up on what was going on with me. We almost never spoke about him, mostly because he gave me the creeps. I imagined him entering his apartment—which I assumed was a shady lair packed top full with sex toys, boas, and cheap, loud makeup—in his sad little man getup, only to transform into a wisecracker queen. I pictured him sauntering drunkenly in an evening gown into the local Pizza Hut and ordering a pie to go in a voice that was, inexplicably, one part Jimmy Durante and one part Minnie Mouse. I had no basis in reality for anything in this image, but its specter frightened me enough to keep away from the topic of his life altogether.

In a completely unpremeditated move, I told him all about New Year's Eve, and how terrifically amazing it was to not be a virgin anymore. To his credit, my father swallowed what must have been total shock and managed to keep his expression pleasantly glazed.

It was a power maneuver on my part just as surely as if I had called check in a game of chess. Dad kept raising the bar of what

Mom and I could accept with equanimity, and I felt justified in doing the same.

After explaining in vivid detail how we had fornicated right in front of the window where we could see if Todd's parents drove up unexpectedly before midnight, Dad, somewhat distastefully, responded, "This is probably a little more than I need to know."

"I want you to accept me for who I am, Dad," I replied, with doe-eyed innocence. "You said you wanted us to be closer." Bait, and reel. Bait, and reel.

"You're right," Dad said, nodding. "If I'm going to throw all these changes at you," he said, glancing downward at his newly hairless arms, "then you are more than entitled to toss some of yours right back at me."

"Okay, then," I said, cautiously. He had surprised me by being reasonable. I was testing him with the sarcasm he had taught me so well, and he wasn't fighting back. Maybe he thought good women didn't attack their daughters. Or perhaps he thought good fathers didn't either.

Larvae

Take heart: the teenage years may be trying, but you only have
to live through them once!
—*Seventeen*

During my sophomore and junior years of high school, I came
face-to-face with the worst rites that the teen years have to offer:
dramatic mood swings, wild hormone fluctuations, physical developments, testing boundaries, sexual experimentation, strange
new hobbies, questioning of identity, and constant fear of social
rejection. However, since I was going through this myself, I was
better able to comprehend my parents' behavior.

In retrospect, perhaps I should have expected it. Dad had
never endured a teen girlhood before, and Mom was mentally
reliving hers, struggling to conjure what it had been like to be a
sexually active single female during her college years, and trying
to forget what it had been like to be a solitary wife ever since.

In my twenties, I heard other horror stories of parents who,
once released from their wedding vows, took the axiom "freedom
is just another word for nothing left to lose" way too much to
heart. "My dad went from Mister Rogers to frat boy," explained
one bemused friend. "My mom wore baby T-shirts with 'spoiled'
and 'naughty' written on the front with glitter pen," choked another, still mortified years later.

Thanks to our ongoing tour of duty in the closet, my parents managed not to distress me publicly. But that may have only prolonged the agony, since nothing seems to make an entire family backpedal to a juvenile state with greater haste than leading a so-called double life. For example, teenagers are so paranoid that if anyone knew about their secret doll collection/third nipple/bedwetting habit they would be ostracized. That fear can cause them to act like complete loons, refusing to let friends enter their bedrooms or shrieking if someone walks in on them changing, at which point the specific eccentricity becomes insignificant by comparison. Closet denizens act much the same way. In an attempt to obscure the shameful secret in question, you act out in other exaggerated ways. You often succeed. Few acquaintances wonder out loud whether you or your husband or your father is a transsexual. What a relief! They just think you need serious therapy, or a vacation.

Before achieving the full blossom of young womanhood, my father was first an androgynous zombie. It was the second time he had been a quivering, asexual, hairless being waiting to morph into pubescence and then full-fledged adulthood. This time, though, my father was determined that his gender was going to stick.

Generally speaking, during the weekdays he was Dick, and at nights and on the weekends he was Dickless. This wasn't merely a crass joke (although transsexuals born with the name Dick are required to make a certain number of those); it had taken my father many years to admit, even to himself, that the snide nickname he'd been called on the playground had actually given him the slightest bit of satisfaction. As much as Dad prided himself on being the Master of Passing, he couldn't help feeling a twinge of thrill—albeit quickly subsumed by massive guilt and inner torment—that he had been caught. They knew my father wasn't just any other boy.

Dickless was the little effeminate boy who hugged his mother, who openly cried, who knew he had a soul. Dickless wasn't a girl, but he was as close as my dad had ever been.

In order to access his larval self more easily, my father shed his prized masculine accoutrements with the deliberate focus of one about to commit suicide. His behavior altered as well. He stopped hanging with the boys after work and bowling with the fellas five times a week. Virtually overnight, he went from being a guy accepted well enough to have a nickname—perhaps the highest echelon of male bonding—to being someone viewed with a touch of skepticism, like Michael Jackson after the second nose job.

The divorce was the first tip-off that Duke was not as together as everyone had imagined. He almost never flirted openly at the office or vaguely indicated that he and my mother fought, so naturally my father's work friends started wondering if he was, you know, *that way.* The second sign of trouble was Dad's sense of humor, which had gone soft—even to the point of causing his work to suffer.

"Dick, I was looking at the radio spot you wrote for Health Spas Incorporated," my father's boss said, in a creative meeting. "It's pretty funny, the guy who wants to lose weight and all that. But I'm confused by this line where he says he wants to go down a couple sizes. I don't think guys talk like that, do they? Getting into smaller sizes? Or is this a joke I just don't get?"

My father cleared his throat. "Where is that? Oh yeah. I see. Well, that is a joke . . . I mean, not a ha-ha joke. You know, I think it could work if . . . look, why don't I take it out?" The other guys at the table glanced warily at each other, perplexed that Duke, the edgiest guy in the office, had lost the art of the comeback.

"Perfect. Taking it out will definitely work. So, uh, you okay, Dick? You seem a little worse for the wear," his boss asked.

"I didn't get much sleep," my father said. "Bachelor life wears a guy out, you know." Dad laughed, weakly, as did his friends, who went out for beers after work without him.

Most of his colleagues also took note of Dad's physical changes, although the full scope of the transformation was unclear because the makeover was so gradual—like watching a film advance one frame at a time over a period of two years. For instance, shortly after telling me he was a transsexual, Dad commenced grueling half hour weekly electrolysis treatments. Although it took a full year and a half to eradicate all traces of five o'clock shadow, some initial change was perceptible from the first several months of treatments. The buzz around the office was that my father was having plastic surgery, in a misguided midlife attempt to stop the aging process.

Many of his friends, both men and women, began pulling away. Lunch invites, once semiregular, came less frequently; dinner offers, already a rarity, became nonexistent. Part of that was typical marrieds' discomfort with newly single friends, but there was also a palpable sense that Dick wasn't quite Dick anymore. The irony, of course, was that as disoriented as my father seemed, life had never been better. Since college, he had fit in as long as he didn't allow himself to feel anything. Having emotions, even negative ones, was a huge improvement for him, and a slightly diminished social stock seemed like a minor concession.

That said, living in the closet fifteen miles from work was only a little less stressful than, say, air traffic control. When my father would venture out in women's clothes—mostly to go to gay bars where no one paid him any attention—it took an average of four hours for him to get psyched up enough to walk to his car. He'd stand at the peephole of his apartment for three of those hours, sweaty palm positioned on the doorknob, and analyze the mathematics of getting to his car.

It was a motel-style lodging, so the door to his unit opened up directly onto the parking lot. His door was about thirty feet away from his assigned spot in a fifty-five-degree line. There were seventy people in his apartment unit. Half had cars, and only a handful had any chance whatsoever of pulling in or out of the lot in the next few minutes. My father would deduce that if someone walked at 10 m.p.h. from his door to the car in a straight line, there was probably only a 3–5 percent chance that anyone would see that person. But then, he'd think despairingly, since this someone was *him*, there was a hundred percent chance that a passerby would point and laugh. "Ha-ha! Look at the weirdo." By the time my father was done with his new math, some kid would skateboard on by, at which point Dad would collapse into tears. Once he made it into the car, hours later, he still didn't feel secure. He recalls that he scarcely took a full breath until he was safely inside the gay bar, way over on the west side of town, where he could disappear.

My mother hated the questions. They reminded her of what she wasn't allowed to say.

People asked her what went wrong in the marriage—"You and Dick seemed so happy! Like two peas in a pod!"—and she answered "irreconcilable differences" or said she and my father were just "growing apart." My mother was not known to be a vague, obfuscating type of person, and so her answers seemed to please no one, including herself.

Living in the closet was not a new or unusually harrowing experience for my father. He had no concept of what it was like to live openly. But my mother had only managed to keep the cross-dressing a secret by playing down its relative importance. Once the fetish graduated to a lifestyle, it was hard to pretend that she wasn't in the closet with him.

Mom feared that if people found out about Dad's secret, they would wonder what was wrong with her. "She was married to a guy in a dress for all those years," she imagined them whispering in hushed tones in the agency kitchenette. "She must be an odd bird, too."

My mother—whose passion above all was to be liked, who forthrightly called herself a "people person" in job interviews—did not want to be exiled from the world of the regular folk. She was one of them! Since her youth she had feared that she would eventually find herself on the outside, no matter how hard she tried to curry favor. As she told the therapist, Mom was frightened that her exile from polite society was now all but inevitable.

It was impossible, she later told me, to try and discuss this matter with my father. My mother's mourning period for the marriage had begun to lift, leaving her with a bitter anger that she couldn't begin to stanch, especially when he showed up unannounced to do his laundry in the basement. She recalls trying to be pleasant, managing to eke out a "hello" or a "how are you?" The conversation sputtered once they got beyond niceties. On the rare occasion that she attempted to discuss her conflicted feelings about their troubled marriage or the transsexualism, my father shut her down as he always had.

"So, I hear from Noelle that you're open to questions and to talking about transsexualism," my mother testily said, as he sat in the living room folding undergarments of every hue and style, from boxers and briefs to thongs and granny-style panties. "She may not have anything to say right now, but I have some thoughts that I would like to share."

"Um, sorry, Dinah, gotta run. I think my socks are done," he said, dismissively, leaving my mother to fume once again.

As nervous as my mother was about my father's impending transformation, she was more frustrated over what wasn't changing at all. My mother had spent decades trying to fix my father, and she finally realized that she had failed. Whether he was a man or woman, boy or girl, he still didn't hear her. In bygone days, his neglect would have driven her to the bedroom, where she would have cocooned herself, but now she told him to go to hell instead.

Dad was not exactly in hell, but he was definitely in limbo.

I never saw his apartment. I had spooked myself about it enough to stay as far away from it as I could. But from what my father had told me of it, it was a perfect reflection of who he was at the time: a one-bed, one-bath disaster area.

The living room was a bachelor-type dwelling, littered with never-to-be-unpacked boxes, empty Diet Coke cans, and a television hoisted onto the top of a tool chest. In sharp contrast, the bathroom was tailored to the specifications of a thirteen-year-old teenage girl, or that leathery type of woman who orders makeup from soap opera actresses on home shopping networks. He had bought a makeup application mirror with tiny lightbulbs encircling the frame—like the ones in theatrical playhouse dressing rooms—which became the centerpiece of the bathroom counter. Surrounding the mirror were a stash of cosmetics (mostly mail-order) that would have rivaled most pageant contestants'.

The kitchen belonged to a man used to having a wife: It was empty except for takeout boxes, vodka, cereal, multivitamin supplements, and twelve types of mustard. The bedroom was decorated with the ultragirly details I had rejected years earlier: dolls propped on lace doilies, satin sheets under silk blankets under velvet throws, an ocean of pink. As my father became ever more devoted to his female aspirations, he passed most of his time in the bathroom and the bedroom.

In an attempt to jump-start his feminine side, my father decided to join a transvestite/transgender club with the docile faux sorority name of Alpha Omega Tri-Ess—the same kind of organization he had ruthlessly mocked with my mother so many years earlier. He says that he had a certain sense of foreboding about returning to the fold: "How could I not? I was going to a seedy motel to meet a bunch of people, several of whom were

250-pound guys dressed up in Little Mary Sunshine pinafores and patent leather shoes." However, my father's irony reflex had been dulled by terror and solitude, leading him to swallow hard and join the sisterhood of true believers.

This group—most of whom were recreational cross-dressers who considered my father one of the more hard-core cases—was as syrupy and supportive as any Tupperware party, albeit way more preoccupied with "feminine concerns." A typical meeting would involve a discussion of how masques should not be applied with a trowel or sandblaster, followed by the "ladylike tips for the week," which ran the gamut from walking with thumbs pointing forward so as to rein in elbows to a reminder of the three H's: hem, hose, heels (two of the three should be the same color, they scolded). My father, along with the other ladies, dutifully took notes in order to practice at home. He had not had the benefit of the beauty education gleaned from slumber parties or a Barbie Styling Head. What he didn't expect was to fall in love: with the sense of community; with the easy, unforced friendships; with a few hours a week during which no one expected him to be wry or cynical.

Once back at the apartment, in the giddy afterglow of a meeting, my father would practice his new hobby, the one that had supplanted bowling: getting ready for his close-up.

Dad applied the same voracious study to appearing womanly as he had back in school, when he was first learning how to ape men. He had no desire to look like a prepubescent girl who went crazy in her mother's makeup box, nor did he desire the cubist look unintentionally obtained by some of the less exacting transsexuals he had met in Tri-Ess. He followed the rules, and was in many ways a more dutiful student in the feminine arts than I ever was.

Whereas my makeup "regimen" by mid to late high school had evolved into dabbing on a few globs of three-hundred-year-old encrusted mascara and smearing a lipstick on without benefit of a mirror, my father followed each instruction to the letter. Unlike me, Dad religiously cleansed, toned, moisturized, exfoliated, manicured, and washed his makeup off at night. Except for being a man, he would have been a beauty editor's ideal subject.

After removing successive coatings of makeup, my father retired to his bed, towel wrapped turban-style around his bald head, with stacks of how-to manuals, ranging from *Redbook* and *Glamour* to transgender newsletters. The beauty advice was usually interchangeable, although the latter tended to babble on more about inner feminine essences (women's mags reserve that kind of talk for douche and tampon ads) and employ carpentry metaphors. The endlessly positive tone of the copy and the breathless product plugs lulled my father into a romantic fugue state. She fell asleep dreaming about cuticle cream, loofahs, body spray: femininity obtainable at retail prices.

In the spring of 1989, the doctor announced that Grandma Schultz's cancer was in remission. Slowly her energy was coming back, and by opening day of the Indians season, she was able to sit up by herself and root straight through extra innings without falling asleep. Right away, Grandma's mood lightened immensely—she eased up on her criticism of the home health aide's cooking just before the insurance company stopped covering her services. She told me every morning how excited she was to be back home and in proximity to her garden, her pantry, her memories of life with my grandfather. Mom, too, was thrilled—for Grandma.

Exhausted though my mother was from playing caretaker in the midst of such emotional turmoil, all she could think was, *There goes another one.* Wife was over. Daughter was ending—in its current incarnation anyway. That left Mother, which would be phased out when I went off to college. She was losing her place in the family, and as a result, was feeling lost and without purpose.

"Danielle," she confided to the therapist, "Dick is the one who doesn't know who he is. I've always held it all together."

"Well, I think, Dick really might know who he—or maybe we should start saying 'she'—is," Dr. Smith tutted. "He just doesn't know how to get from point A to point B."

"I know this is a pointless thing to say," Mom grumbled, "but I'm mad. I spent ages taking care of that man, and I don't have anything to show for it. I don't even know who I am anymore."

"Interesting," Dr. Smith said, jotting notes on her legal pad. "Maybe you can try to remember."

It's no easy task to become a woman, as any biological girl can tell you. But it's a little harder when you have to unlearn being a man first. Fortunately, years of making a dollar to a woman's seventy-five cents had given my father the necessary resources to train for womanhood like a champ.

He worked every week with a vocal coach who taught him how to inflect like a natural-born female. "You speak in monotone," the coach pointed out. "Women's voices move up and down. There is variety." For three weeks, my father repeated phrases like "Samantha wants to buy some laundry detergent" over and over while driving to work, making sure he was infusing similarly fascinating sentences with the appropriate inflection of interest. Satisfactory completion of his inflections meant that my father was able, on cue, to sound as preposterously iambic and soprano as Lamb Chop the sock puppet. It sounded silly to me when he would accidentally slip into his upper register during one of our lunches, as though his voice was cracking in reverse, but Dad seemed satisfied. Now he could fool telemarketers, who then apologized to "Ma'am" for asking for "*Mr.* Howey."

Just as I had once feminized my handwriting in order to attain an ever-elusive social status, so too did my father practice writing each letter of the alphabet twice as large and adding curly flairs to the "y's" and "j's," even checking with a few friends to make sure that the writing did indeed look girly. My father breezed through this de facto transsexual finishing school, until he ran into facial expressions. There were no hired hands to assist him in "expressing" like a woman. On that point, he was on his own.

When my father entered University School back in the fifties, one of the first things he had learned was not to smile. Forget boys don't cry: There were (and are) few taboos of boyhood more insidious than the unspoken ban on smiling. Dad noticed that boys eagerly, gleefully offered up toothsome smiles in elementary-school photos, but once their voices cracked, their lips turned down. And if anyone ordered boys to smile—a frustrated class photog or a harried mother taking vacation snapshots—the correct response was to flare their lips upward and bare their teeth in caricature, which made them look more miserable yet. Thus, from puberty on, my father coached himself not to smile, even on command, which made his task of becoming more womanly that much more difficult.

Nightly, he crouched in front of his little trusty makeup mirror and practiced curling his lips up. He was able to do it when he could see his reflection, but once he took Polaroids of himself, trying to "smile for the camera," he fell apart. Oftentimes, he was certain that he was grinning like a fiend, when his lips were actually in a pursed straight line. Like an amputee who thinks he's moving a leg that has already been cut off, my father had totally detached himself from his body. After several weeks of frustrated mugging, and dozens of discarded photos, at last he was able to achieve a full smile. It was his first sneak peek at his inner girl, the one he'd always known was there.

The memories would alternate in quick succession.

Think of Chuck. Dinah, you are so beautiful. Do you want to . . . you know?

Think of Dick. Can you wait until after this movie? After this game? After I'm done with this ad? Can't you see I'm doing something here? Can't you see I'm busy?

Think of Claude. American women want to look like boys, but you are voluptuous, you know? You look like a woman.

Think of Dick. I might get a little more turned on if you tried a little harder. Would it kill you to do some stomach crunches or something?

Think of Chuck. Claude. The guy who took her virginity on the coats at the kegger.

Think of Dick. Did you hear me, Dinah? I said no.

My mother got off her bed and wrapped a thick terry cloth robe around her bare body. "You fucking bastard," she murmured, rubbing her eyes with the tip of her sash. "This is ridiculous," she muttered. "Forget about it."

She went downstairs to watch TV.

Dad rushed it. Once he had conquered smiling, he thought he was ready for the world. He was wearing a very nice knit top, an attractive denim skirt, white sneakers, an off-the-rack wig and heavy foundation plastered over what was left of his stubble. It was bright white and sunny, hot and humid, the kind of day you can see spittle cooking on the asphalt. He parked his little sedan, and after trying to quell his rising blood pressure and squinting downward at his feet, darted in a straight line—that strategy had worked so far—toward the May Company department store entrance. He didn't make it there.

Out from nowhere, a pack of six or seven teenagers saw him and read him flat. "Holy sheeeeeit!" one boy yelled, dropping his cigarette. "A fucking fag in a dress!"

"Eeeww," shrieked his girlfriend. "That's so . . . eeewww."

Their faces were contorted in disgust. They laughed, and pointed, and howled, in what seemed to my father like slow motion. They were only a few years younger than I was.

My father knew he was dead. The teenagers would shoot and kill him on the spot, and the newspapers would write of it—if at all—as "Man in Dress Shot at Mall." He cannot remember running into the bushes, nor cowering behind a store sign, but he knows that's where he ended up, anywhere from ten seconds to twenty minutes later. Those heated moments replay in his mind from time to time: his stockings torn from the bushes, trickles of sweat running from under his wig, the hands that wouldn't stop trembling, the memory of a pamphlet with hate crimes statistics, the fear of a death wrung of its tragedy because of what the victim was wearing.

He ran back to his car, never happier he had purchased an automatic instead of a stick, bolted out of the lot, and drove around for three hours. The next day, he locked his door at the office, and in a hushed voice, made an appointment with the Case Western Reserve University Gender Identity Clinic for in-depth gender dysphoria counseling. If he was really going to do this, he decided, it was time to go all the way.

The "big house" had never seemed bigger. My mother was suffering from a combination of empty-nest syndrome, self-pity overload, and plain old cabin fever.

Many of her old, still-married friends had initially sympathized with her plight, then drifted away. Mom decided, at last, to form her own trio of newly single women, all of whom were recovering from their travails with men as well.

In comparison to these other women's sob stories, my mother's situation was relatively stress-free, and not only because she and my father were not actually divorced yet. One of them, Jessica, had survived a troubled childhood only to be left with nothing except herpes simplex II after splitting from her abusive, philandering husband. Another, Carole, was dealing with mean-spirited speculation for the reasons why her husband, a successful neurosurgeon at a hospital in southern Ohio, packed his lunch one day, went to work, and leapt off a parking garage.

My mother, Jessica, and Carole were inseparable for a time. They went to movies together, smoked cigarettes, and traded wincing stories about mothers-in-law. Rarely, but more often than before, I would come home late from Todd's house where I had stuffed myself with pizza and good, nuclear family bonding, and was greeted with the sight of my mother and Carole swilling wine and smoking Merits in the outdoor hot tub. Afterward, they loudly retired to the den for a lustful viewing of Kevin Costner in *Bull Durham* and late-night gab sessions about whether Bush was as bad as Reagan.

I had since grown out of sleepovers, so the spare bedroom was usually free for guests. I loved the sound of my mother's easy giggle emanating from that room, as she pointed out where the guest towels and the bathroom were. I loved hearing her brush her teeth and wash her face, gently close her own bedroom door, and immediately click off the light. She didn't read her pulp paperbacks when she had visitors. Briefly, escape was unnecessary.

After Dad's first session with the therapist at the gender clinic, which consisted mostly in giving an extremely brief version of his life (both as a man and as an aspiring woman), he found himself stopping at a Sears, where, without hesitation, he purchased a pot holder of a small thatch of yellow daisies. Back at his apartment, he hung it up in what was his bachelor kitchen. Such a silly thing, a pot holder. Yet he stared at it for five minutes or so, absolutely enthralled. It was the first bouquet he had ever had.

EIGHTEEN

Losing It, 1989

The divorce papers were delivered by messenger to my mother's office as she was getting ready to leave for the day. She left the thick, legal-sized manila envelope sealed on her desk, just next to an overflowing ashtray of cigarette butts.

She called me to tell me she wouldn't be coming home right away. I said something like "uh-huh." Todd was straddling me, moving his hands to the front of my chest and then hurriedly to the back, trying to figure out which kind of bra clasp I was challenging him with today. I was preoccupied.

My mother hung up the phone and walked to her car. Driving the red convertible was an experience. Teenagers would pull up, à la *American Graffiti*, in their assorted rusty boats, gape, and yell out laughable monetary offers. Every now and then, one would smirk at my mother, silently, and she would fill in the dialogue just like she did year after year with my dad.

Idiot Teen: Hey, what's a middle-aged hag like you driving that fine vehicle for?

Mom: Go to hell. It's my car.

Idiot Teen: Man, you can't pull off that car. Why don't you get a, like, Oldsmobile?

Mom: Shut up, shut up, shut up. Stop talking inside my head, goddammit.

This night, a cool, pitch-dark one just before daylight savings, my mother ended up at a hotel bar. She was seeking a nice brushed brass table, a comfortably upholstered chair, and endless white wine carafes. (For her, that meant two.) Instead, she saw someone she knew hunched at the mahogany bar stirring a Bloody Mary. She knew him a little bit: He was a friend of a friend, an attorney, an attractive, tailored white fox type. He was one of those guys she would always see at parties and spend a few minutes laughing with over cheese cubes before gasping "Lawrence!" because she had just remembered his name.

He said he was getting divorced.

"You look how I feel," my mother said, with a gentle smile. She told me later that he didn't seem to be surprised to see her there. He grinned back, without missing a beat.

They got a booth and talked. It's not worth reciting what they discussed, and my mother, easily snockered, wouldn't have the slightest idea anyway. The point is the quantity, not the quality: A man was interested enough to sit and talk to her until hours went double digit, and then single again.

He asked her to come home with him, an invitation that Mom has assured me (no fewer than a dozen times) was not an effort to take advantage of her vulnerability. She says it was an act of kindness, of generous compassion. While I think my mother, in her relentless self-effacement, might not want to classify a sexual pass in the same terms as a bequest to UNICEF, she has a point.

She said yes.

Back at his house, Lawrence made love to my mother. He touched her, in more ways than one. He asked her for status reports along the way: how she was feeling, whether she was enjoying herself. He asked to see her, undressed, by the light of his night-table lamp. When she agreed, trying not to shiver, he told her she was beautiful, feminine, womanly. He never balked or joked. He said the kind of things that sound really good during sex, but embarrassing later. The lines that, from my father's

mouth, would have been meant facetiously—like "You are a Bot-
ticelli," "You are kissable," or "I want you."

"I remember doing this," she said, at some point.

He laughed, and made that old joke that it was all like riding
a bicycle.

She said she was very relieved to see that was true.

When she prepared to leave a few hours later, muttering apologies and explanations that she should have called home if she
was going to be out until 5 A.M., she kissed him good-bye on the
cheek and promised, jokingly, to remember his name at the next
cocktail party. When she arrived back at home, I was still in bed,
and my mother stayed up, too rushed with adrenaline to sleep.

My mother spent the next day reveling in the ache and linger-
ing quiver of her legs and pelvis, and smiling at herself in the
mirror as though she had pulled one over. Terry McMillan would
say she had gotten her groove back. My mother called it losing
her virginity, part two.

NINETEEN

Girls Get Emotional

January 12, 1989: I gave a little lecture today to two of my friends on how to give blow jobs. They're all virgins, so I'm the big "expert" now. I felt sophisticated until Kerrie asked me whether I spat or swallowed . . . I said neither, you should make him run to the bathroom. They said they were amazed I had dated anyone for so long.

When I was little, I felt inferior because the little girls in my favorite books kept diaries tied with satin ribbons or an elaborate overlapping series of rubber bands. They entrusted the names of their favorite boys and their innermost thoughts to "Maura," "Ashley," or "Calico." By not keeping a diary, I was certain I was missing out on one of the essential experiences of girlhood. But the only times I tried writing in "Caitlin," I ended up with fascinating insights along the lines of February 14, 1982's entry—"Out of Cheerios. So hungry!!"—or the one from May 26, 1985—"Boys suck my butt. Ha!"

As I grew older, I felt increasingly worse about not keeping a journal, as it came to be called in high school, because this was something Real Writers did. Real Writers, many of them of the cumudgeonly male persuasion, constantly jotted down an extraordinary turn of phrase, a deft landscape description, a memorable quotation. Real Writers' journals could later be preserved with their equally impressive letters at Prestigious Eastern Seaboard University.

I didn't want to miss out on this opportunity for future en-shrinement. At the beginning of junior year, I had made a trip down to the mall bookstore, bought a composition book with the more sophisticated "college lined" look, and started spilling right there in the food court. I wrote and wrote about the burdens of keeping a big family secret; I ruminated that this is what it must feel like to be a Mafia princess. I bled ink over the travails of divorce. I made a top ten list of my favorite pizza toppings. I was tethered to the journal for several weeks, until my busy schedule left me little time for extracurriculars that would not go on a college application. Over the next year or two, I would return from time to time to that book, to scribble either something so meaningful or so stupid that it needed to be kept under tiny pad-lock. Now it is a helpful archive of my latter-day teen thoughts, but at the time it was not the source of as much catharsis as I had hoped. The problem was that I didn't want a private confes-sional. I wanted a bullhorn and an audience.

Our closeted lifestyle had forced me to lie to friends, relatives, everyone. Why did your parents divorce? The boozing, the women. What's your dad up to these days? Same old. Why are you crying? Allergies. Why is your father wearing a toupee? Long fingernails? Lavender pants? Uh, it's for a part in a play. A cos-tume party. Like I understand anything my *father* does. Strangely, all the lies and fibs, omissions and fabrications made me driven, with the zealotry of a born-again Christian, to give testimony in every other area of my life.

I kept nothing to myself. I rambled on every subject that I was able to broach. Casting aside my remaining vestiges of shyness, I became a talker, a wild gesticulater. (Is it just a coincidence that closeted people like gays and transsexuals have a reputation for flamboyance and melodrama?) I blamed my urge to purge on being an ordinary girl. Girls get emotional.

I recounted in-depth scenarios about my sex life to my parents and a random assortment of friends. My boyfriend, Todd, was not thrilled about this development; I told him it was normal girl talk, which seemed to perplex him sufficiently to close the subject. More and more, I wanted to be *seen*, sexually. I coaxed my embarrassed boyfriend to worm his fingers past my belt line on a bus packed with choir members on a field trip. I dolled myself up in my own newly acquired stash of lingerie and paraded around in my basement for Todd's viewing pleasure—and, quite possibly, that of the lawn-mower guy. At the video store, I fingered the boxes of thrillers about men peering at women leisurely changing in silhouette behind open venetian blinds, and I didn't think, "Shut your curtain, you idiot. He's going to kill you!" I thought, "That's me! Only with bigger boobs!"

Ironically, as though my quota was one secret per lifetime, I felt completely unable to keep quiet about anything. No matter how many times I crossed my heart or hoped to die at the plea of a confessing friend, I tempted fate. I told. Once I had unburdened myself, I repeated the admonishment to "keep this a secret. Don't tell anyone because I really shouldn't have even told *you*."

I spoke truths the listeners didn't want to hear—my mother swallowing hard over bacon and eggs as she heard me describe the first throbs of orgasm might be a case in point. I talked about things even I didn't want to say (the blow job reminiscence, for instance). I thought if I somehow emptied myself of all other nascent fears and cultural taboos, and virtually eliminated my own once sacrosanct sense of privacy, that I might feel less alone.

My father had no such concern. Thanks to his cross-dressing club, he had girlfriends for the first time, with whom he would exchange articles about obscuring typically masculine features like Adam's apples (think turtlenecks and ruffled collars!) and thick wrists (a silver cuff works nicely) much the way other women of his imagination might swap recipe cards. In truth, they all had little in common except a diagnosis of gender identity dysphoria, but that was of no matter since Dad didn't want to talk about anything else anyway. Although the presence of burly men in dresses recalls images of drunken lodge initiations, my father's group was more like an inverted consciousness-raising group: compulsive gender discussions to raise awareness of just how *feminine* one could become, rather than how to break out of stereotypes. If Marabel Morgan had run a CR group, it might have looked like this.

My father was reveling in his perky new world. Every day was cause for a new superlative. He used exclamation points without irony. Everything might still be a mess—Mom and I might keep him at an arm's length, his colleagues might be bewildered—but he finally was starting to feel right in his body. In a world where people spend millions on diet programs, plastic surgery, beauty products, spa treatments, and myriad other ways to make their bodies feel like *home*, perhaps the fact that this overwhelming need could trump all other concerns shouldn't have been all that shocking.

His mind was slowly made up for him. The more he inhabited a female's body—and increasingly, a female's apartment—the more he became that female. The male "costume," as he called his masculine clothes, started to feel more constricting. He felt like he was holding his breath all day until he could come back home and be his woman self again.

And who was this lady exactly? She was kinder, nicer, tidier, better with children, interested in flowers and birds and chick flicks. She had less of a penchant for one-liners—too snippy—and didn't like alcoholic drinks unless they were garnished with an umbrella. If Dick was in the details, then he had nearly been eradicated. Although my father never referred to his male and female incarnations in the third person, separating the former self from the current and relevant self as some transsexuals do, he still insisted he was a new person. A new woman, to be precise.

To me, it sounded like the transformation of Mr. Hyde into Miss Jekyll. I tried to sort the whole confusing business out with my mother over Sunday breakfasts. We couldn't understand how becoming a woman would make someone a totally different person. We wouldn't be completely different if we were men, would we? And if all these wonderful traits were inside my father all along, why was gender the only means to let them out? Why wasn't loving me—or my mother—enough? And who said women can't handle one-liners and a single-malt Scotch?

That year, Dad went to Provincetown's Fantasia Fair, one of the largest gatherings of transgendered people and cross-dressers of every stripe in the nation. After he got back, we convened for pizza dinner. He looked more feminine than ever, in pink pedal pushers and open-toed sandals. The electrolysis treatments had recently finished up, so his face was cleansed even of peach fuzz. Over half sausage (mine) and half dieters' deluxe (his), Dad tried to explain to me how freeing it felt to be able to walk out in the open in women's clothes.

"It's the most liberating feeling ever," he said.

I associated *liberated* with marching on Washington for rights of some sort, so I was confused. I said, "I can't imagine."

Which was true. I couldn't imagine feeling like I couldn't wear what I wanted to outside. I couldn't imagine how wearing my female clothes could be some great thrill. I couldn't imagine feeling okay with my body.

For the next twenty minutes, Dad told me about gabbing with the other girls, taking classes in deportment and speech, and even participating in a talent show where he sang "When You Wish Upon a Star." (One of the favored songs of the trans community, along with the ever-popular "Georgy Girl" and "Somewhere" from *West Side Story*.)

"It must sound like a cross between finishing school and summer camp," he noted, making light. I shrugged.

When he finished his breathless recitation, I realized that he had never told me so much about himself in one sitting before. Usually, he was content to sit back and watch me talk, which always made me feel self-conscious and caused me to babble at a greater velocity.

"Wow, Dad," I said. "I feel like I'm getting to know you or something."

Tears gathered at the corners of his eyes. "Sorry, hormones." He laughed. "That's all I ever wanted, you know. To know you." My old anger roiled inside, briefly. "Although I know I didn't do much to show it."

He'd read my mind.

Dad told me that Fantasia Fair had encouraged him to take the next step, to come out and live as a woman full-time. (For some reason, during my father's transition, we always described him living "part-time" or "full-time," as though being a woman was gainful employment.) This should have been a major moment, I suppose, but it felt anticlimactic.

"There it is," I said, reflexively. "I figured that was coming any day now."

"I'm not much of a guy anymore, huh?" Dad chuckled.

"Well, there's the Dick part," I pointed out. "Are you going to call yourself Dickette or something?"

"That name might leave a little to be desired, wouldn't you say?" He smiled, still a little weepy. "I thought I could try Rebecca Christine instead." He explained that he chose Rebecca so he could keep his monogrammed stuff and not confuse the mailman, and Christine just because. He planned to go by Christine. "What do you think?"

I had no idea. A dad named Christine. I watched him drum his fingernails on the table—they were long enough to do that now—while he returned my gaze with those eyes that once had seemed so impenetrable and frightening.

"Are you getting it removed?"

"I'm in no rush."

"So if we tell everyone, does that mean we're going to be poor outcasts like you and mom warned me?"

"I hope not. But as scary as this still seems to me, I don't feel like I have any choice at this point. This is something I have to do in order to live." Dad spoke in a lot of dramatic absolutes.

"Does this mean I have to call you mom?" I asked, panicky. "Because I really don't think I can call you Mom. I don't think Mom would like it, either."

"Noelle," he said, in his newly honed soprano, "I'm your dad. I will always be your dad."

"But you can't be a girl and my dad at the same time, right?"

"I don't see why not."

March 12, 1989: I was thinking that Picasso had a blue period. So maybe this could be my brown period. Brown is how I feel. Not happy or sad, not smart or stupid, not black or white, not good or bad . . . I think, starting tomorrow, I will only wear earth tones.

I was of approximately five minds on the issue of my father's impending womanhood. I was scared of having to sleep in the sports car, of maximum allowable Stafford loans (coming out is never part of a good college money-savings scheme). I was worried about eggs being smashed on the living-room window, sugar in the gas tank. I was pleased this would embarrass Grandma Howey, distressed it would upset my mother. I was horrified that no one would think I was normal anymore. And I was relieved that no one would think I was normal anymore.

Like my father, I was in the midst of an identity crisis, albeit

a more low-key one, and my inconsistent feelings about his coming out depended on which Noelle I was inhabiting that minute:
lavender me or sienna me.

Lavender me was happily ensconced in a multiyear relationship
with the nicest boy in the world. Since Todd's acne was yesterday's Buf-Puf and my braces were off, we might possibly have
been the blondest, skinniest, horsey toothsome white people in
Ohio.

Starting junior year, Todd and I were cast opposite each other
in several successive school productions. I was the Laurey to his
Curly; the Marian the Librarian to his Music Man. We strode the
hallways on the opening nights of plays with hay in our hair,
adorned in period gingham frocks or suspenders and chaps, looking like Young America as depicted in a Republican National
Committee advertisement. In the evenings, Todd and I attended
one choir rehearsal, where we sang songs about the joy of singing
while plodding through innumerable jazz squares; and then yet
another, a church-sponsored ensemble where dozens of talented,
svelte kids culled from the 'burbs sang *42nd Street* medleys while
dressed like bridegrooms and hookers. Lavender me was a gentle
conformist, a plucky go-getting National Honor Society type of
gal.

Sienna me, on the other hand, despised popularity, even the
tepid kind that a lead in a school play conferred. Sienna me was
responsible for my daily uniform: Dad's hand-me-down men's
brown blazers and oversize white button-downs with peasant
skirts. (When Todd asked why my father seemed to be giving away
so many of his clothes, I said he was redoing his wardrobe.)

I scoffed at pop, instead preferring the brooding music-to-kill-
yourself-to by the Smiths and the Cure. I joined the National
Organization for Women. I discovered coffee, weaning myself on
Maxwell House instant before moving to high-grade java, and
made myself drink it even though it made me flinch. I started
using SAT vocabulary words in actual conversations.

Sienna me was serious. I had begun to think of myself as "the daughter of a transsexual," almost as though it was a major characteristic of my identity. I also thought of myself as an aspiring actress and writer. I wanted to convey the insouciant sophistication of a young Joan Didion or the wry, cigarette-choked humor of a Dorothy Parker. I wanted *gravitas*.

Often, these two parts of me would bleed into each other, as when I tried to apply Stanislavski to line readings in *Oklahoma!* or when I informed the other Democratic Party phone bankers that lucky me had gotten a prom dress on sale because there was only one size two left on the rack.

I thought of myself as schizo during this period although I probably was just *eclectic*, and hell, maybe even average. But at the time, perhaps following my father's lead, I felt a desperate need to become consistent, to have all my interests, tastes, and lifestyle choices jibe with the same image I was trying to present. It had not yet occurred to me that cultivating such an image might not be required.

Undated, spring 1989: I started crying again in front of Todd. I was thinking about Dad coming out and getting tormented or attacked or something. I couldn't use the old PMS excuse again, he's going to think I'm a nut job. So I said I had gotten this obscene phone call, and it was really horrible. I made the whole story up about it. Todd tried to make me feel better all afternoon, which just made me feel worse.

Apparently, all my mother had needed was a good lay. After her rendezvous with Mr. Hotel Bar, that was how good she felt: If she were a movie heroine (and had liked to shop), she would have scouted for a whole new wardrobe on Rodeo Drive in montage as a sassy, life-affirming anthem played in the background. *That* good. Since it was real life, though, she bought herself a new set of aluminum pans. Money was a little tight after the divorce.

Gradually, her de facto First Wives' Club dispersed, as my mother stopped wanting to talk about feeling sorry for herself. She joined a ladies' golf club, and even spent the occasional evening by herself. Instead of merely huddling in confessional whispers on her bed, she and I were even doing actual activities together: driving to D.C. to agitate for abortion rights, and hitting the road for prospective college visits.

Because of the psychic space he occupied, as well as our weekly meals, Dad was ever more a part of my life. My mother, on the other hand, was thinking less about my dad, as well as less of him. She was unimpressed by his decision to go public, as she considered it an act of self-preservation more than pure courage. "After all," she said, "he can't hide in his apartment forever, and there's only so long you can get away with fingernails like that without coming out." She changed the locks, and coolly told my father he would have to phone before he came over with dirty laundry. After that call, she looked at me, and said, "I am over this. Really."

"So you don't care if he comes out?"

"No, I care," she allowed. "Of course, I care. I'm concerned for you, and your father, and what people will think of me . . ." She trailed off. "But look: I'm ready, really ready to have my life back again. If this is the only way to do that, then so be it."

Hey, kid, your dad's just decided to become a woman! What are you going to do next?

In May, Dad and I took our first vacation together, courtesy of his agency landing the SeaWorld Orlando account. On the plane down to Florida, we were as jittery and overly considerate as new lovers. Dad kept insisting on wrapping the airplane blanket around my sandals, and when I had to move so he could get to the bathroom, I leapt right into the aisle, rather than just lifting my feet for him to pass. He made too many jokes, and I giggled at them too uproariously. We were making an effort.

We were in Orlando for four days. Dad shot promos for Shamu while I slept, and we headed out to Magic Kingdom in the afternoon. Todd had carefully listed for me the top twenty things one must do at Disney World and Epcot Center, but I was a little distracted. It was before the era of Gay Days, so all I could think, as my father and I walked from Mexico to Italy to Norway, where we watched a panoramic film about fjords and ate authentic Norwegian french fries, was that the park would kick us out if they knew what social deviants we were.

We tended to keep the conversation on easy subjects we could wittily whine about—say, how overrated the ride in the big silver ball at Epcot was, or what a mistake it had been to eat at the Norwegian food pavilion. Both of us were delighted to realize we were developing repartee; it was a lot more fun than stilted questions punctuated by awkward silence, the only other conversational style we'd ever perfected.

Only after accidentally catching a cartoon short of Mickey Mouse aping Minnie or some other big-lipped, puckering, eyelash batting, skirt-wearing rodent, did we even venture close to the subject.

"Can I ask you a really stupid question?" I asked afterward, as we sat in a food court behind Cinderella Castle. "Is that what you look like?"

"It's worse," he said, deadpan. "Picture Pluto with lipstick and a mincing sashay."

"Daaadd," I moaned.

"No, I don't look like that," he said, gently. "But why would that be stupid? You have no way of knowing what I look like when I'm dressed. I can tell you this much: Whatever you've pictured is probably a lot scarier."

"Yeah," I said, "you're probably right. I'm scared, I don't know. What if I can't handle it?"

"Then let me have it. Point. Scream. Throw things. I can take it."

"Dad, I would never be that horrible."

"I know," he said.

On our last night in Orlando, Dad was called to the studios for a last-minute editing session. I stayed in the hotel room, ordered four courses of room service on Dad's expense account and watched *Tootsie* on cable. I studied Tootsie's every nuance, especially the opening sequence when Dustin Hoffman plastered on false eyelashes and slipped into panty hose. I watched the movie intently, as though I was studying a cheat sheet. Tootsie seemed so unthreatening to me, so unlike my nightmares about some bizarre hallucinogen-induced version of my father. Tootsie wasn't a drag queen: She was too regal and secure, and not nearly hot enough. When Tootsie tore off her wig at the end and Dustin Hoffman reverted to being a guy, I missed Tootsie. But what frightened me was how relieved I was to see him back as *him*— certainly that was not the ending I foresaw for my own home movie.

It reminded me of Shakespearean comedies I'd studied in school in which all the crazy cross-dressing heroines trade their knickers for corsets, and with feminine docility, marry themselves off to appropriate male suitors. The teacher called that "wrapping things up for the happy ending." If Viola, for example, had stayed a guy, it wouldn't have been a comedy. All the sources of knowledge I'd ever trusted—school and drama and movies and the media—were indicating that my family was inching toward tragedy. But then why did my mother appear to be content? Why were my father and I closer than ever before? If we were on the edge of a precipice, then why did my family seem so damn pleased with itself?

The day before Todd left for summer camp with his parents, we sat together on the campus of Ohio University, where we had attended a drama students' colloquium, and he led me through an in-depth analysis of Arnold Schwarzenegger movies. I didn't hear most of it, as I was very involved in grasping clumps of grass with my hands and watching the blades sift through my fingers.

By the end of junior year, I think I was hanging on to Todd out of some sense that we should finish out our four-year term as well as a dependence on having regular sex. Or perhaps I needed the stability he provided me: He was kind and predictable, unwavering and present. I joked with him that he was the only male role model left in my life, now that Dad had moved out, and in many ways it was true. He was the only guy I had left.

That day, we kissed good-bye with only a smattering of tears. I went to immerse myself in advanced esoterica at Oberlin Theater Institute, where for four weeks I would roll back and forth for an hour in movement technique class and do interpretive dance to the *Jeopardy!* theme song while wearing a plaster cast mask. I spent the summer smitten with a snide, philosophy-spouting boy from a private academy in the Northeast. But nothing happened, and at the beginning of the fall year, I returned to the safe, open arms of my boyfriend.

October 17, 1989: I got so close. In AP govt. today they were talking about gays wanting to adopt kids, and everyone seemed to act like it was the grossest idea in human history. "They'll recruit their kids!" one guy said. And that dipshit I had a crush on—what the fuck was I thinking—starts talking about how gays shouldn't be allowed on the streets, much less near innocent children. The teacher didn't say a word, he just acted like "yes, well, everyone has their own opinion." I got really mad and asked if gay parents couldn't raise normal kids then what about transsexual parents. And the same stupid guy I had sex with in the shower in my mind like one billion times said, "They'd be sick. Put them out of their misery." At that moment I didn't even care who knew. I was so angry. I was so close. I was so so so so so close it scared me.

That fall, in a continuation of their redux adolescences, Mom started dating and Dad became queen of the queens.

In September Mom had penned a list of the top five men she'd

like to "get to know better," and called them up one by one to
ask for a date. The first, she confessed to me, was "a boor and an
asshole." The second was a nice guy, though admittedly unstable,
who charmed her on their only date by recounting his previous
relationship failures. But the third, a friendly attorney, took. He
was "light and loose," full of those chortling anecdotes my mother
had come to favor over my father's biting wit. He complimented
the care she had taken to choose her blouse and slacks, and the
effort of dabbing on a bit of pink lipstick. He opened doors and
pulled out chairs. He reminded my mother how to giggle.

I was happy for her, and relieved to see her out of the house,
especially since I had planned to go away to Oberlin the following
year. Nonetheless, I feared she was dating with such ferocity in
order to quell her fears, ever-lingering from childhood terrors, of
being alone. To that end, I smiled cautiously as she went out on
date after date, and spoke in hushed, qualifying tones when she
rhapsodized about her latest beau. I didn't want to see her (or
me) get hurt again.

In the following years, I came to realize that in true parental
fashion, I was being overprotective, for my mother was hardly a
shuddering mouse. She had cut her ties with Wyse Advertising,
the agency where she had been employed for several years, and
had launched her own design firm with two male partners. She
was spending lots of time browning her freckled face in the summer sun, on fishing expeditions and golf trips with friends.

Truth be told, although I had grown to expect constant change
on the part of my father, and of myself—I was still young after
all—I had assumed that my mother would remain solid, static,
always the somewhat melancholy, devoted figure off on the sidelines. Although her changes were more subtle than the rest of
ours, she was changing from a wife and mother to, simply, an
independent woman. I found that image change the most threatening of all—even more so than the exultant news from my father
that he had been crowned Miss Paradise 1989.

Amidst steep competition from four other Cleveland-area cross-dressers, my father had been granted the tiara. He was so thrilled that he couldn't help but gush about it to me. I was stupefied. This was the person who had mocked me for watching the Miss America pageant as a child. At those moments, I wondered whether taking his daily dose of estrogen was somehow siphoning off brain cells.

But in fairness, for my father, the crown was a validation that he truly embodied Christine, and could pass in public as a woman. After the champagne had been poured and the cake consumed amidst titters of whether it had lo-calorie frosting, my father celebrated that same afternoon in private by heading for the mall where he had been so cruelly taunted. That time, no one even noticed him. (There is no more triumphant a coming out for a transsexual than to be completely ignored.)

Having changed into a comfy pair of slacks and a suede blouse much like the ones my mom wore those days, Dad walked straight into a shoe store. Salesclerks were handing out silk roses to each "lady" who walked in the door, as part of a grand opening promotion. Without issuing a second glance, one saleswoman handed my father a flower. "Welcome to our opening!" she said, smiling. "Let us know if we can help you, ma'am."

"All that day," my father gushed to me the following weekend, "people said 'she' and 'her,' referring to me, and 'ma'am' and even 'miss.' "

I wanted to say *then I should see you, too. Let me try to accept this for real.* But something stopped me. I was still too frightened.

I hadn't seen Grandma Howey in about seven months when she called. In fact, I'd probably only visited her ten times since high school began. Dad brought her to my plays, during which she hung on to his arm like he was still—or ever—the prodigal son. It seemed strange seeing her in the lobby after the shows, admiring my thick pancake foundation and ridiculously over-the-top musical theater costumes as though I was still her feminine protégé—flitting from one costume to another, forever disguised. Far from still craving her approval, I would rather have had her see me in my combat boots with my trusty men's undershirt and Guatemalan folk skirt.

I was not subtle. I was angry. I was so set against her that I won a statewide poetry contest for writing about how much I hated her. The last line, in feverishly purple prose, stated "Grandmother was a beautiful girl/But her heart was painted black."

I didn't want to see her that day to talk about Todd and whether I had any pictures of the handsome couple to show her. I didn't want to hear about the lobster she and Rusk ate at Pier W. (Since marrying him, she, too, frequented only one restaurant.) I did my best to sound gruff on the intercom when she buzzed me in, and made every effort to look put out when I got to her swanky apartment with the white-on-white living room. I didn't want to feel bad that she didn't have any hot chocolate because she had been feeling too tired to go buy any. Or guilty when she inquired about having heard from Dad that I'd won some type of award for something. I didn't want to reach for her hand when she suddenly started blinking back tears, while both hands seemed tacked to her knees as though she might fall apart if she moved a muscle. But I did. I had to. She knew.

For the next hour, she leaned against me on the sofa, as though I was the only thing propping her up. She said she couldn't talk to Rusk about this; if he couldn't understand why she might want to take a vacation, she said, he wouldn't get anything this outlandish. She said it was her fault. Either she had neglected the signs, and was therefore a bad mother, or she didn't see any signs, and therefore was a bad mother. She didn't know what people would think. "What if some old friend of mine sees us while we're out? What should I say? This is my niece, Christine? 'Hi, this is my niece, Christine.' "

I asked her how my father had broken the news. She said it happened at a seafood restaurant, a week earlier, between dinner and dessert. She had been so distraught that she had barely been able to finish her bowl of Tin Roof. That night, once she was able to get her bearings, she'd taken control of the situation and wanted to tell me about it.

"I made a list, just so it was all on paper," she told me, and pulled a tattered memo sheet out of her white linen pants. "Okay, the pros are . . . if he lives as a woman, he'll be happier, he says. I couldn't think of another thing. Now the cons: He may lose his job. How will he support himself? You're starting college. How will he pay for it? He may lose some of his friends. The neighbors will wonder. Health insurance may be difficult. And what about AIDS? And you know, dating? Who's going to want to be with someone like him?"

"Have you given this to him yet?" I asked.

"No," she said. "I don't want him to bite my head off. He has such a temper, you know."

"Yeah," I said, "well, for the record, it's getting better."

She looked down at the list on her lap. "I don't want to lose him," she said, sniffling. "Which is funny, don't you think? Since, you know, I know he can't stand me."

"Grandma," I said, in a hushed tone, and put my arm around her shoulders, "that's so not true."

"This is a hard one for me," she mumbled through her tissue.

"I know," I said, and we sat together on the sofa for a while, holding hands.

The next day, I called my father to chide him for not giving me advance warning. I remember telling him that he was one surprise after another.

He explained to me that it was time. He was going to be out within the year, and the family needed time to adjust. So he told Grandma H. I asked if I could tell Todd and my other friends.

He was silent, for a long, uncomfortable moment, before clearing his throat and in his best little-girl voice, said he'd rather I didn't just yet.

But Mom and I had stopped listening to Dad. That, as she and I had discussed ad nauseum, was our secret, too. *We* were ready to spill. In quick succession, Mom confessed to Grandma Schultz, and I told Todd.

As expected, Grandma Schultz, struggling with the relapse of her cancer, took the news very well. "He'll make a beautiful woman," she said, chirpily, from her bed at home. "I still don't see why the two of you couldn't work things out." My mother shook her head, and changed the subject to the cretins at the insurance company who were denying adequate cancer care coverage—something they could both agree on.

Breaking the news to Todd was less intimidating than I had ever imagined. We were at a point where our relationship was so lackadaisical that I wasn't risking too much.

I told him in the midst of a basement makeout session. He was on top of me, going through the motions, when I pulled my shirt down, and said, "We need to talk."

"Um, okay," he drawled, looking confused.

"We're not breaking up. I need to tell you something, and you can't tell anyone."

"Noelle, I'm not really comfortable with hearing other people's stuff."

"No, no." I sighed. "I'm not breaking a confidence. Well, I am. It's about me, though, so it's okay. I think." Todd looked dour and silent, as though he was steeling himself.

"My dad's a woman," I said. "I mean, he's coming out as a woman. He's like, you know, one of those guys on *Donahue*."

Todd's eyes widened slightly. "Okay," he said, shuffling off of me.

"That's why my parents got divorced. It's why I, you know, get emotional. I wanted to tell you, but I wasn't allowed to. I hope you understand. My family was nervous that something bad might happen if we told people. I might get teased, my dad might lose his job."

"So why are you telling me now?" he asked, concerned.

"Because we're going public kinda soon, and I thought you had the right to know first, being my boyfriend and all."

Todd slumped back, looking shocked, until a smile broke over his face. "Wow," he said, and hugged me fiercely. "I thought, when you said your dad and you had this secret about this bad thing he had done and it was hurting you and no one could know and it would be terrible if it got out . . . I thought—do you know what I thought?"

I blanched. "Oh my God, I had no idea. You must have been so worried."

"I thought—well, it doesn't matter. I had no idea, obviously," he said, laughing. "You have to understand, though, this is *so* much better than what I thought you were upset about."

"I guess in comparison to that," I smiled, uneasily, "this is no big deal."

He held my face and kissed me, and despite our growing older (and apart), I loved him more at that moment than at any other.

Once Dad moved into a new house—one with a functioning washer/dryer—he and Mom barely saw each other anymore. They didn't burden me by communicating through me, but their phone calls were as brusque as those of any other recently divorced couple—especially after the "girlfriends" debacle.

Shortly before my graduation from high school, they decided to get together for coffee (Dad in his female clothes) and hang as "girlfriends." Dad's garb was nothing Mom had to prepare for, since she had gotten a sneak preview over several decades. Dad desperately sought the old friendship they had shared, the one that had puttered on through all but the worst times of their marriage. Mom was less enthusiastic about seeing Dad. As she told me, she didn't know if she would ever get over what he had done—not the cross-dressing, but the cruelty. But she missed him, too, in a less avid way, and figured it would benefit them both if they were able to maintain a relationship.

It didn't work. From the moment they sat down in the dark-paneled Arabica coffee shop at Shaker Square, they felt ill at ease. Whereas once they had always been able to talk, now their conversations replicated the way Dad and I used to not communicate.

"So you're dating?" Dad said, awkwardly. "That fun?"

Mom nodded, and launched into a girlfriend-to-girlfriend description of the date. When she was finished, Dad was red-faced and clenching his paper cup.

"I thought you wanted to be girlfriends," my mother said sharply.

"Yes, but I was your husband," Dad whined, in her high-pitched voice. "What do you expect me to think?"

"Well, do you want to be my ex-husband or my girlfriend? Pick one," my mother snapped, "because I can't keep track."

"That's not fair," Dad pouted.

"Then again," my mother snarled, "if you want to act like a little girl, you're on your own." She dabbed her mouth with a napkin and excused herself.

I did not blame my mother for her fury against my father. I wouldn't have blamed her if she had never spoken to him again, given the insecurities he had saddled her with over the years. The hardest part for me in dealing with my father was getting over the damage he had wreaked on my mother in the name of gender identity. It was vastly easier to forgive Grandma H. for hurting me than for hurting my mother. The same rule applied with my dad.

But unlike the way I had swiftly cut Grandma H. out of my life for years, I had no intention of following suit with my father. Mom didn't want that. As much as she pondered having my father surgically excised from her life, she wanted me to have a real relationship with him for the first time. It would mean I was happier. It would also mean that she had fixed something after all—albeit just one part of our dysfunctional family. She hadn't been able to save her husband for herself, but she believed my father could be saved for me.

July 9, 1990: I decided to do it. On my birthday, actually. I thought I'm eighteen and Dad came out like four years ago, and I still haven't seen him, which means I'm being kind of babyish about this. Dad was so happy when I told him. He said he was so proud of me, and he cried (again!). So that was cool. I guess he's coming over this weekend. I'm not as freaked about it anymore as I thought I would be. I keep telling myself he's going to look like Tootsie.

Dad did not look like Tootsie, but he was close. He had hair! A brown curly wig. And a nautical-themed blue-and-white shirt, with white pants and sandals. He had breasts! Small ones, though. A wristwatch on one arm and a gold bracelet on the other. He was attractive! Not scary sexy attractive, but cute nonetheless. The kind of approachable woman who might be offered phone numbers scribbled on napkins at a clambake.

He had no sooner walked up to the front door of the house than I collapsed into peals of laughter, walking backward into the mantel and doubling over.

My father just stood there, next to my mother, with a plastered-on smile. They both stared at me as though I had lost my mind.

Quickly, feeling like I might be hurting his feelings, I recovered. "Oh my God," I gasped. "I'm sorry. You just look so . . . so . . ."

Dad's face was pinched, prepared for incoming insults. "Normal," I sighed. "Who could have expected that?"

He came over and hugged me, the hard little bumps of his breasts pressing against mine. I didn't know if they were real or not, but I wasn't going to ask.

We meandered together into the backyard. "You might not believe this," he said, "but I am coming out for you.

"If I didn't do this, you might never have had a father. I could just see this future, you know, I could see you grown-up, thirty or thirty-five years old, and saying to someone, 'Oh yeah, I haven't seen my father in fifteen years.' It killed me that you didn't know how much I loved you. I needed for you to know. Maybe that's selfish." He sighed. "It wouldn't be the first time."

"It's not," I murmured. "It's not selfish. I need you, too."

"Now that I'm a woman," he said, "I think I can finally be a real dad." He started laughing. "Boy, that sounds fucked up, doesn't it?"

"Yeah," I said. "So we'll be fucked up together." We embraced again, standing under the shade of a maple tree, and I could see my mother standing in the window, arms folded, with a wide smile as though she'd seen the happy ending to her favorite movie.

TWENTY

Coming Out, 1990

Dear Tom,

Hi! How's your new house? Hope you're not getting saddle burns from your riding mower this summer. I know the last thing you expected to receive is a letter from Dick Howey, but here it is.

I'm sending you this letter to let you know about something that's going on in my life that's very positive, very challenging, and just a bit (ahem) unconventional. What I'm going to tell you may seem rather personal, and I apologize for not discussing this issue in person with you, but time and schedules didn't permit.

My mother, my father, and I decided to throw a "coming out party," inadvertently borrowing the language of debutante balls. We planned to hold it at a country club–type setting, with black tie waiters serving fussy hors d'oeuvres, in honor of Dad's ascension to womanhood. The gala would be hosted by my mother and myself, along with close friends and advertising colleagues of Dad's who had been gently approached some months earlier, widening the circle of Those Who Knew to an unprecedented ten. It may seem surprising that my mother didn't simply absent herself from the whole affair, given the borderline estrangement between her and my father, but she held firm to the principle that we were all in this together.

"This isn't just your father's coming out," she told me. "We're a family, and we support each other." She wasn't trying to sound as feisty and selfless as Mother Jones. Nor had she abruptly forgiven him for his failings as a husband—and even a friend. She might have wanted to kill him, but she loved him. She might not want to share regular coffee klatches, but there was no way that she was going to hang him out in public.

My mother wasn't falling back on old patterns then, standing by her woman come what may. She had grown weary of being on the sidelines while my father spoke for her from the spotlight. She wanted to explain why the most normal woman around would have married and remained faithful to a wanna-be female. She wanted, at last, to speak for herself.

I was looking forward to the occasion. I had graduated from high school, and would be buried in midterms at Oberlin College by the time Dad hit the local gossip transom. As a college freshman, I was excited by the prospect of chaos in direct proportion to the degree I had feared it as a high school freshman. I didn't know if I would be joining any music or drama clubs at school, but I planned to become at least an occasional participant in the most popular extracurricular: shaking up the bourgeoisie. Unlike my mother, who was rehearsing a rotating set of gentle explanations followed by a FAQ at the end, like Transsexualism for Dummies, I was ready to be pissed. I planned to be in-your-face supportive, and I only hoped that someone would tell me exactly what I had once feared: You're not right. You're abnormal. You're going to hell on a rail.

I wasn't altogether honest with myself when I tried to pretend that I (or any of us) was fear-free. Mom and I were still scared that Dad would lose, well, *everything*. Dad himself was afraid of the clear and present dangers, as well as the insidious forms of discrimination that might emerge two months or two years down the road: the slow ebbing of his career and personal life. But the coming out had long since become inevitable, for all of us, so we held our breath and hoped for the best.

First, a brief historical perspective about an individual struggle I've had for the past four decades. Ever since I was five or six years old, I've had strong feminine feelings and a feminine role identity. Over the years, I submerged and denied those feelings in order to meet the expectations of society. This process became more and more difficult, to the point where I had almost destroyed my emotional existence and, as a result, a good part of my life.

I decided to change course and finally determine who I was and how I should live. I was accepted into the Gender Identity Clinic affiliated with Case Western Reserve University. Gradually, over many months and several revelations, the person who was me began to emerge.

In August, Dad wrote a letter to two hundred family friends and work acquaintances. He wrote to old teachers from Kent State University, acting partners from Dobama, art directors from various agencies. We had realized that the only way to keep the rumor mill from churning on overdrive was to come clean oneself—to everybody simultaneously. Selective groups wouldn't have worked; it would be the best watercooler fodder that anyone had heard in years.

One week after his forty-fifth birthday, Dad stood by his mailbox with a basket of letters for two hours. *What the fuck are you doing? Get the fuck back in the fucking house and get a goddamn suit on.* He was so terrified that even the mailman, winking from his little cart and saying, "Can I get those for you, ma'am?" didn't make him feel better. Trembling, he handed the basket over, and watched as the mailman dumped the pile into a white corrugated box stamped "Official Property of the U.S. Postal Service."

It was a felony to retrieve the letters, and Dad didn't want to go to jail. "Man in Dress Arrested for Attacking Mailman." Comforted by the thought that he had no choice, he turned to go back inside the house.

That's a roundabout way of saying I discovered that my true gender is: woman. This is the gender where I feel natural, comfortable, and happy. This is where I function best and relate best with others. Therefore I have chosen to live the rest of my life as the woman I am, namely: Rebecca Christine (Chris) Howey.

Grandma H. called me when she got her letter in the mail. She said that she couldn't come to the party because she didn't know how she would explain it to Rusk. I told her, a little sharply, that that was a ridiculous reason.

"I know," she said, mournfully. "But you know I love him, her."

"He, she loves you, too," I said.

Well, now that you've picked yourself up off the floor, I would like to assure you that this is a decision which I did not make easily. I have, in fact, fought against this for many years. But a personal identity is a hard thing to ignore or defeat, and serious life consequences were awaiting me had I not resolved to face the truth.

The day the letters went out, I got on the phone and told all of my good friends. I answered all their questions: No, he still had one; yes, even waiters can't tell.

Each friend peppered me, asking questions I had not yet considered, like "Is he attracted to men or women?" and "What do his genitals look like?"—as though my Dad being a female meant we all hung around naked now, comparing equipment.

By and large, though, my friends were understanding. "We love you," they said. "Of course, we'll support you."

It wasn't until I heard their soft words of encouragement, one after the other echoing through the phone receiver, that I realized how fast my pulse had been racing. When I finally hung up for the day, I wiped my sweaty palms on my jeans, and cried.

As of September 1, 1990, I will begin living full-time as a woman. I hope to maintain my existing friendships and relationships, both

*personal and business, since I am essentially the same person I was—
although functioning better and in an admittedly different package. I
hope you will be able to accept this important transition in my life,
and I stand ready to offer any explanations or assistance in helping
you (or anyone) cope with this change.*

*I must take a moment to mention that I haven't arrived at this very
significant stage in my life by myself. Many close and caring friends
(some of whom are mentioned below) have been there for me when I
needed them, and I offer them my eternal thanks. And as for my
family, my remarkable daughter, Noelle, and my ex-wife-and-always-
best-friend, Dinah—I am forever indebted for their wonderful love
and support.*

The majority of the letter recipients responded in kind. They
called my mother. They wrote my father. For Mom, they offered
clucking condolences and words of praise. For Dad, they murmured clichés like "Well, you have to do what you have to do."
A few on the fringes told my father he was going to burn. Several
on the opposite edge thought he should be canonized. By the end
of the following week, 100 people said they would come to the
soiree.

The party went something like this: I drove the hour from college,
bellowing along with an old Tom Lehrer cassette to make believe
that I was feeling sassy and defiant. I sat in the parking lot, and
carefully applied my makeup by inches in the rearview mirror. I
ate too many little spinach phyllo turnovers. I watched my father
enter the room, simple and elegant in a black turtleneck and long
skirt. I expected people to turn slowly, clutch each other's arms,
and pass out or shriek. I expected time to slow down. As usual, I
had been ready for cinema.

Instead, no one noticed. Dad had to tap people on the shoulder
and explain that yes, she was the person formerly known as Dick.
Many laughed, anxiously or with happy surprise. One admitted

he had been checking her out. Dozens of the curious clustered around Mom and me, whispering how shocked they were that she looked so great, and complimenting us for our fortitude as though we were the lone survivors of a natural disaster.

I was called brave, courageous, and the best daughter in the nation. My mother was compassionate, kind, and the best ex-wife in human history. I had never been subject to so many superlatives in my life.

My father didn't notice much of that. She was radiant, basking in the experience of being with friends as herself for the first time. She glided across the room, from person to person, instinctively working the room the way she had when I was a child. Her approach wasn't the same; there were fewer jokes at others' expense, and more at her own, in what one might call the Phyllis Diller effect. She was less commanding, and more conciliatory. She wasn't exactly the woman I sought to be, but she had become an actual—if not actualized—person.

I'll be taking a few weeks off from in-person contact, to tend to some of the details of this transition (although I will continue to work from my home via phone and fax). But I hope to see you on October 5. In any case, I look forward to seeing you soon, and maintaining the excellent relationship we've had in the past.

Thanks very much for your attention to this rather unexpected letter.

Very sincerely,
Chris Howey

TWENTY-ONE

She Thing

"There's a story going around my hometown about a man who decided to be a woman and two years ago began a series of operations. Today he is a she. To celebrate, he/she had a coming out party given by—of all people—the woman to whom he/she was married.

A bit bizarre?

My son thought so when he told me. My daughter said she'd always believed those kind [sic] of stories were made up for TV talk shows."

—Lois Wyse, *Good Housekeeping*, May 1991

In the days following my father's party, I half expected calls from journalists seeking my titillating take on "alternative family" life, or mocking late-night monologues about how the Howey family constituted one more example of American zaniness. In my lucid moments, of course, I remembered that we lived in Ohio: another vowel-heavy state, difficult for the French to pronounce, located in the region officially designated by bicoastals as "one of those middle states." Ohioans only popped up in stories about tornadoes in trailer parks, or when the bigwigs wanted to see how controversial ideas like, say, health-care reforms or *AfterMASH*, were playing in the heartland.

So imagine my surprise when we did presumably make the

national media, in the unlikely form of a column in *Good House-keeping*. Lois Wyse, impresario of a mini-empire of bathroom books with titles like *Gee, You Don't Look Like a Grandmother!*, cofounded the advertising agency where my mom had previously been a division vice president. Lois also just so happened to be a monthly purveyor of family values aphorisms in the home of the Seal itself.

More of a *Consumer Reports* reader herself, my mother saw the column by pure chance and immediately called me at school to tell me that we were apparently the scourges of housewives everywhere. She said she was so pissed that she wanted to carry the magazine to the trash with kitchen tongs. I asked her how it felt to be officially abhorrent. She sighed and said it was not as bad as she would have expected, and almost funny.

In truth, the hard part about coming out was not at all what we thought it would be. We expected to run a gauntlet of aspersions, discriminatory actions, and, from the nicer folk, condescension. As a former speech therapist and bookstore manager and an aspiring actress and writer, my mother and I might have thought language would be the least of our problems. But as it turns out, you never know how far you've *not* come until you try to talk about it.

"Noelle's father has started living full-time as a wo— . . . a female," my mother might say, all the while trying to explain how much she had fully accepted and comprehended the magnitude of this life change. "He, she wants to be known as Christine," I muttered, not much more deftly.

Even as both of us had adjusted to calling my father a "female," we had trouble with raising the bar to "woman," and adding in the appropriate pronouns. For some reason, "female" sounded clinical, and relatively free of cultural baggage, whereas "woman" seemed more selective and rarefied, as though you should have to apply for admission. I don't know my mother's reasons, but I associated the word with fertility goddess figures, all plush breasts and ample hips; or conversely, lithe supermodels, radiating sex appeal with pouts. Personally, I felt that I was neither buxom nor well accessorized enough to be a woman. Certainly if I was too embryonic in my own mind to have earned that titular promotion from girl, certainly my father, with all of a month or two worth of genuine female experience, wasn't qualified either.

Friends asked me again and again, "So do you think of your dad as a woman?" yet I was never sure what the prerequisites for womanhood should entail. The ability to menstruate? To bear children? Lots of bona fide XX carriers had no uterus, no eggs, no periods, no desire to procreate. Was being a woman just about having a vagina? If that was the case, then Women's Studies should consist of just one class: Anatomy 101. Or was that word really shorthand for an amalgam of cultural experience, from giggling at slumber parties to being wolf-whistled at on the street? These, of course, were rhetorical questions.

"She" and "her" were more rife with complications, partly because I still had to revert to the masculine pronoun when people—like, for instance, a financial aid officer—didn't know my life's story and it seemed a trifle personal to go into depth all for the sake of using the appropriate three-letter word. Then again, so many vestiges of tradition still cling to language—as when older men called me a lady, or Miss Howey—decades after the world they embodied has all but disappeared. All appearances to the contrary, I guess I was being traditional.

Our relatively good humor about the not-so-*bons mots* of *Good Housekeeping* was engendered in no small part by the fact that the attitude of my mother's former boss proved to be an exception. Sure, a few people told us we were dead wrong. They said it just like that, which made it easier to shrug off. A male friend of the family regretted to inform Mom that, had she been more feminine, Dad would have had "incentive" to stay the way God made him. I can't say that sentiment didn't hurt my mother, since it's one of the few interactions from that time that she recalls with high-resolution clarity, but she made it through—largely because the enormous, albeit unexpected, bounties of coming out out-weighed the negatives.

The day after the party, no fewer than five people called up my mother at her office and exposed their own skeletons: My husband is an alcoholic; I was raped two years ago; My uncle murdered my aunt. "I've never told anyone this before," they said. "I knew you'd understand." My mother spent half that afternoon and the next on the phone, watching the ashes of her cigarette waft in the shaft of sunlight across her desk while she listened, smoked, and advised. She was the recipient of so many phone confessions that she got "violin neck." She told me that in a giddy rush, crowing like someone who had won a major award.

Thanks to not abandoning Dad, she was being recruited to rescue dozens of other people who vaunted her compassion, em-pathy, and other stellar maternal qualities—just as she had always wanted. Before the news was broken to the public at large, I had been more frightened for her than my father; she wasn't nearly as accustomed to bouncing between popular and peripheral as Dad was. I didn't know if she could bear it, and I was relieved that she wouldn't have to find out.

Still, the goody bag my mother took home from the coming out party paled next to the riches I reaped. I was a freshperson at a school where so many people affixed pro–gay rights pink ribbons to their backpacks that I was initially terrified I'd never get a date. Where I was given a Welcome, New Student! kit con-taining a pack of dental dams—which I mistakenly thought were hygiene-related, like some sort of elaborate plaque-removal sys-tem. Where I was taunted in the coed bathroom on my third day of orientation for shaving my legs. Where I had not the slightest chance of maintaining my image as an artsy granola girl, because there were about fifteen hundred womyn willing to nail my mascara-wearing, white-flour-eating ass to the co-op floor in a feminist death match. Until, of course, I mentioned my dad.

I fell upon that strategy by accident, as I was wandering around the campus, a small, slightly illogical maze of buildings ranging in style from Ivy League brick to sanitarium cellblock. Dad's confessional letters had gone out a week or two before I headed to Oberlin, and no sooner had I unpacked my microwave, halogen lamp, and other fire hazards, than I started coming out to random strangers.

At first, this truth-telling binge wasn't calculated in the slightest. Having survived the hothouse years, I felt compelled by a primal force—one unhindered by concepts like *tact* or *timing*—to tell people immediately upon meeting them. Call it catharsis. Call it emotional masturbation. Call it a by-product of reading Carol Gilligan over the summer, and therefore believing, as all earnest undergraduates must, that I had been silenced for years and needed to speak out—again and again and again. Whatever the nomenclature, it felt really good. Coming out was probably the second biggest high readily available at my college, and I was so intent on engaging in it that I was willing to shed all social niceties like asking someone his name *prior* to announcing my unusual genealogical history. It's a fascinating statement about my alma mater that I can't recall anyone who seemed all that surprised.

"Hi," I said to one cute guy in a Ben & Jerry's T-shirt. "I'm a first-year student, and I'm really happy to be here because it's such a liberal place. See, my Dad is a transsexual."

This is not an exaggeration.

"Cool," the guy said. "Wanna hacky sack?"

I told my new roommate, Jenn, even before we had exchanged the names of our hometown boyfriends and compared the "So long but not farewell" mix tapes they had both given us. I wasn't sure how she would react. Jenn, a pert overachiever with long blond ringlets had told me she'd liked high school, and adorned her bed with a giant stuffed purple character from *Where the*

Wild Things Are. She was perhaps the only person at Oberlin more mainstream than I was.

But she, too, seemed pleased to hear my revelation. "That's really great," she burbled, like she had been dying to meet someone related to a transsexual, and asked me probing questions on the biology, sociology, and psychology of the phenomenon.

On the second week of classes, I bared my family tree to Introduction to Acting. We had to perform a monologue on a topic important to us. One guy talked about his scruffy pet beanbag. I held up a photo of my mother, my father (as a guy) and myself, and talked about what it was like to have a female father. Afterward, the professor gave me kudos for the courage to be so honest and asked me to audition for his upcoming production. Another classmate, the guy who rhapsodized about his beanbag, asked me out.

I quickly deduced that being related to my father, and not acting like a bigot about it, elevated me above all the other upper-middle-class white chicks in thrift wear roaming the commons. (Strange that this would be thought an unusual virtue in a school so casually accustomed to cross-dressing that on any given afternoon, men in Tibetan print skirts played Frisbee in front of the library, and the annual Drag Ball was as avidly attended as, I suspect, the Harvard/Yale game.) Being "the daughter of" legitimized me. I might not have been an Arab-American lesbian or a half-Jewish bisexual, but I was the daughter of a transsexual, and that meant something. It meant I got into every class in which a preregistration application posed the question: "What unique perspective can your background bring to the discussion?" My answer, dressed up with fifty-cent vocabulary words, was always the same: Daddy.

Unfortunately, as is too often the case, coming out didn't materially improve life for Daddy herself. Her friends *were* calling less, the bowling league *wasn't* thrilled about welcoming a former man (with a two-hundred-plus average, no less) into the women's league, and she *did* lose work (in a collective societal effort, perhaps, to inch her toward the average women's pay scale). Fortunately, thanks to her blind state of euphoria from finally going public and not being pilloried or dying in the process, she didn't care. Her psychic space was occupied. After all, merely being female wasn't enough. She needed to know what species of woman she was. Decidedly uninterested in the "butch" side of the spectrum for obvious reasons, she elected to give *über-*femininity a try.

The catering bill for the coming out party was barely settled before I started hearing about the changes. She didn't just buy flowers—she arranged them. She crafted her own dining-room centerpiece: a tiny wicker basket filled with walnuts hand-painted gold. She perfected her own recipe for shiitake mushroom soup and mailed it in to *Bon Appetit*. Breakfast cereal was served with linen napkins and accessorized rings.

Far from the gender dysphoria of her old apartment, Dad's new house was hundred percent Girl. Everything was mauve: bathroom towels, an assortment of guest soaps, the random ceramic vase. Here and there you'd catch a sentimental trifle: a faux sepia-toned photo of a little boy and girl in period dress smooching over a baby carriage; a pencil holder I made in kindergarten; a spray of pussy willows arrayed on an end table; a half dozen eau de cologne spray bottles artfully arranged on a dresser, as though a photo shoot was imminent. The books, too, had gotten softer in subject matter. Calvin Trillin, Hunter Thompson, and Fran Lebowitz, the old acerbic favorites, had been shunted aside on the built-in bookcases in favor of *Entertaining* by Martha, and most egregiously, *14,000 Things to Be Happy About.*

Over fall break, I saw all that for myself. I had never been inside my father's apartment, or her new house before, so I drove around the block about three times before parking in the driveway and walking oh-so-casually up to the door.

I shouldn't have been nervous. Beaming in an apricot-colored apron lightly dusted in flour, Dad ushered me through the door. Dough clung to every last crevice of her hands, making them look like the appendages of gigantic old people. She was sweating, and a trickle of foundation was seeping into the collar of her white T-shirt. "Sorry," she said, grinning. "I just got done with my second rising." We hugged briefly, while she waved her dough-caked hands in the air away from me. And as usual, I tried to deduce whether her chest bumps were regular implants, hardened implants, or a stuffed bra. I could have asked, I suppose, but the query had become part of my solitary parlor game: guess what's real.

It was a lovely evening, and at first, I couldn't have been more uncomfortable. Dad made a mesclun salad, her now-famous mushroom soup, homemade white bread, vegetable lasagna, and chocolate pie. She dabbed at the corners of her lips after each course and at the end, reapplied her lipstick.

"Um, are we going somewhere?" I asked, watching her peer at her face by inches in the compact she kept in her pocket.

"No, no," she said. "I just like to look nice."

I nodded and we sat quietly, stealing glances at each other. I wasn't wearing any makeup. I had tossed it all out after about a week at school. She looked so rosy and well coiffed, like a picture from one of the advertisements she wrote. I wished I had at least put on some concealer.

After dinner, we sat in the living room and relaxed into the big fluffy pastel-flowered sofas that, according to my father, you're allowed to have when you're a girl. We flipped the remote (I was glad to see she still did that) and mocked a home shopping network anchor trying to sell a youth-replenishing mud masque allegedly from the grave of an ancient Roman who maintained a perfect complexion—even a full goatee—three thousand years after his death.

"Boy, am I glad I didn't put that shit on my beard," my father joked, blowing her nose into a paper towel. "My electrolysis really would have been a bitch. And that corpse has an amazingly modern hairstyle, don't you think?"

"Well, that's not fair, Dad." I smirked, feeling a hundred times more comfortable whenever she revealed a side that was more recognizable as my father's. "It's a Caesar cut."

She looked at me, pleased to see I could smirk alongside her—maybe reminding her that being female and snarly were not mutually exclusive traits. Then she sweetly offered me a mocha sundae with a coconut tuile and mint sprig on top. She apologized for not having yet bought rings to match her dessert napkins, like the most particular Southern hostess.

"I'm still in transition here," she explained, with a heavy sigh.

"It's okay, Dad," I said. "I got that."

Once I was a little more settled at school, I finally ended my "marriage." Todd and I broke up during college after I hooked up with a short, no-nonsense astronomy major who promised he could never love me.

I had missed the early jolts of seratonin when Todd's eyes first started to glide over my body, pausing at the curvy parts; my surge of quick, breathless, completely self-absorbed thoughts like "oh-yes-Noelle-see-you-are-sexy-see-he-wants-you-you-are-hot-and-beautiful-and-desirable-and-babelicious." I wanted to feel that power again—the unmistakable feeling of victory that came from being watched, and wanted—and I figured the payoff would be bigger if the boy was more unattainable.

I was looking for a guy who was a dreamboat of emotional inaccessibility, as congenitally unable to show me kindness as any Marlboro man. Fresh out of cowboy suitors, I imagined myself with an Artist; preferably one with trendy wire-rimmed glasses, who would correctly pronounce "Proust," drink Scotch straight up, and with whom I would always come second—after his poetry, painting, or organic gardening. But that guy already had a girlfriend. So I hooked up with Josh.

Josh diverged in most respects from my well-drawn stereotype. He was a petite man who favored a casual preppy style of soft cardigans over T-shirts and jeans, which were cuffed at the ankle. He wore contacts. He was not overly intellectual, especially by Oberlin standards, since his tastes tended to run more to pulp fiction authors, and he was a teetotaler who'd never even smoked pot. To his considerable credit, however, he was a brilliant puzzle solver and music buff who sighed knowingly during jazz concerts. He considered himself a deeply rational and logical person—"I don't make decisions with my heart," he once announced—which seemed very guyish.

Moreover, he had the core quality of aloofness that I was going for. What proved to be the ultimate turn-on for me was the moment, after a month of dating, when he took me aside and informed me that his best friend was the closest female in his life. No matter what I did, he said, he could never care about me as much as her. He made the speech matter-of-factly, holding my elbow, in a stairwell just a few steps shy of two highly amused sophomores smoking a bong. I ran away to my bedroom and cried, and swore I would never speak to that conceited jerk again. That cinched it: I wanted him *bad*.

That year, as I began to cart around 100-level feminist tracts like *This Bridge Called My Back*, I nonetheless made myself completely available for Josh, meeting him after classes, surprising him with candles and dinner in his monastic dorm room, and most of all, fashioning myself into a submissive sex fanatic so that he would never contemplate breaking up with me. It seemed to work. After a few months of paying undivided attention, he swore he was in love with me. I'd bagged the big prize.

I told myself that getting what I wanted meant I had to keep up my all-sex-all-the-time routine. I looked for inspiration to keep me primed for sex as often as possible. I studied the small cache of soft-porn mags a friend kept squirreled away in his sock drawer, and memorized the models' positions, the way they craned their backs and spread their legs like slo-mo gymnasts. I didn't know what Josh's fantasies were, specifically, but I figured I'd happen upon them in time.

I wanted Josh's approval, but his disdain came in a close second. Just as my father's moments of softness—amidst his general mood of sarcasm and displeasure—used to appease my mother for days at a time, so too did I find new kicks by pleasing Josh. When I could coax his sullenness into tenderness, it gave me a bigger charge than if he had been gentle all the time. Finding ways to trigger his mood change became a pleasure almost as heady as sex itself.

Intellectually, I told myself that all my efforts were toward the eventual goal of total reciprocity. At night, after making love in variation #62-A, Josh would fall asleep spooned behind me, his breath making moist "O's" between my shoulder blades. I would stare out the window, and wish that we would stay together forever—that Josh would love me as much as I loved him.

Sometime during the middle of my first year, Grandma H. called me in a tremulous voice to let me know that she had left her husband and was filing for divorce. She asked me to come visit her at her new place soon.

After making lame excuses for a week, I obliged her and drove up to what Grandma had called her "old folks home" in the University Circle area of Cleveland. Foolishly, I had expected (and dreaded) a run-down sort of institution, where the slightly used condition of the seniors matched the flickering overheads and yellowing bedsheets. The kind of place at which my fourth-grade choir was forced to sing Christmas carols, while the glazed-looking residents in the front row peed quietly on the linoleum. But despite her considerable emotional distress, my grandmother had retained her panache. She had somehow, within a month or two of deciding to abandon her second marriage, leapfrogged up the waiting list and gotten herself a primo apartment in Judson Manor, a "retirement facility" so swanky that I would have gladly moved in there myself.

Upon greeting me at the front desk in the atrium, I noticed her ladies-who-lunch look had softened. Her hair had gone grey in the several months since we'd last seen each other, and her hands were unadorned. Taking me on a tour, she pointed out the mahogany library, the myriad Tiffany lamps and stained-glass windows, and the pedigrees of the residents—"more Ph.D.s than any other retirement home, I've heard," she said—until adjourning to her living room, still crammed with framed art in bubble wrap, where we sipped colas and picked at her candy dish.

"You're not wearing makeup anymore?" Grandma finally asked.

"Nope," I said. "You're going grey?"

"Mmm," she said, sucking on one of the mints she always had at the ready to fight dry mouth. "Change is going around these days."

I asked her if she wanted to talk about it. She asked, "Which it?" I said her husband. She snorted, and said, "Well, yes, I guess there's that, too."

The previous weekend, she had gone over to Dad's house for dinner. She told me she was expecting to be a little uncomfortable, especially worrying who might see them if they needed to go out together, but reported that she'd had a fabulous time. "Not like what you'd think at all," she said. She especially appreciated my dad's stellar taste in guest towels.

"Well, he, she, probably gets it from you," I said.

Grandma H. smiled. "Yes, I guess so," she said. "Whatever you think of this whole crazy thing . . . and don't get me wrong, it *is* crazy, you do have to admit that he, she, has excellent taste."

After a brief chat, I was taken aback to realize that Grandma H. was—in spite of her obvious ambivalence about whether the gender change was right, or whether the coming out party was a little too in-your-face—more comfortable with Dad's new image in some ways than my mother and I were. (Mom had seen Dad only a few times since the party, and each time, called me to guffaw about her latest hyperfeminine affectation. "You can't believe the way she holds a teacup," she had said. "Like a little porcelain angel.") But Grandma H., perhaps to her own consternation, seemed secretly pleased. My father and she were finally simpatico, at least in aesthetics, and she hadn't had that kind of feminine bond since I'd doffed girly pretentions years ago.

"I think it's great that you guys are getting closer," I told her. "You need each other."

Grandma blushed. "Closer?" she blurted. "Well, that might be a little premature."

After an hour or two, and about a half pound of M&Ms, Grandma confessed to me why she left her husband.

"We were growing apart," she said. "Either that or we were never really in sync." I moved next to her on the sofa and slung my arm around her shoulder.

"I'm not so sad, though," she said, enveloping my hand in hers. "I'm not sure why I was there, with him."

For the shrimp cocktails? I thought. The swanky apartment? The warm body in bed? "He never understood about Christine, anyway," she said, and looked at me. "You know, I mean your father."

"I know who Christine is."

"Either maybe I wanted my husband to be someone he couldn't be," she said, "or I wanted to be someone I wasn't." She stared at nothing particular, before bursting into a smile. "You know, I've taken up painting again."

"Great!" I gushed, trying to shake the memory of her eyesore canvases. "It sounds like you're finding yourself."

"Yes, well, that seems to be going around as well," she said.

✿   ✿   ✿

While I was tending to Grandma H.'s growing pains and accompanying heartaches, my mother was tending to my other grandmother's cancer, which, this time, was terminal.

My mother, who had adjusted to the quiet rhythms of an empty home and casual outings after work, now spent the better portion of her "leisure time" visiting the hospital, nursing her mother. Grandma's hair was gone; she was as swollen and flushed as a pink water balloon; she had energy to smile when the Cleveland Browns made a touchdown but not enough to reach for her own water glass. She was dying a little each minute, and in the absence of her family, Mom bore the brunt of the pressure. Fearful of putting any more stress on me, my mother had no one to speak to about her anger toward my grandmother for defending Dad, for helping to build the expectation that my mom was indeed a superwoman capable of handling any problem without assistance. Mom turned inward in an attempt to squelch all her less sanitized emotions. It didn't always work. Sometimes she'd slam the water glass down on the bedside tray instead of handing it over to Grandma, and after visiting hours, she wolfed down a huge bowl of ice cream as succor.

My mother felt not merely alone, but lonely. She was the source of support for others, from my dad to me to the many people seeking a second mother in her, but hadn't mastered the skill of soliciting comfort. While Grandma Schultz was sick, she called few friends, and spoke rarely to me on the subject so that I had no idea how much it devastated her. It was years before she told me that she'd been depressed not so much because Grandma was dying—after all, she was old, in pain, and unafraid—but because she was losing one more person whom she'd been unable to save.

In the waning days of Grandma's life, my mother found solace at last with one of the most unlikely men for the job. At the very same time, my father surprised us with the announcement that she was heterosexual (i.e., attracted to men) and dating someone. In yet another unlikely coincidence, my mother and father had each found companionship with two burly, testosteroned hunters named Michael.

The convergence of the two Michaels upon my parents' lives, and mine by proximity, was arguably the strangest development in my family yet. All my parents' revelations paled in contrast to a mondo bizarro universe in which my dad was dating a claims adjuster with anger management issues, and my mom was falling for a lifelong Republican who extolled the virtues of an anti–flag-burning amendment.

My mother didn't expect to fall in love with her Michael. A paper salesman with whom she'd had a passing acquaintance, Michael was the spitting image of Ted Turner: a white-haired, moustached, bespectacled good ol' boy on the other side of the spectrum from my father in every single way. After their first date, Mom called me to say he'd brought her an American flag as a gift.

"You're kidding me," I deadpanned.

She laughed, too, but unconvincingly. "Yeah, weird," she said. "But he's so *nice* to me."

To my mother, *nice* was what counted. He brought her flowers, and sprinkled their conversations with compliments. Unlike my father, who was mostly a no-show during Grandma's hospital stay, Michael lodged himself in an uncomfortable green room chair, thumbing through old copies of *National Geographic*, and fetching her weak coffee in paper cups at regular thirty-minute intervals without complaint.

As for Dad, I hadn't been aware that she had heterosexual inclinations. I wasn't sure I wanted to know. I kind of liked thinking of her as an asexual ascetic, beatific and content because she was allowed to wear hose and heels to work. It's not that I wanted her to be alone, but I didn't want to get into anything that smacked of genital talk any more than we already had to. She had said once that you had to know what your gender identity was before acquiring a sexual orientation. Apparently, she had moved on to phase two.

Before I met Mom's Michael, she spent the better part of our thrice-a-week phone calls constructing his pedestal. According to my mother, he was the nicest, sweetest, most romantic, compassionate, kind, smart, funny, thoughtful, empathetic, likable, popular person in the world. I was alarmed by the proliferation of adjectives, as it reminded me a bit too much of her incessant protests of Dad's goodness and greatness—"and that he really does love you!"—back in the day. I kept wanting to reply, "But what are you doing with a Republican duck hunter?" But at least in the beginning, I didn't. I bit down hard, hoping that he was the second coming indeed.

But when I met Mom's Michael, I was not nearly as overwhelmed with his goodness as Mom would have liked me to be. I sat miserably through a dinner of BBQ chicken at a restaurant with too many neon beer signs as he made a few jokey references to his rockin' love life with my mother and fumbled for more benign conversational topics. I don't recall saying more than a few impassioned words in favor of Robert Mapplethorpe and the National Endowment for the Arts. Completely put off by the image of my mother having sex, I was probably horribly rude.

I was no more enthralled by my father's paramour, a stocky man built like a mailbox with the warm conversational cadence of Norman Schwarzkopf. Oddly, the push-pull of our dinner talk—over another of my father's famous four-course meals—made me feel as though we were the soldiers at Iwo Jima, struggling to claim her for ourselves. For one thing, he was enraged that I wasn't calling my father "mother" which, he said, "was the only polite thing to do." (A fact which probably upset him because it reminded him that my dad was once a full-blown guy.) Upset, I excused myself to bed.

Of the two Michaels, my father's version worried me more

because he seemed significantly more capable of having a homophobic freak attack. But both flummoxed me. In fairness, I'm sure neither one knew what to say to the smarty-pants hippie chick with the large chip on her shoulder and the penchant for calling her parents every other day. Personally, I felt I had been as flexible and accepting up until now as anyone could have expected, and I thought my parents were ready for some tough love.

For the first time ever, I was close to both my mother and my father. Although the two of them were generally steering clear of each other, except for occasional financial aid discussions, they were at worst, civil, and at best, friends. I could rely on them both: Mom for our deep talks, her excellent—if sometimes unrequested—advice, and bitching about my father; Dad for our growing ability to have witty repartee and her wonderful unwillingness to give advice because, as she put it, "like I'm the expert on how to deal with life." They were my best friends. And as far as I was concerned, it was as though suddenly my beloved parental pals were missing some essential testosterone in their RDA and were drawn to these men like a deer to a salt lick. Of course, they thought their teenage daughter shouldn't be the only one getting some action (both had certainly gone without long enough). They were ready to work off some sexual steam, and so be it if the objects of their affection happened to be Alpha males. They both vaguely understood my misgivings, but neither was going to lose any sleep over it.

Perhaps it shouldn't have felt like a betrayal. Maybe I shouldn't have taken it personally. But just as I realized I might share some traits with my father, she was inching toward docility and dating a manly man. And just as I felt like my mother and I were free to play girlfriends without an ornery fellow to get in the way, there another one was again. This time, though, it was worse. If Michael was everything my father wasn't, as my mother often said, then he was probably everything I wasn't as well.

✿ ✿ ✿

I took refuge in my boyfriend, following my tried-and-true road map for navigating chaos. Josh was an easy way to lose myself, if for no other reason than the fact that he could be distractingly high maintenance. He liked to engage in dialogue via the Socratic method, firing questions at me until he obtained some sort of conclusion, or decided to call it a night. (It was a slightly stressful way to have a discussion.) We once tried to talk about abortion—I was pro-choice and well-read on the subject, he was decidedly ambivalent and clueless. After answering rapid-fire questions (some logical, some only tangentially related to reality) for twenty minutes, Josh motioned to stop. "I need to do some more reading before the conversation can continue," he said, in a calm, supercilious tone that made me want to rip all the hairs out of my head. From time to time, he also liked to have a check-in about the Relationship, which just so happened to be my least favorite thing to do. Talking about Us really meant talking about Me, which entailed listing my faults—mostly some variation on the theme of "you're too emotional." Afterward, Josh, always the rational arbiter, would say, "It's your turn. Tell me whatever about me is bugging you." I would think: This. This is bugging me. But I didn't want to hurt his feelings, and I didn't want to lose him. Five minutes later, I'd try to win him back by having sex, and when we'd lie there, entangled in a sweaty pretzel and staring up at the overhead light, he'd say, "You love me too much. I can't keep up. I don't think I can give you everything you need." I'd try to make him feel better, by saying, "That's okay. I love you enough for both of us." To my credit, I never believed that. I assured myself that I was waiting for him to catch up.

I loved him with a white-hot ardor that was based largely on feeling agitated and uncomfortable. Sure, I liked the fact that he wept at chick flicks, and volunteered to work with housebound seniors. I appreciated his passion for the science of music and the art of logic. But mostly I was in thrall to his fury, his insistence on having a conversation the most difficult way possible, his hyperrationality and accompanying impatience with my flare-ups. His most unappealing traits, after all, were the ones that kept me enamored.

Still, whatever his own flaws, Josh should have qualified for hazard pay for being my boyfriend during the summer of 1991 and the following fall. I did not have the best stress-management techniques in the world.

Monday: Mom called. We argued about her boyfriend. I hung up. Screamed at Josh.

Wednesday: I called Mom. We talked about everything but her boyfriend. I hung up. Screamed at Josh.

Friday: Mom called. I returned her call once I knew she was out at a barbecue, or on a golf outing. Left a conciliatory message. Repeat. Repeat.

Josh tried to help me with my growing alienation from my mother, but I didn't want to be reasoned out of my irritation. I wanted my family back. Not the boy-girl-girl template from the photo album, but the girl-girl-girl incarnation, dysfunctional but whole, so briefly on display at the coming out party.

I had probably little reason to feel so abandoned by the mere fact that my parents' lives were evolving. Even at the time, I had a hunch that my angst was not proportional to the actual events of my life. I wasn't ready to let go of the sense that it was me and my parents against the world, the three of us alone in the closet. I had become resistant to further change, given all the tumult that had already occurred in such a miniscule period of time. All my other friends seemed to have dull, static parents who changed eyeglass styles in a particularly wacky year. Unfortunately, I had expected, and hoped, the coming out party would signal the end of the parental revolution.

✿   ✿   ✿

My mother's Michael helped her through the passing of Grandma Schultz, and moved into our house a few months later. My father's relationship didn't have that kind of staying power. They split, and my father confessed that his Michael "was a real loser. Not put together right." I asked her what she'd seen in him in the first place.

"I wanted to fit in," she said mournfully. "A normal man-woman couple out on the town. You don't know how good it feels to be accepted without question."

I was glad, personally, that she got out of the whole mess without a shiner or worse.

Instead of engaging in awkward small talk with her macho man, Dad built herself a flower garden. Alongside her, pulling weeds, spreading mulch and planting begonias was Grandma H.

In between her latest trips to Chatauqua, New York, for senior learning seminars and her classes on charcoal painting and collage, she was parked at Dad's. Together they gardened, and then stole catnaps on adjoining couches in the living room. They talked: of me, Dad's work (and was it still coming in okay?), Grandma's divorce settlement (was it enough to pay the rent on her spread?), the attractive professor emeritus types at the retirement home. They shopped together. It was convenient since they liked many of the same stores.

"Dic . . . Chris," Grandma would call from the shawl section. "Do you like this wrap?"

"Very nice, Mom," Dad said. "What about this pendant to go with?"

Once, Grandma told me with unbridled glee, a saleslady complimented her on having such an elegant offspring. "I wish," the lady had said, "that *my* daughter dressed so nicely."

After years of distance, of being as dissimilar as any two people sharing the same genes, Dad and Grandma began to connect. Dad steadied Grandma's gait when they walked down the landscaped steps to the backyard garden, with a gentleness that implied love rather than obligation. Together they watched the flowers they planted bloom, and die, the leaves turn red, then brownish, then fall onto the barren lawn. With each month, I swore they became closer, and even grew up a little bit, too.

I still spoke to Grandma mostly of silly things: Josh, school, why I wouldn't put on a little blush to get some color in my cheeks. I didn't ask her why she became so interested in volunteering for a Democratic governor from Arkansas; nor why she had taken up books and advanced learning again; nor why, in the most shocking change of all, her art—now black-and-white monographs—had actually become *good*. I didn't ask why she asked about my mother—something she had never done while my parents were unhappily hitched. For obvious reasons, I couldn't say, "Hey, Grandma, why do you appear to have a little depth all of a sudden?" Fortunately, when I saw her with my father, I thought I might know the answers. Maybe she had longed for a girl and had finally gotten one. It would have made sense, given her excessive doting over me. Or once my father, advertising creator par excellence, shattered his image, perhaps he gave her license to follow. Maybe she was emulating yet another image: the earthy, progressive sort of elderly woman depicted in news-weekly lifestyle stories. Maybe it was something else.

For Christmas 1991, I made the decision to give my father a Barbie, since she had never had one. Following in my father's footsteps of Christmases past, I liked to impress her with grand gestures of acceptance that she could extoll to all her other transgendered friends. Plus, she was still so ultrafemme, that it would go with the pink doily and smoked-glass decor she'd set up in her bedroom.

I was upstaged. My mother, who was only on the most tenuous of speaking terms with Dad, had me cart over a box that contained a delicate baby doll with hand-painted lips and curly ringlets. "I love and support you, always," the card read.

Once my father had dried her eyes, Grandma H. handed her one gift: a slender, neatly wrapped volume. It was a book entitled *To My Daughter*.

The moment told me that my family might have been a little road-worn and fractured, but it was not truly broken. I watched my Grandma H. and Dad embrace, both of their eyes squeezed shut, and their arms tightly wrapped around each other. None of us was alone.

TWENTY-TWO

Schisms

In the beginning, there was a teddy: the gold hand-me-down with snaps on the bottom reminiscent of toddler jumpsuits. Then in high school came simple satin slips in cheery pastels, purchased in answer to the question: If Cinderella wanted to get Prince Charming's knickers in a bunch, what skivvies would she choose? Spaghetti-strap negligees were supplanted by men's-style pajamas unbuttoned for maximum yet casual flesh exposure, then again by Merry Widows in bridal white and midnight black with suspension systems of buttons and hooks custom-designed to entice a horny scientist.

But by the end of my sophomore year of college, store-bought lingerie of any kind smacked to me of mass-market sexuality, particularly distasteful since I was seeking "authenticity" everywhere: in my CD rack, my spice rack, and my sex life. I bootlegged friends' Joni Mitchell cassettes, cooked complete proteins from the curry-yellowed pages of *Moosewood*, and crafted my own sultry clothes. As always, I borrowed from the movies: slicing ovals out of the front of a rayon blouse in mimicry of the Droogs cutting boob holes out of their rape victim's pantsuit. Or I freelanced it, slashing a T-shirt and boxers with a razor blade and tousling my hair in a style one might describe as either "untamed," "ravaged," or "camping with raccoons." On one occasion, when Josh asked me why I was draped against his headboard looking like the victim of a rabid attack, I said I wanted to try something new. I was ready for grown-up sex: raw, real, and occasionally chafing (at least after unwrapping the nylons from my wrists). I told myself my new yen for the rough stuff was another ploy to attract his attention, and told him it was one more means to keep our sexual fuse smokin'. Neither was true. I was earnestly trying to keep us from achieving equality in our relationship, and playing tops and bottoms was the only thing I could think of.

The problem was that my boyfriend had recently gotten in touch with his so-called feminine side. Out of nowhere, he began sending me a love note every day. He scrawled impassioned poems with inapt metaphors, then apologized, saying he hoped I knew what he was getting at; surprised me in bed with eggs fried up in the kitchenette; and treated me with total kindness. I left three of his notes sealed in their envelopes, and became belligerent when he waxed lovey-dovey. I soon realized, with trepidation, that my love for Josh only flourished when it remained unrequited.

I was disgusted with myself. Forget Phyllis Schlafly, I thought. I was the ultimate antifeminist. I was fetishizing male rejection at the very same time I was chirpily marching for choice. Once I made this connection, I felt really, really bad. But nothing changed.

While I was embroiled in mind games of my own devising, my mother was immersed in what she considered her first healthy love affair. In stark contrast to marriage with my father, her current relationship involved comparatively little character analysis. Her liaison with Michael was plot-driven, one verb after another: they *went* fishing, they *drove* to Maine, they *rented* a boat, they *walked* along a beach, they *made* love. I got to hear about all of it, and in my better moments, was happy for her—and relieved that my previous guilt over cavorting with a boyfriend while she lounged alone in the den could now be put to rest. Predictably,

Mom became the de facto counselor for the younger of Michael's adult sons, who was drug-addled and prone to a martyr complex. Over cigarettes and salami sandwiches, she talked to him for hours on everything from etiquette—why one shouldn't use a spit cup during supper—to current events—why the "three strikes and you're out" laws could someday mean big trouble for him.

Mom assured me that ideology, of which she shared precious little with her new family, had become the least of her considerations. "Democrat, Republican, what-have-you," she announced, "doesn't matter. You can always educate them. What matters is if people show you love, not just talk about showing it." She was referring to my dad, but I feared she meant me, too.

Like my father, I'd become a blank card snob—taken to writing weepy paeans to her every holiday in lieu of wrapping up store-bought gifts. I, too, was more likely to compose a villanelle than to shellac the front porch as a token of my affection. My mother's attitude change also alarmed me because I had become increasingly politicized at the same time that she had decided it wasn't so important after all. I'd sworn off red meat and had signed up to move into a women's collective in the fall, thereby joining the ranks of the upperclasswomen who'd intimidated me a year or so earlier. I was a little touchy in those days: A cosmetics commercial could suck me into a horror spiral. *Basic Instinct* made me weep for humanity. I could pass hours flagellating myself for my own shortcomings as a feminist. I wasn't prepared to hear my mother say that love conquered politics.

She listened to me a bit warily, then proceeded to do exactly what she wanted. "This is my life," she told me again and again. "I love you, but I'm going to make my own decisions." Just my luck, I thought. She gets empowered right now when I need her to listen to me.

The rift with my mother didn't compare with the gulf between me and her man. He had an unfortunate tendency to make off-color jokes: fags walking into a bar, women lying back and enjoying it, that sort of thing. I wasn't well balanced enough to handle such comments. Interpreting them as assaults, I developed a habit of shrieking a response, running out of the room, or, once, picking up a heavy object from the mantel and, not being crazy enough to throw it, dropping it on my foot.

It wasn't entirely his fault, Mom said. He was from a completely different cultural background than us, one in which boys guffawed at bra-burning knee-slappers while driving their dead deer to the taxidermist. (My caricature, not hers.) I told her that I understood what being from a different world meant, but whenever I looked at Michael, I thought: These are the people that want to ship my dad to Mozambique. I managed to gloss over the fact that Michael and my father, in casual conversation at a dinner party or two, actually got along tolerably well.

Like everything in my life, my fear of Michael was, of course, at least partly about my father. Dad had created me as surely as if I'd emerged whole from the crown of her head. My insecurities, talents, foibles, and quirks were patterned after her or in response to her. Seeing Mom defend her boyfriend in the same manner that she had pumped up Dad pushed all my buttons. "Michael likes you, but he doesn't know how to express it," she'd say. "Why don't *you* go talk to him? Why don't you ask *him* how he's feeling about such-and-such?"

"Why doesn't he learn how to talk to me?" I'd snap back.

As anyone who's survived a coming out can probably attest, families band together through the scrutiny and fall apart only when the dust settles and a sense of privacy is restored. My anger had waited, biding its time so quietly that I barely knew it was there, until our lives were calm enough to withstand another bout of upheaval. That said, I had no use for my own righteous fury. All I wanted was some peace—and my mother, my friend and confidante, whispering her good advice in my ear.

✿ ✿ ✿

It was a classic pattern: I pushed my mother away, then wanted to crawl into her lap and cry. But I was twenty, shoehorning in a bout of adolescent rebellion in the nick of time. At age forty-six, my father, a late teen herself, was behaving much the same way. Dad tittered over decaf and Triscuits with Grandma H., whom she treated like a long-lost friend, but saved her whiniest antics for occasional interactions with Mom—still and always the biggest authority figure in her life.

"Jesus, Dinah, can you let me know when the tuition bills are due?" she raged every semester, when I got the notice that I'd be summarily tossed out of school if my "parents' portion" wasn't fully paid up. "You know how bad I am with money."

"Chris, you get the notices from school just like I do. I paid my part months ago."

"Am I asking for so much, just to have a little help here?"

"Yes, you are," Mom replied, puffing agitatedly on her cigarette. "You're a big girl now, aren't you?"

He's back, my mother thought. Maybe this gender change was merely extensive cosmetic surgery.

"I honestly, truly, don't care if I never talk to her again," my mother informed me. "I don't know what I'm waiting for. She's never going to change."

"I think Dad is angry because she needs you too much, and doesn't know how to deal with not having you there for her all the time," I said.

"She keeps it up, and I won't be here for her any of the time," she muttered.

"Try to be patient. She's going through a lot of changes right now."

"I only signed on to raise one teenager."

"If you say this to a lot of people, you know, they'll think you're really not okay with her being female," I said. It had recently come to my attention that once a big show has been made of accepting your transsexual dad (or ex-hubby), any problem you have with that person will be seen as a sign that you're not as kosher with the girl thing as you claim. No amount of denials will convince anyone otherwise.

"Woman or not, I don't care. The only difference is she's either a bitch or an asshole."

When one member of a divorced couple finds a new lover, and rhapsodizes about her new relationship in front of anyone who will listen, it might be readily apparent why the ex might act less than perfectly *thrilled* about this new development. That thought never occurred to Mom and me. However, that idea—accompanied by clenched fists, pursed smiles, and unfortunate rejoinders—had occurred to my father.

She was jealous: both of losing Mom to her new boyfriend-cum–pet project, and of having few romantic prospects herself. Having moved on from her own Michael, the pickings of middle-aged straight men capable of carrying on intelligent conversation were slim enough without having to inform each of them, come second date, that nothing resembled a Georgia O'Keeffe painting beneath those silk shantung slacks. The most chivalrous in the beginning—who held out single long-stemmed roses and made reservations at French bistros—were the most put out in the end, depositing her at the front door with little more than a "see ya." The most open-minded—who suggested foreign films followed by rijstafel—were the most inadvertently condescending. "I'm sorry," one attorney told her, as though she was soliciting money for Greenpeace at his door. "I applaud you for your statement, but I'm not brave enough to tackle your issue." Because of a careful screening process involving the casual mention of "don't ask, don't tell" policies on the first date, at least she never encountered any truly terrifying homophobes, the possibility of which kept me up many nights tossing and turning and wishing Dad didn't have any more second dates.

By mid-1992, I had basically been granted my wish. Dad pulled back on dating, fatigued by the process of endlessly outing herself and waiting for the man's minor-key response. She also began pulling out of her few other social commitments as well, most notably transgender clubs.

"Talking about all this *girl* stuff is well and good," Dad said. "I like a number of people in the group as regular friends, but with some of them there's not a whole lot to say."

I wasn't too surprised. She had recently stopped glorifying all aspects of the female experience—in part because she was a test case for how men and women can be treated differently.

Here and there, she'd started dropping sociological insights. She told me how clients who didn't know her back story would cut her off in meetings, or speak right over her. "People used to pay attention," she said. "They were too scared not to." She noted how more people on the street would ask her for the time, as well as for a lay. Once her daily dose of estrogen began to pad her hips a little, she came to realize that no saleslady in a clothing store would ever say something that would not offend her to the core, in one way or another. I heard all these stories with a bit of awe; it was confirmation of something I'd always suspected to be true, but couldn't quite prove. That spring, when a flyer for a NOW rally in downtown Cleveland caught my eye while waiting for the bathroom in a coffeehouse, I didn't ask my mother. She and Michael probably had plans to go do something. I took along my father, and we got all worked up together.

During the hot summer months, I slept in the bedroom down the hall from Mom and Michael, and made frequent escapes to the haven of my father's house when the teenagers-in-love routine got out of hand. They gazed at each other on the patio. They sneaked out late at night to take a skinny dip in the hot tub. He brought her gifts. She cooked him dinner. There she was, laughing and kissing as though she'd always known what constituted a normal romance. The straightforward happiness my mother shared with Michael seemed suspect to me. It looked a whole lot easier than the mental calisthenics I was performing in my ever-rocky relationship with Josh.

Nothing was that simple when Josh and I kissed. Back at school that fall, Josh was one romantic gesture after another: wanting to kiss in the rain, that sort of thing. I tried to love him as much as ever, but the whole affair had become too sweet, too *equal* for my liking.

I decided that if Josh couldn't be snarly to me in the cafeteria or the commons, I could coax him into being like that in private. I thought that forcing myself into a submissive position would be mutually satisfying, and that by being degraded—pretend degradation, mind you, followed immediately by egalitarian conversation and perhaps a pizza—I could allow Josh to be sensitive while sating my need for excitement, for submission. After getting him to relent and play along, I would plead for Josh's attention and attempt to fulfill his wishes as long as he would dominate me. In fact, I usually told him exactly what to say and do and became cross if he deviated from the script, which, I suppose, made me a bottom only in terms of where I was literally positioned. Regardless, I couldn't make love unless I was being play-humiliated. When I returned back to my room later, with sore, quivering thighs, I read my Women's Studies homework.

In the fall, I sponsored a talk by my father on transgender issues at the collective. Dad was a little reticent at first, having resisted the pull to become a professional transsexual several times already, but relented once she realized how supportive the audience would be. I introduced her, and launched into what had become "the spiel": Dad was an alcoholic (sorta), who neglected wife and child (mostly), who needed to become a woman in order to survive (true enough), and thanks to her being a transsexual, we were all one big happy alternafamily (except for all the baggage). I kissed Dad on the cheek and took my seat.

Perched on a plush armchair in front of seventy people, my father began to perform. She spoke truthfully about whether she'd get a sex change (answer: she wasn't sure), and how she felt about the Michigan Womyn's Festival kicking out transsexual attendees (she thought lesbians, of all people, should be a little more accepting of people who break gender stereotypes). The room was completely quiet before bursting into unadulterated applause and a standing ovation at the end of the forty-minutes. Not since the coming out party—where she'd wowed a tougher crowd—had she seemed such a perfect balance of my two fathers: the great communicator with the witty turn of phrase and the straightforward truth-teller able to give comfort to an androgynous teen who'd sniffled through the Q & A.

"I am so glad I did that," Dad gushed, as I walked her to her new car. My father spoke so fast that she tripped over her words, as giddy as I'd seen her back in her acting days. In those days, he'd ride postshow buzz, the actor's methadone, all the way to the after party. "I miss talking like that to people, in a forum."

"Maybe you should take up acting again," I said, and hugged her good-bye.

Her face was flushed and rosy. "Maybe so, maybe so," she said.

Later that day, dozens of talk participants around campus showered me with the usual ooh's and aah's. "It's so great how out you and your dad are," one person commented.

"Yes, well, it's kind of old hat by now." I smiled, trying to sound casual.

But the truth is that, no matter how many times I came out publicly and proudly, I continued to fear that someday I or my family wouldn't be accepted. It was much less stressful, after all, to make the political personal on a campus dubbed a "gay and lesbian mecca" by *Newsweek*. It was harder to hide when I had to come out without ceremony, in the most unlikely of places and without preparation.

I would never have thought about how many documents require "father's full name" on them until father's full name was Rebecca Christine Howey. Financial aid officers stared at me, befuddled and embarrassed, every single year. "No, not your mother's partner," they said, trying to sound tolerant. "Your *father.*"

"She is my father."

"Your father's name is Rebecca?"

"It used to be Dick. Does that clear things up?"

That's nothing compared to the post office, where in the course of getting a passport, I had to repeat my abbreviated life history to two clerks and a manager while a woman in line guffawed each time I said the word "Dick." It was very restoration comedy, but I nearly ran out of the post office feeling like a felon and convinced the passport agency either would not let me leave the country—or come back in.

I shared those awkward moments with Dad, mock-scolding her for not picking a nice unisex legal name to make my life a little easier. She, in turn, told me about her own coming out foibles: the time she had to apply for a new driver's license—the DMV clerk laughed so hard she popped out her contact—and getting her official name change. In the latter case, the judge, an old white-haired man, had shaken his head with one of those "look at these modern times" kinds of perplexity before granting the new name. Then, as though he wasn't being paradoxical in the slightest, he told her that Rebecca was a lovely name and reminded him of his granddaughter. Dad smiled stupidly, not knowing what to think.

Around this time, I came up with another new name for my father. Names, like pronouns, had always been a challenge for us.

This conundrum might have been solved by defaulting her title to "Mother," as most children of transsexuals are inclined to do. Call us old-fashioned, but my father and I had little intention of altering the name of our relationship, regardless of peer pressure. I already had a mother, who was a bit proprietary about the title and rightfully so, as she had virtually raised me solo. Also, I *had* a father. She might have changed her gender, but that didn't change who originally brought the sperm to the party.

Of course, calling her Dad was a bit of a mind bender: every image I had, from a smirking Bill Cosby in his rainbow-bright geometric sweaters to illustrated dads slinging burgers over a grill on the cover of special-occasion cards, was incongruent with this attractive lady in her ultrasuede pantsuit. Father's Day circulars always displayed keyhole saws and paisley ties on sale, not discounted bath beads and personalized bouquets.

It also seemed unlikely that I would ever adjust to calling her Chris. No matter how liberal we were, I couldn't deal with abdicating titles entirely. After obtaining no help whatsoever from the thesaurus, I shortened and softened my father's appellation into "Da." Not as frontier woodsmanesque as "Pa" and not as baggage-laden as "Dad," but still fatherly all the same.

During my Junior year I was a residential assistant, a job that entailed stomping until the rats scurried away so I could put boxes in basement storage, handing out leaflets on depression, and keeping extra pairs of room keys in case of an emergency—like surprising my boyfriend in his dorm across campus. After borrowing the dupe key from the R.A. on duty there, I let myself into Josh's room with the intention of serving a bunch of his favorite microwavable dishes on paper plates as an apology for having been distracted and demanding.

When I got inside the room, I found several stuffed plastic bags from the mall piled up on the bed. Shirts and cardigans, nothing special, until I saw the tags. They were from the women's aisle.

I ran over to the wastebasket, feeling as though I was going to dry-heave. My mind sped through rationalizations: He bought them for me—a gift!—and here I've spoiled it. It's for the drag ball; only two months to go! They were out of men's sizes. What, did I want him to go around campus shirtless?

I wanted to rip one of the sweaters into shreds. I blanched and dropped it into a heap on the bed.

"I'm a hypocrite," I said, out loud. "I'm a complete and total fraud."

When Josh arrived at his room an hour later, I was sitting on the bed, having hung his new clothes in his closet.

"Hey, I got some new stuff. Did you like them?" he said, cheerily.

"Yeah," I said, slowly. "So, some women's clothes, I saw?"

He was unpacking his backpack, looking unaffected. "Yep," he said. "It fits better, since I'm a small size. The material's softer."

"You like wearing women's clothes?" I blurted.

Josh looked baffled. "Um, *no*," he said, a little sternly. "I like wearing *comfortable* clothes. Who cares? They don't look any different."

I said that it made me a little nervous. It reminded me of my father, and I wanted to make sure that Josh, wasn't a, you know, a person inclined in, okay, that direction. That women's clothing direction.

Josh laughed, and pushed me back against the bed. "You're worrying for nothing," he smiled. "I thought these sweaters would be more comfortable. Period. I swear. I won't wear them if it upsets you."

"No, no!" I shouted. "I would be fine with whatever you wanted to do. How ironic would it be for me to have a problem with this?"

"It's really no big thing," he said, and leaned in for a kiss. "Are you in the mood?"

I wasn't. His chest seemed bonier, more pubescent than only

hours earlier; his eyes too pretty, framed by the kind of eyelashes that make mascara redundant; his frame, which I'd often extolled for mirroring mine as though we were matching parts of a hinge, struck me as unnervingly small for a man. But perversely, I thought that if I didn't make love to Josh right there and then, I would be betraying my father. If I was intolerant of a few gender-neutral sweaters, how could I blame the inconsiderate men who had hurt Da's feelings again and again? I leaned in for a kiss, and closed my eyes.

"Did I ever tell you I almost went deaf?" Grandma H. asked me one afternoon that spring.

"Um, no," I said. "My parents told me about it at some point."

"There's a reason for that. I thought people would look at me differently, and judge me. It's what I was afraid of for your father, you know."

"I know."

"So I've started giving workshops here in the Manor to people with hearing loss. Old people like me don't like to admit that they're not going to live forever. They don't want anyone to know they're frail, which," she said, "is so sad. You can't hide being hard of hearing—or aging."

"I don't think I'd be able to do that if I were older. I can't keep a secret to save my life."

"You say that now," Grandma said, "but it's amazing what you're capable of hiding if it really embarrasses you, or doesn't go along with how you want to present yourself to the world."

"So they're lying," I said.

"No" she said, impatiently. "They're people. Imperfect and scared like the rest of us."

In July, I attended Oxford University for a month-long summer session in English Lit. It was a mostly solitary month for me, spent perusing Jane Austen first editions in the dusty, grandiose Bodleian Library and writing letters halfway around the world to Josh, who had graduated and moved to Tacoma, Washington. By the night before my flight back to Cleveland, I had exhausted all my traveler's checks and was sustaining myself on chocolate bars from the Cadbury machines. While waiting for my plane, I slept in fits under a row of seats in the Heathrow Airport terminal. Around 4 A.M., inexplicably, I had the sudden notion to call Grandma H., whom I hadn't spoken to since leaving for England. I called her on my father's calling card, but hung up after the machine picked up. I crawled back under the seats, chastising myself for calling her after bedtime.

Shortly after Da picked me up at the airport the next day, I found out why Grandma H. hadn't answered the phone. She wasn't asleep after all.

"When?"

"This morning."

"What?"

"A stroke."

"Who?"

"The cleaning lady. She let herself in."

Da held me to her breast, and I shook. I didn't say anything.

We held the memorial service that following weekend in the ballroom of Judson Manor. My dad's brother, Bill, and my cousin Steve whom I'd seen only a few times in my life, flew in. My mother and Michael both attended. I tried to give a eulogy, but I kept punctuating my sentences with incoherent sobs. The only thing I remember choking out between blowing my nose and wiping my cheeks was saying, "We were so close." A lot of people took that statement to mean that Grandma H. and I were cross-generational best buddies. I meant it another way.

My father was the last to speak. She said that this was a celebration of the independent life that Grandma H. had begun to lead. Da displayed some of Grandma's artwork (several pieces of which were sent immediately afterward back to the galleries that had purchased them), and passed out sheets of colored construction paper to the dozens of people present.

"When I came out," my father announced, with a dazed smile and wet, pink eyes, "my mother helped me plant a flower garden. She helped me gather up freesia, chrysanthemums, marigolds, daisies, and whatnot to put around my house. She said 'I don't know a woman who can live without color in her life.' So everyone, please hold your piece of construction paper up in the air, and let me return the favor by giving my mom her own bouquet."

I signed for the ashes a few days later, which came in a plain cardboard box Scotch-taped shut. In pink crayon, across the top, it read "Howey remains." The undertaker was clearly not pleased that we had passed on the three-thousand-dollar porcelain "In the Style of Greek" urn.

My father and I had bonded over dissing bad TV; helping each other through the mourning process was new. I can't recall that we did anything particularly special, like have a deep profound talk about what Grandma H. had meant to us. I took that as a sign of how far Da and I had come. We didn't need to talk about it.

Before I went back to school, Da bought Malaika, a six-week-old female German shepherd, to keep her company. She joked that it was the reincarnation of Grandma H. "Puppies are high-maintenance, too." She laughed. She also let me know that she was auditioning for a show at the local Unitarian church, a production of *Same Time Next Year*. She was trying out for the female part.

I asked her how that would leave time for flower arranging and meal planning. She said she was getting a little tired of domesticity and was missing some of her old hobbies. It occurred to me she might be worried there was no one left to cook for.

✿   ✿   ✿

During my senior year of college, Mom and Michael informed me of the inevitable: they were getting married, and the big date was July 2, four days before my birthday. Mom wanted me to sing at the ceremony, a backyard potluck affair.

I had initiated a campaign to prove that I could accept Michael unequivocally, and I was taking all the olive branches I was offered. I didn't like his politics any more than I ever had, and it seemed like it would always be a struggle to make it past "Hello" with him. (The only complete conversations we'd yet been able to have were on the relatively limited topics of inclement weather and cake versus pie.) I just didn't want to fight with my mother anymore. She was never going to understand my anger about her being with Michael, so I figured it was easier for me to give in. I figured most families made nice-nice, amidst feelings of deep residual rage. Why should mine be any different? When Mom asked me to participate in the wedding, I cordially agreed. She mentioned that Da had agreed to come, too, as incentive for my good behavior. However, the prospect of faking more emotion, pretending that we were all one big, happy family made me a little queasy.

Not many people turned out for the *Same Time Next Year* tryouts in the suburban church basement, but Da blew them all away and landed the lead female role. I couldn't wait to see her perform, since her acting prowess had become a family legend, and I had been too young to really glean how good she was.

I brought Mom along to opening night, where we shifted in folding chairs along with twenty or so other spectators, awaiting greatness. "No matter what your father does, and what I think of it, she's a great actor," Mom said.

As it turned out, Da was thoroughly *okay*. She garnered a few laughs, and even made her way through a sweaty, panting childbirth scene that was no less realistic than anything on a sitcom. Meryl Streep she was not.

After the show, when Da appeared from behind what appeared to be a tacked-up sheet, I breathlessly proclaimed her brilliance. She was having none of it, though.

"Thanks," she said, sniffing the flowers I brought her, "but it's gone. I don't have the thing anymore. The urgency. I suppose I'm better at pretending to be a man than pretending to be a woman."

"That's because you *are* a woman," I said.

"Yeah, I guess," Da said, and turned to look at my mom. "It means a lot to me that you came."

"We're family," Mom said, and they embraced for a good ten seconds, before my mother ran off to meet up with Michael back at home.

Da told Mom of her decision first. They still weren't close, exactly. Mom's irritation over Da's tantrums of a year or two ago wasn't dissipating anytime soon, especially since she believed there was a very good chance that another one could erupt at any given moment. Da, for her part, tried to be conciliatory, asking Mom how she was feeling, and making every effort to be friendly with Michael, but she had few delusions that Mom was ever going to forgive her completely. In a way neither could completely understand, though, they continued to rely on each other in times of distress. Da called Mom first when Grandma H. died. Mom called Da initially to announce her engagement. Now Mom was first in line to hear that Da was changing the answer to everyone's number one question: Did she have the operation?

Da had never seen her penis as the ultimate signifier of manhood. Vying to have it hacked off—in Brussels, Belgium, where a well-regarded sex-change surgeon had a practice—was not a symbolic gesture. "That's a lot of suffering for symbolism," she once said.

Her decision was wholly pragmatic. Boyfriends who could work up a lustful lather after being confronted with a shriveled penis were few and far between, and Da had visions of being elderly and having a cadre of home health care aides disdain her for having the wrong parts.

"I'm doing this for my own protection," she said. "I'll admit, though, it's a little scary."

Mom couldn't resist someone in need, even when that person was Da. "I'll be here for you, and so will Noelle," she said. "We'll send postcards, do whatever we can for you. It's a big step. So when is the big day?"

Da sighed. "Well, it looks like the available opening with this doctor is less than a week after your wedding," she said, and reached across the table for Mom's hand. "Don't think I won't be there to throw rice and whatever you'd like me to do. See, I want to be there for you, too." She laughed nervously. "Hope that's not too little, too late."

Mom squeezed Da's hand. "It's late," she said, nodding. "I'll work with it."

For Christmas that year, I gave Da a mix tape with songs like "Dude (Looks Like a Lady)" and "Lola." Da gave me the Barbie board game. We played it twice later that day, and she won both times, sweeping the good boyfriends and killer gowns to become queen of the prom. Later, after we collapsed in front of the TV, she pressed the mute button and said she had something to tell me.

"Boy, is that a familiar phrase," I said, lightly. "Should I be worried?"

"Not in the slightest," she said. "It's all good."

TWENTY-THREE

Vagina Monologue

Every time I closed my eyes, I saw genitals, disembodied and floating in a sky of cumulus clouds, like a Magritte painting. Vaginas in concentric shades of ever-lighter pink. Aristocratic penises as slim and regal as Doric columns. Vulvas pursed and purple-brown. Stubby dicks bulging with blue veins. Obviously, I tried to stay awake.

It was my first night alone in the hotel. There were only seven channels on the television. Two in Dutch, two in French, two were pay-per-view European porn, which left me with nothing but CNN. It came down to a choice between twenty-four hours of O.J. or another viewing of Franz and Ilsa meet the new nanny. I would have read, but since arriving in Belgium three days earlier, I hadn't much of an attention span for books. To make matters worse, the only reading material I'd brought was a Norton anthology, the complete works of Nietzsche, and *The Fountainhead*. All to impress the flight attendants.

I killed a few minutes by ordering room service. I would have preferred to order an appetizer, main course, and dessert separately, in order to waste as much time as possible, but that would look really conspicuous. A young guy with rumpled black hair and Gauloise-stained teeth brought in my dinner tray. Politely, he queried after Mrs. Howey—was she my mother or maybe my aunt?—and asked if we were enjoying our stay.

"Yes, yes," I said, signing the bill. "She's on business."

The pleasure of requesting room service was far greater than that of consuming the meal. Everything I ordered tasted the same, probably because both the *salade verte* and chicken à la king featured a thick piece of salty ham. All I had previously associated with Belgium was chocolate, lace, banking, and beer. The fixation with all things porcine came as a surprise.

There was much, in fact, that I hadn't prepared for. I wasn't prepared for Belgium's first summer heat wave in decades. I wasn't prepared for the hotel, billed as a Small Luxury Hotel of the World and decked out with a marble bath, minibar, and twenty-four-hour valet. Ideal for a honeymoon, and a gigantic nuisance when you are trying to remain anonymous. I wasn't prepared to feel so far away from home.

I wrapped myself in the thick white terry robe provided by the hotel and wedged myself under the bedcovers. The air-conditioning was ratcheted up to the max, so I buried myself under all the extra coverings, including the down comforter. Since I couldn't sleep—even after the somnolent effects of the bath—I called Josh. He asked me, in that delicate tone people use when they ask about a terminal illness, how everything was going. I answered good, fine, things have been better, but hey, that's life.

In the middle of the night, I ran to the bathroom and threw up. My throat burned for a half hour, and I berated myself for being so overwrought.

Eventually, I fell into a sleep so shallow that I could still hear the whir of the air conditioner, the swish when the bellhop slipped a fresh *Ne Dérangez Pas, S'il Vous Plaît* sign under the doorjamb. At 9 A.M. I got my wake-up call.

"Bon jour! Good morning!" the operator trilled. I dropped the phone back into its cradle.

Da's surgery was in three hours.

❖ ❖. ❖

I had been champing at the bit to go to Brussels with my father. It was our first real vacation together since going to Disney World when I was back in high school. Besides, I reasoned, no one fresh out of college and headed for a temping job should pass up an all-expenses-paid sojourn in Europe. Admittedly, two weeks in Brussels where the average tourist was about sixty wasn't as jaunty as traveling the continent with a knapsack of dirty laundry and a Eurail pass. The fact that Dad was traveling there in order to have her testicles sliced off, and penis inverted into a vaginal canal was also a bit of a downer. But we had already been through so much already that I thought mere surgery couldn't possibly faze me. It seemed anticlimactic.

I was so positively convinced that the operation was going to be a mere pit stop on Dad's journey to total womanhood that I booked the rest of my summer in Europe. I applied, and was accepted for a fellowship to teach English in Prague, where I hoped I'd have a fling or two. Following that, I banked on cheating on my boyfriend by paying a brief visit to a gorgeous, single friend of mine who was studying in Berlin. Why I thought that nursing my father through genital surgery seemed like the perfect precursor to working out my latent sexual energies across the European Union is a mystery to me now, and all I can say in defense of this plan is that I was completely insane—and naive.

Not surprisingly, my mother vehemently disapproved of my plan, particularly the first stop. "You are not going," she said, firmly, and flicked her cigarette butt defiantly into the kitchen sink. "This is not your responsibility. If your *father* wants to do this . . ." She never said "father" with that clipped tone unless she was just this side of exploding.

"Noelle," my mother paused, "you don't know what it's like to see a parent go through surgery. Your da and I have never been sick," she said, "and it can be very hard to watch someone you love in a hospital." Her voice trailed off. I knew she was picturing

Grandma Schultz, her mind already gone, body swollen, eyes bulging and vacant.

"Mom, with all due respect, I appreciate what you're saying, but it's not your choice," I shot back. "Besides, if I don't go, who will? Who of Dad's friends can take three weeks off work to go to Europe to help her?"

"If your father got out a little more . . ." Mom muttered.

"I'm not going to let her go through major surgery in a foreign country by herself. You shouldn't either." I sat back in my chair, feeling slightly flushed, proud that I loved Da so much I was willing to defy my own mother to help her.

That was my first warning. I was too puffed-up about my plan to nurse my ailing transsexual father back to emotional and physical health. I told anyone who would listen about my plan to play Florence Nightingale, and watched their eyes widen as they nodded approvingly, respectfully. I saw this trip as an opportunity to support my father, and to prove, at long last, that she had won my trust. Less altruistically, this gesture would also reinforce to everyone else that I was selfless, impressive, the perfect daughter. I might even believe it myself. If I could fulfill that role and get a European vacation to boot, so much the better.

Shortly after arriving in Brussels, we found the doctor's office several blocks away from the hotel, in a brownstone building framed by two fat old oak trees that couldn't have been indigenous to this pert little square of front lawn. My father rang the bell. "Ahem," she coughed. She was nervous, shifting her weight from one foot to the other, clearing her throat repeatedly. "Um, ahem." She sucked in her breath when the door opened.

"Christine? Wonderful. Come in, yes?" the doctor said in halting English. He gave me a quick glance. "Ah . . . and who do we have here?"

"My daughter, Noelle."

The doctor arched his eyebrows, looking a little dubious. "I've never seen a child come with her parent to a surgery here. You must be *very mature*," he cooed in a syrupy tone, as though he was about to offer me a lollipop.

He led us through a narrow hallway to his office. It was an untidy affair piled with journals, books, ashtrays, a few coffee mugs. The doctor grabbed a feather duster and wiped the thin layer of dust off both wooden armchairs set out for us in front of his desk. I noticed his fingernails were caked with dirt. Not, perhaps, the best sign.

For the next hour, I tried to pay attention to the doctor's explanation about how the surgery would work. First, he said, they detach the skin from the penis and disentangle the urethra and web of blood vessels inside. Then they remove the testicles. Finally, magic time: they invert the penile tissue and create a vagina. Remaining tissue would be used to form a clitoris. Even a gynecologist wouldn't be able to tell the difference, he announced proudly. "Unless they go look for the eggs!"

My father nodded, taking notes in her little Mead notebook, gazing with an approximation of the bovine state she usually only attained in front of the television. It was astonishing. Da, as a man or woman, was liable to swerve her car into a ditch if a bee flew in the window, and barely functioned when felled by a minor stomachache. She was not known for stoicism in the face of physical discomfort. Here the doctor was discussing *serious* pain, the kind that would dope my father up on morphine for days and force her to sit on an inflated donut for two months. Frat boy halfbacks would double over at the thought of a scalpel in their southern regions. Even I, penis-free, shifted in my seat every time the doctor mentioned what would be sliced, added, and reconfigured. Still, there Da sat, jolly as Mrs. Claus.

An hour later, we headed back to the hotel to pack up her stuff for the hospital the next day. She seemed blithely calm, pointing out the lovely bookshelves in the hotel, admiring the nice hand towels in the bathroom. Just as I was wondering who had stolen my father, she cracked. By the time we ordered room service— baked beef stew with ham, and lasagna with ham—her pretense of worry-free equilibrium evaporated.

"I don't know if I have enough," she said.

"Enough . . . money?"

"Enough penis," she blurted. "There's almost nothing there, from all the hormone treatments. What if they don't have enough to work with?" She began pacing back and forth in front of our suite's matching beds.

"I've heard about certain transsexuals," she confided. "Their vaginas are only three inches deep because they didn't have enough penis to work with. Because of hormones and whatever else, it was all gone by the time they got the surgery." She started to gesticulate wildly. "What if I'm one of those people?" she said, her voice rising with panic. "What if my vagina isn't deep enough?"

My father was only getting warmed up. For the rest of the evening, she walked in a circle, yanked at her wig, blinked back tears, swore. For the rest of the evening, I tried to listen without going somewhere else in my mind. I focused on her problems, and being a good friend and confidante, instead of the daughter who had second thoughts about getting *this* close.

I thought if any life-altering event during the first week of July 1994, was going to be traumatizing, it wasn't going to be my father's sex change, but rather my mother's nuptials. My mother had been planning the wedding for months, trying to work out the details of where precisely in our yard to put the bales of hay, the rented plastic cow replica, and the line-dancing band. Mom's bubbling enthusiasm over the cowboy theme made me wonder if, someday, without prior warning, I would morph into one of those middle-aged ladies who decorate their houses with frog-themed statuary or put plastic slipcovers on their living-room furniture. My worries about the affair going downmarket nearly obscured what I was truly concerned about—that this event would finally sever Mom from what I thought of as my true family: the original party of three.

When the big day itself rolled around, I sang an Irving Berlin ditty during the wedding ceremony as promised. Mom wept. The happy couple exchanged vows. The clustered audience dabbed their cheeks.

Later that evening, as the newlyweds and a handful of stragglers convened in the living room with plates of BBQ chicken and potato salad, Da and I walked arm in arm in the shadows of the nearly empty backyard.

"You know, I really miss her," Da said. "She'd never believe it, but I do."

"Is it hard to see her move on?" I asked.

"She deserves to be happy."

"That's not what I asked."

"I lost the right to answer that question a long time ago," she replied.

When I came back in that evening and kissed Da good night, I sat and talked with my mother for a few minutes. She told me that the wedding had been the best day she'd ever had, that she was thrilled to share it with me and my father. Michael was upstairs changing, and she lit a cigarette in the dark of the kitchen.

"I know this is bad timing," I ventured. "But if Dad had stayed a guy, would you guys still be together?"

"I don't think so," she said. "I know you don't understand Michael, but I can be the person I am around him. I don't question whether I'm attractive enough, lovable enough, sexy enough. He needs me and lets me help him, which your father could never do." She held my hand across the table. "I love Christine, and I always will. But now you're the person she needs, not me. Amazingly, she allows you to be close to her. She could never do that with me."

I told her that sometimes I thought of her and Dad—two peo-

ple who adored each other, but could never quite communicate—
as star-crossed lovers. Mom shook her head.

"Never lovers," she corrected. "She's my friend, my pain in the
ass. Call her my sister, maybe."

In the hospital the night before the surgery, Da didn't sleep much
better than I did, although not for the reason one might think.

That evening, she was standing in the bathroom, staring at the
back of the toilet and realizing how much was about to change,
when she noticed a pink disposable razor sitting on the counter.
Hot damn, she thought. I forgot to shave the way the doctor told
me to.

Five minutes later, she rinsed her hair off the razor and, as she
stood there, holding the blade under a stream of water from the
sink, she froze. I don't know who used this last, she thought.
Statistics of the disproportionately high HIV transmission rates
among transgendered people reeled through her mind as though
she were watching headlines unspool on microfiche. She threw
the razor in the biological-hazard trash.

She walked back to her bed, feeling suddenly lost in her own
body, absolutely certain that she had infected herself with the
slightly rusty razor. It's so unfortunate, she thought dolefully, that
when everything in my life is finally coming together, I have to
die.

She never told me about this incident until several years—and
three negative HIV tests—later, but as selfish as it may sound, I
was relieved to hear that the sex change hadn't just made me
crazy. As copacetic as she claimed to be about all things surgical,
something about it had obviously scared the bejesus out of her,
too.

It took me twenty minutes to walk to the hospital. Thanks to the
lack of trees along the way, I felt the beginnings of a sunburn all

along my part; by the time I arrived, my scalp was bright pink and hot to the touch. I was evenly coated with sweat as though it had been applied by aerosol, and had never felt less attractive.

Not that it made any difference. The reception clerk smiled widely at me and called me "Mademoiselle" until I told her who I was here to see. She tersely informed me of the room to which my father, whom she called my mother, was assigned. She's going into surgery in ten minutes, she told me in French. After consulting my dictionary for a translation, I said thanks and scurried down the corridor, alarmed by the chipped paint, the blinking fluorescent lights, the small piles of soot awaiting a dustpan.

My father was already lying on a gurney when I arrived, looking like a train wreck. Her wig was off, and I could see her bald head, the one I hadn't seen since she started living as a woman. I was startled to see a few wisps of silvery grey hair, which had changed color while tucked beneath her wig. Her breasts, made of a padded bra, hung from a hook on a closet door, allowing her Tweety bird nightshirt to lie flat across her chest. Her nails were immaculately manicured, with acrylic tips. She was a brilliant shade of red, from the arid heat inside the building or from mortification at having been stripped down to her gender-conflicted essentials, and clearly terrified, even though she smiled when I walked in the room.

I leaned down and kissed her on the forehead. Her skin, soft from lotion, was damp and cool. "I'm going to be fine," she said in a quavering voice. "You should go have fun tonight."

"I'll go out to eat," I said, holding her hand. "I'll see the city. Pick up some guys for us."

Dad grinned and pulled her hand away to wipe the perspiration on her nightshirt. "You do that," she said.

The nurse hovered at the door, glaring at both of us as though we were infectious vermin. "Time," she said in heavily accented English, and started maneuvering the gurney, banging it on either side of the doorframe in the process. "We go now."

"I love you, sweetheart," my father whispered. "I'll see you later."

"You bet," I answered. As Da squeezed my hand and stared up at me like a lost child, I had never been so aware of what this surgery was really taking away.

I never said good-bye to my father—the original model. I never ran alongside a train waving a tissue, never pressed my lips to window glass as a car sped away, never gently closed his eyes with my fingertips. I never knew he was leaving until he was, finally and inexorably, gone. I don't wish to strain the analogy by calling it a death, but like everything else related to this issue, the available language is inadequate to the task at hand. How do you label the sensation of losing not a person, but a *persona?* It seems trivial compared to real ashes-to-ashes death, and yet there's something profound about it. My knowledge of early-childhood development is meager at best, and yet as far as I can tell, babies learn who their parents are through sensing them—the tenor of Mom's voice lulling them awake, the feel of Dad's chest, the strength of his hands, the whiff of her pheromones. What if all those sense associations were suddenly to cease? Would we recognize our parents anymore? Would we think someone else had taken their place?

To this day, as much as I love my da, I have a recurring fantasy about my male father, Dick. I imagine he's somewhere in an infamous penitentiary, wearing one of those orange jumpsuits he seemed to covet back in the days when *Midnight Express* looped on our VCR. I picture being in the outdoors visiting area, surrounded by barbed-wire fences, amidst pockets of scruffy lawn, mounds of cigarette butts and several rickety, splinter-ridden picnic tables. He isn't any nicer than the last time I saw him, and he tells me I shouldn't have come. He looks haunted and remote.

The dark circles are back under his eyes, and he has no hair at all. The few wisps left are deep brown, the way they always were. He looks youngish, still about forty.

We sit in awkward silence, and I wish I hadn't come until we exchange a perfunctory hug. He smells like sweat, cinnamon, iced tea, and something cloyingly sweet. The aroma is too strong, like he's trying too hard to smell appealing. His hands are rough and indelicate when they push me away. His accordion-style watch-band tugs at a few of my arm hairs along the way. I tell him not to kill himself in here, and I walk away.

In the dream, I then clamber into Da's car, where she holds me for hours. Da tells me I don't ever need to go back, and I can tell from the tone in her voice that she wishes I wouldn't. She says that it pains her to see how much he can get to me. I know, I say. I don't want her to know that I'm not crying over our history of hurts. I don't want her to know that I miss my male father and love him, and that as wonderful as she is to me, sometimes all I want are *his* arms wrapped around me, his sickly-sweet smell making me feel dizzy and nervous and home.

Surgery was scheduled to end by noon, but Da was not permitted visitors for the rest of the day. I tried to kill time by roaming around Brussels, attempting to work up some fascination for the Tintin museum and the home of Victor Hugo and all the while not imagining my father's sex organs being stretched, inverted, and stitched together like she was some sort of pornographic rag doll.

I spent another night filled with baths and room service and regurgitation, and made it to the hospital the next day ten minutes shy of visiting hours. Da was still pumped up on morphine. She lay on a cot just beneath a window, sopping wet from the sun. An IV tube ran directly into her groin, where her shirt had been bunched up to show a massive pile of crusty-brown bandages. She said, "Hiiiii, honnnneeeey" in a slurry voice, like an ESL student on a bender, and promptly fell asleep again. I sprayed her with cold water and dried her off with a washcloth, and even tried to stand in front of the window, to give her the approximation of shade while she slept. I didn't want to leave: The nurses didn't come around much, and I was afraid she'd catch sunstroke or worse if I left.

I passed the time glancing at a *Newsweek International* from the hotel, and talking to China Christie, my father's roommate and, in all honesty, one of the most disturbing people I'd ever met. China ("after Chynna, the Wilson Phillips girl") and Christie ("after Christie Brinkley because people say I look like her") was a swimsuit calendar model from Southern California. From afar, or if you squinted, she looked gorgeous: six feet tall, huge eyes, perky breasts, legs built for business class. She was the celluloid image that teen girls vomited for, twentyish women dieted for, middle-aged women nipped and tucked for. She was the most femme woman I had ever seen and, naturally, a biological male.

She was also an optical illusion. She reminded me of those Magic Eye paintings that had gotten popular in mall kiosks: The longer you stared at one of them, pixels quivered and altered to form a new picture. Since she refused to wear a stitch of clothing in the hospital room under any circumstances, I had a lot of opportunities to revise my estimation of her body. Her perfectly rounded breasts had deep, jagged valleys beneath them where it appeared that she'd been operated on by someone with a hacksaw. Her lips were enlarged by collagen, her cheekbones constructed, her eyes tucked, her Adam's apple shaved. Her pubes were shaved as though she was prepubescent or a porn star. Like a baby doll who can only repeat the same five phrases, China only seemed capable of doing five things: filing her nails, painting her nails, tweezing, reading *Vogue*, and telling me I should do something with my hair ("After all, you're a real girl!" she exclaimed, "make the most of it!").

In between her various activities, China regaled me with her life lessons.

Why She Became a Woman: "Because I'm weak and I can get more being a weak girl than a weak man."

What Men Look for in Girlfriends: "Someone fishy-smelling."

How She Had Found True Love: "My boyfriend doesn't know I'm here," she told me. "He thinks I'm a girl and that I'm on a photo shoot. I go down on him when he makes me, but we haven't done it because I tell him I'm not that kind of girl." She told me this while lying entirely naked in bed, filing her nails.

"Did he buy that?" I asked, trying to repress incredulity.

"Men are so gullible," she said, without a hint of irony. "They believe anything a pussy says. He'd kill me if he knew. He'd slash my throat and cut me up or something."

"Mmm," I said, resisting the urge to hand her battered women's hotline information. As would be the case with China quite frequently over the next few days, I had no appropriate rejoinder.

China had several friends, other male-to-females from the club scene in L.A. who were all staying at the same hotel, a cheap joint down the block from the elegant retreat my father had booked us into. They stopped by the room to bring flowers to China, and clutch their skirts at the ready and ask me (repeatedly) if I wanted to check out their "snatches."

"It looks so real!" they exclaimed.

It's true that I felt enormous sympathy for China and her strip-club comrades. They were obviously poor, all of them had been sexually assaulted, repressed, treated like dirt, and exiled from their families in the most despicable fashions. But I also had my fair share of reactionary thoughts like: You aren't women. You're chauvinists in dresses. I felt guilty as soon as I thought them because I'd been so busy convincing other people that "woman-hood" was a big tent and all of us could fit beneath it. Of course, in the cold light of day, I had probably meant people like my dad.

That whole trip, I never wore any makeup. I avoided skirts. I fantasized about being neutered. The prospect of the sexual she-nanigans I had planned before leaving seemed preposterous; given the events of the last week, I determined that I wanted nothing to do with sex, maybe ever again. I heard China talk day after day about wanting to become genitally female before "it happened"—meaning getting raped by her boyfriend—and it made me rudder. I had to remind myself that China and her sixth-grade education hadn't come up with these theories all on her own. She simply watched, listened, repeated.

What I was repelled by in China was exactly what I despised about myself: her need to please, to seduce, to prove her wom-anliness by being sexually demeaned.

My father was released from the hospital after one week. She had lost about five pounds in water weight from lying in the sun. I wasn't doing much better. Despite my unfortunate ritual of nightly stress-induced vomiting, I had gained ten.

The next week passed in a haze. We took long, quiet walks, the most strenuous activity Da was up for, and talked about any-thing other than the operation. I remember only one conversation about it. As we were taking a break at a café, I asked her if all this pain in the ass had been worth it, and she looked quite serious and said yes, I think so, then shifted on her rubber donut.

After several days, I left for Prague to go on the teaching fel-lowship. I asked Da if she was sure she'd be okay. She said of course, and not to worry—she was on the mend. It was true; except for walking at the pace of a ninety-year-old woman, she was looking comparatively spry. It soon became obvious that she wasn't the sick one.

It happened as soon as I left the station.

Snippets come back: Screaming irrationally at the ticket clerk who couldn't tell me when I'd get into Dresden. Writing letters to Josh that started with complete sentences and ended up in doodle. Crying too much, and too loudly, without provocation. Falling asleep and forgetting where I was when I woke up. The one fact about getting to Prague that I know for sure is that it almost didn't happen, not after I got off the train in Dresden, missed my connection, and immediately determined that the world was ending right then and there. Using my calling card, oblivious to time zones, I phoned my mother in the States. It was the middle of the night, and I must have terrified her, calling in a torrent of tears and claiming that I didn't know how to get to Prague. I remember hanging on to the phone booth, clutching it with both hands, as though to remind myself that I was in the real world, amidst tangible objects. I remember seeing in blurs, because my vision had gone fun house on me.

Thank God she was calm in a crisis. Mom talked me down, in her usual common sense way. She told me to look at the schedule, and that she would call the people in Prague to let them know my new arrival time. Somehow I gained my equilibrium again, and made it onto the new train. But my panic attack in Dresden was a precursor of times to come.

I lasted in the fellowship program for exactly five days of orientation, which mostly consisted of drinking Czech beer and learning where the textbooks were locked up, and one day of actual teaching. I taught a single class, peopled by middle-aged Czech blue-collar workers who threw spitballs and called me "Skipper."

At age twenty-two, with zero experience and a resolute strain of perfectionism, teaching a daily five-hour class without training to people who made fun of me might have caused me to lose it anyway. Considering that I felt like I was held together with a bit of tape and some dental floss, it was a certainty that I wouldn't last until the Friday night teachers' hang at the local expatriate bar.

I had no idea what was happening to me. I wanted to cry all

the time. I was frightened of everything except, for a change, death—which suddenly seemed overhyped. I couldn't eat. I couldn't sleep. I wanted to get drunk. I was bone tired in that first-trimester way, and I was losing my mind. My summer plans of frolicking with random boys and seeing the countrysides of Europe had never sounded so impossible and unappealing. I sought only to crawl under the covers and sleep until 1998.

I wouldn't have left, either, until my mother virtually ordered me to do so. "You need to come home now," she said, as though I'd been out too late. "Let me help you," she said, as though she thought she could save me.

I quit, although I was mortified about doing so. I canceled my summer plans and went home to spend long afternoons walking the dog with my father and eating quiet dinners with my mother. After a month or so of solitude, we all thought I was getting better—that what we called "my mood" was lifting. My parents, both of them more confident and self-assured in their own choices than they'd been in years, were sure I had just needed some downtime. They might have been too preoccupied by their own unprecedented levels of contentment. Now that they had finally established their own identities and settled with some comfort into their lives, I was losing myself completely.

TWENTY-FOUR

Snapshots from My Trip

The brain is the only organ that tries to make sense of its pain. It is as if the bone were trying to understand the break, as if the blood vessel could comprehend its rupture. But this is also its greatest impediment to understanding. The mind clings fiercely to any alternative to chaos, even if that alternative is self-destruction.
—Tracy Thompson, *The Beast: A Journey Through Depression*

I had always been self-conscious about my wrists. Weighing no more than ninety-seven pounds at any previous point in my life had resulted in having wrists that looked like dresser pulls. I had always refused to wear a watch because I'd have to force a new hole in order to keep it from dangling off my arm like a bracelet. Maybe it was all the ham and beer in Europe, or a gradually slowing metabolism, but my wrists no longer looked so gaunt to me. They were thicker, and less delicate. I spent a lot of time looking at them, and wondering what was happening to me.

Cleveland, August 1994. Da knocked on my door to wake me up. I stayed with her instead of Mom to avoid breakfasting on awkward-silence-and-toast with Michael. Da said, "Hey there, about time to get up yet?" I growled something in response, and rolled out of bed.

I took a shower so hot that my butt shaded to pink, and so long that my fingers wrinkled up like jerky. I patted myself down with a towel and stared at each visible body part in the medicine cabinet mirror, taking inventory, rendering verdicts—a new habit I'd picked up, inadvertently, from China Christie. I scrubbed my teeth, especially the ones that my dentist had recently warned would probably fall out before I was thirty, thanks to orthodontic malfeasance in my youth. I pinched the new ounces of flesh around my thighs, my waist, my breasts. I weighed myself. I was an unprecedented 108 pounds. I dressed myself in a sundress that blew upward in the wind like those Marilyn Monroe cardboard cutouts in novelty stores.

Da had laid out the corn flakes, the 2 percent milk, the bowls and spoons on the dining room table. She was already there, sitting on her donut, talking about buying a new outfit at the mall for a lesbian-gay-transgender barbecue that evening.

"I didn't think you were doing that stuff anymore," I said.

"I wasn't," she said. "Hey, I need to get out of the house now and then."

"Okay. Well, that's fine because I need to start packing."

"Are you sure you're ready to go anywhere?" Da asked.

"It's already been a month, and I'm doing much better," I said, dryly. "I need to get on with my life. I miss Josh, anyhow." That wasn't precisely true. I missed his validation; since I'd returned from Europe, he had called me every day to tell me how much he loved me and couldn't wait until I moved to the Pacific Northwest to resume our relationship. I owed him.

I drove by myself from Cleveland to Chicago, where I was to meet up with Josh, who would keep me company on the westward stretch of the trip. It took me about twenty miles to feel homesick, seventy to revisit the scene of the sex change, one hundred ninety to shake my head, turn up the radio, and tell myself to stop being such a goddamn baby about everything. I had never been more grateful for the flat, open roads of Ohio and Indiana.

Even once I met up with Josh at his parents' home, that drive remains sketchy in my mind. I remember seeing him bound down the front steps of their bungalow, a pastiche of spindly legs, long record-store-clerk hair, and wide grin. I hadn't seen him since my graduation weekend, a few months earlier, but he looked more petite than ever. I remember having that ominous sense that I had fucked up, big-time. I was suddenly cognizant that it didn't make much sense to move across the country to be with someone just so you could mourn the end of the relationship together.

My greeting was probably underwhelming. I hugged him, pecked his cheek, and ran inside to say hello to his parents. On the rest of the trip, through the Badlands, the Black Hills, past the arid prairies of Wyoming and the nuclear power plants of eastern Washington, we made small talk and slept on separate sides of the bed. I froze when he tried to get near me, explaining that I was going through a hard time right now, with all the changes that had been going on.

"You're always going through a hard time," he grumbled, and stormed into the bathroom. It was true. He was right. I had nothing to say.

Seattle, October 1994. I was only allowed fifteen-minute breaks twice a day working as a receptionist in Human Resources at the HMO. Fortunately, I could pee as much as I wanted. By noon, I had worked three and a half hours and taken approximately seven trips to the lavatory, where I rested my head on the toilet roll and stared at the scuff marks on the stall door.

I spent my afternoons retyping file labels and instructing seemingly baffled neurosurgeons on how to use the Mr. Coffee. When no one was looking, I completed graduate school applications for Ph.D. programs in English—fourteen in all. If this sounds horrifically dull, I have to admit that I didn't notice. I had attained the state of autopilot, easing through my days with little stress, joy, or anger of any kind. It occurred to me that lots of other people lived like this all the time; I thought I could get used to it. Being numb was preferable to being a fount of torrid, dramatic emotions. I wasn't exactly happy, but I figured this was what people meant by being "well-adjusted."

I was managing, at least, to make the relationship with Josh work—largely because he was the only person I knew within a five hundred-mile radius (he lived in Tacoma). I willed myself into being in love with him again.

It wasn't easy. Although he had begged me to come to Washington state since moving there himself the previous year, now that I was there, making pasta in his kitchen, sleeping on the right side of his queen-size, he seemed constantly irritated with me. One night, after dinner, he berated me for facing the soup bowls the wrong way in the dishwasher. Another time, styling myself after *Cosmo* articles of the midsixties, I greeted the hardworking man home from the office by donning a black teddy purchased at the mall (my standards were easing up vis-à-vis authenticity, now that we weren't in college anymore). He took one look at me trying to preen and burst out laughing. I ran into the bathroom, locked the door, and sat there, completely mortified, for twenty minutes.

"It's hard having you here all the time," he said.

Or, "You need me too much."

And the occasional, "I'm feeling crowded."

In an attempt to give him a little space, I moved out of his apartment into a rental share. I learned which direction the plates should face. I strained to recall whether he liked the toilet paper coming up from under or over the top. I reminded myself how sexy I'd always found dominant guys with some edge. I remembered all the love letters from him that I'd never opened. I tried not to say anything most of the time; I wasn't quite ready to lose anyone else.

Seattle, November 1994. Josh and I finished making love. He rolled over, staring at the crack in the wood paneling next to my futon.

I rubbed the small of Josh's back and nuzzled his neck. "Josh," I asked, "do you think I'm pretty? Do you think I'm beautiful?" For three years, I had asked these painfully insecure questions after every time we had sex.

"C'mon," I begged, my voice crescendoing, "please say it. Please?" For three years, I had asked these questions in a plaintive, meek voice nearly frantic for approval. But this exchange, too, like our dirty talk, was scripted. Josh knew to expect the questions; he knew what answer to give. Thereafter, I would lean back, newly relaxed, as mellow as if I'd smoked the clichéd postcoital cigarette. After his compliments, fished-for and planned-out as they were, I would feel comfortable in my body—at least for a day or two.

On this night Josh was mute. He rolled back over to look at me, his eyes as hard and unflinching as marble. "No," he answered. "Frankly, Noelle," he said, wearily resting his head on his hands, "I think you've gained too much weight. Your thighs look so fat that they repulse me. I can't bear to look between your legs. It's disgusting."

I drew a sheet over my bare body. Without warning, we were off the script. I had always dictated the insults Josh would hurl at me during sex. I called that being submissive. I suddenly realized, with a shudder, that this improvisation was an altogether different story. I always picked out insults I could handle, ones that functioned as backhanded compliments, like "slut," or "bitch." "Fat" didn't make the cut. "Disgusting" and "repulsive" didn't either.

I leapt from the bed and threw on the first sweats I could find. I layered myself twice on top and bottom, in a desperate attempt to shield my body from his words. It wasn't like being cold; it was like being emptied out.

"Josh," I muttered, "I'm 108 pounds. That's skinny."

"Look," he said sternly and slowly, like a nineteenth-century schoolmaster, "if you didn't want to know what I thought, you shouldn't have asked me."

Seattle, January 1995. For the next few months, Josh and I had occasional dinners. We also had infrequent, passionless sex during which I thought, triumphantly, "ha-ha, guess I'm not so disgusting after all." I told friends, far away in Chicago, Washington, and Tokyo, that we had broken up. In order to "get past" what Josh had said to me, I told them, I would have had to chuck all my self-esteem entirely. At moments, I think I sounded convincing.

I joined a gym for the first time. Every day after work, I climbed an imaginary seventy-story building, then pedalled through an animated park. I took the fit test on the Exercycle once a week, and jotted the results on an index card. In a manner of speaking, I had never been healthier. I had my hair chopped off and dyed, then purchased my very first makeover at a local spa. The makeup artist, a part-time art student at the U, told me that she was thrilled to "get at me with the tweezers," since my unmanicured brows made me look "a little too Frida Kahlo." People at work complimented my new look, which lasted for three days, at which point I, already feeling fatigued much of the day, decided that sleeping in was preferable even to vanity.

One day at work, my supervisors asked me to attend a seminar they were hosting about the obstacles to high levels of achievement. I was pleased. I figured I had impressed them sufficiently by tacking up gift-shop postcards of Maya Angelou, Hillary

Clinton, and a Matisse on my cubicle wall, meant to signify my extracurricular interest in Smart Things. Or maybe it was my scoring on the personality test they made me take, which informed me that I was an ENTJ, the psych profile of generals, presidents, and according to one of the human resources managers, "aggressive women who sometimes are seen as abrasive by others." After getting my coffee and muffin and settling into the third row of chairs, however, it became apparent that the seminar was for low-level workers who needed to learn the *secrets* of truly talented go-getters. We were each required to make a list of five things we could do to "stand out from the crowd." I excused myself to go to the bathroom and didn't come back.

My parents had always been the ones with the identity crisis, I thought, not me. I'd always picked an image and stuck to it with resolute fervor. Yet here I was, another drone struggling not to be invisible. While it's true that I conveniently overlooked the fact that a plethora of college grads—creative writing majors, especially—don't immediately step out into rewarding careers, it's also true (if a tad melodramatic) to say that I didn't know who I was anymore. I felt like my superlatives had been stripped away from me. I was no longer the tiniest girl, like in high school; no longer the most accomplished, not compared to my friend getting her biochemistry Ph.D.; not the nicest, like my mom; not even the most fascinating, like Da. I was me, which did not seem like enough.

Berkeley, July 1995. I had gotten a sense of identity back when I was accepted into the UC-Berkeley's combined MA/Ph.D. program in English, which was ranked #1 in *US News & World Report*, a fact I managed to worm into every conversation. I did not particularly want to live in California, nor to attend graduate school, but as I told my parents "I have no choice. It's the best, and so I'd be an idiot not to go there." In actuality, for the next ten years or so I probably would have been happy just telling people I would be going there in the distant future and watching them rejigger their previous estimations of my intellect. Attending school was an afterthought, and thus, it's not surprising that I lasted exactly three days in the program.

From the point at which the plane from Seattle touched down on the tarmac in San Francisco, I knew I had made yet another huge mistake. I moved into one group house in Berkeley, and packed my bags three days later because the throb of the neighbor's boom box made me weep. I moved into a gorgeous white stucco bungalow, but informed the other graduate students I was leaving because the house was on a hill and I wasn't physically fit enough to put up with the walk to school. I picked a third place to live and once I purchased all my pressboard furniture and a futon so thin that I woke up with red horizontal slat marks down the length of my body, I proceeded to go into my room and watch soap operas for hours at a time—a fact that horrified my very serious, holistic, vegan roommates.

I was deeply frustrated with myself. I had been priming to become the very embodiment of an academic scholar for the last year or so, and had spent much of my receptionist salary acquiring T-shirts emblazoned with chortle-worthy Dorothy Parker epigrams and impressively obscure Balinese folk music CDs for my rack. Now I was here, amidst the aspiring literati as I had wanted to be, and at orientation cocktail parties, I inexplicably changed the subject from the subversive comedic subtext of Aphra Behn's Restoration-era comedies to what happened on *Melrose Place* last week. It's as though I was setting out to sabotage my own image.

Plenty of people have written about depression, its myriad cruel symptoms, the perplexity of not being able to trust your own judgment and feeling betrayed by your body (though that feeling was hardly an unusual one for me, or for most women). My experience was not unusual. In a nutshell, I stopped eating, and started sleeping fifteen hours a day. My state of numbness had come to a crashing halt, as I began to moan and cry a great deal to people

I knew, and to an embarrassing number that I did not. I knew what was wrong with me, intellectually. From glimpsing a self-help book in a used bookstore near campus, I learned that I wasn't merely crazy because I had every single symptom in the book for severe clinical depression. As textbook as my case was, so too was my denial. Depression was a malady for people who couldn't deal with life, not competent academic strivers like myself. To my feminist mind, it seemed too easily connoted with "hysteria," that peculiarly feminine disorder. I left the bookstore and couldn't remember how to get back to my house for several hours. I sat under a bush with tiny little red berries on it trying to puzzle the directions out. Once I finally made it back, I locked myself in my room and played the first movement to Mussorgsky's *Pictures at an Exhibition* over and over for hours until I fell asleep. When I spoke to my parents the next day, I didn't mention a word about the fact that I might have depression. I kept saying that I was fucked up, which seemed a preferable self-diagnosis.

By the time the first day of orientation rolled around, I could barely speak in complete sentences. I forgot to bring a pen and paper to class, which went over well with the prof.

I spent a lot of time looking at my wrists, wondering what was happening to me.

Throughout that summer, my parents conferred several times a week about my worsening condition. Each of them was receiving phone calls two or three times a day from me, always the same: a litany of complaints about minor issues (noise pollution, a bad haircut) blown up into cataclysms, punctuated with guttural sobs. My mom thought I might be schizophrenic, or manic-depressive, and my father worried she had finally destroyed me after all. But in clucking like two mother hens together, setting their own grievances aside, they figured out a way to help me.

They decided that one of them should go out to California on a rescue mission. My mother, having considerably more experience in the field, was the designated caregiver. Before her departure, I protested that coming out to see me was unimportant, a waste of her time. I said I was going through a difficult life change. I told her to stay at home with her family.

"You *are* my family," she sternly reminded me, and gave me her flight number.

Berkeley, September 1995. My mother took one look at me, runny and mottled in the noonday sun, slumped on the front stoop of the group house, and said, "I thought you said that you couldn't keep a secret if your life depended on it. I guess you were wrong." I was worse off, apparently, than I had let on.

"I don't know what you're talking about," I said. "I'm feeling emotional. You know how I am."

"Yes, I do," she replied.

Power of attorney transferred from me to her in a moment. Within hours of her arrival, she was packing my bags, carting my brand-new, crappy furniture out to the curb for pickup and making a one-way reservation for me on her same flight back to Cleveland.

I told her over and over that she was being unreasonable and ridiculous. Who ever needed to be rescued from sunny, beautiful California? "Go home," I said. "I'm fine now. Go take care of Michael and his sons. They need you more than I do," I said. Undermining my argument, perhaps, was the fact that I wasn't able to pull myself out of a fetal position, or consume solids.

In my addled mind, my several weeks–old association with graduate school was the one remaining element of my identity I had left. Without my Ph.D. program, I was nothing. My logic, so corrupted by a dearth of seratonin, rattled and perplexed my mom.

"Where did your confidence go?" she asked. I didn't have an answer. I wasn't even sure what she was talking about.

❋   ❋   ❋

The next day, I went to school to fill out withdrawal papers. My faculty advisor shook his head and scolded me for my impatience. He chewed thoughtfully on the edge of his ballpoint pen. "The first year is always tough," he said. "It's only been a week." I was sure he was going to go home to his wife that night, and tell her that *some flake dropped out after three days of classes if you can believe that. I thought we were more selective than that.* I couldn't meet his face. I looked down and folded my arms, in the hopes that a sheepish pose might mitigate his obvious contempt. And then, I withdrew anyway.

Walking to a campus parking lot, where I had parked my mother's rental car, I grew angry at her. She wants to play nurse-maid and save people, and she hates how together I am, because then she can't save me, I thought. I got in the car. I peered at the knobs on the radio, the steering column, the cruise-control button. I put my key in the ignition and turned it over, but I couldn't go anywhere. I sat there in a stupor for twenty minutes. I had forgotten how to drive.

My mother took me to a therapist—who deduced I was clinically depressed in ten minutes flat—and then to a nearby motel in Oakland. She purchased us two adjoining rooms, just for the night. They were standard singles with sliding glass doors that opened up on a swimming pool. The beds were tightly made; the air conditioner was cranked up. It was freezing and sterile, like an infirmary, which felt more soothing to me than I would have expected. I curled up on the bed to sleep, and when I woke up in the orange haze of the late afternoon, my mother was doing a sweep of my room for sharp objects. "Better safe than sorry," she told me, in unconscious mimicry of the fire-safety placard on the back of the door.

For the rest of the day, she held me while I cried. She murmured "shhh" and rocked back and forth when, suddenly, one of my irrational fits of panic spewed forth. She held me close, and as I lay my head upon her breast the way I always had back in elementary school, I remembered that my mother didn't take care of people only because of some sort of pathological need to be liked, or to draw attention away from her life by focusing her energies on others. Perhaps that was part of it, sure, but during recent years, I had somehow forgotten how bountiful her love was. How fierce her devotion to the ones she cared about. Her arms were so strong that I almost felt that she *could* put me back together piece by piece, just from sheer willpower. I nearly basked in the wreck that my life had become, simply for the chance to be cared for by her again.

Later, I swam laps outside in the dark, feeling oddly soothed by the repetitive motion. My mother sat on a lawn chair. I could feel her eyes on me, watchful as a nervous baby-sitter. I didn't want the night to end.

Cleveland, September 1995. It was an unusually frigid, but golden fall day when Da walked me through a tiny corner of a nearby Metropark. The wording is no accident; I was not ambulatory on my own two feet. (Those who see depression as merely a mental illness neglect the fact that it tends to shut down a good number of physiological functions as well, rendering even a youthful sufferer as delicate as an octogenarian recovering from a hip replacement. I walked at such a slow plod that, had I been a character in a movie, I would have expired in the next scene.) I hung on to the leash for her German shepherd, Malaika, and Da hung on to my arm, occasionally propping me up as I went. She placed the donut from her sex change recovery down on a bench in a gazebo, and bent with me as I sat.

"Here you go, Methuselah." She smiled.

"Hey, you weren't walking so well last summer," I weakly reminded her.

"I had gotten some major cutting-and-pasting done," she joked. "What's your excuse?"

She sat down next to me, holding my hand, while Malaika curled at our feet.

"You scared me and your mom a little there, you know," she said, in a little voice. "You were sort of slipping away from us."

"I'm sorry," I said, leaning on her shoulder. "I know what that feels like."

"I hope you can forgive me for whatever part I've played in all this," Da said, sadly.

"I can't," I said. "You've been the best friend—the best *fa-ther*—I could ever have wanted. There's nothing left to forgive."

I got better. It was a group effort: Mom, Da, me, and the pharmaceutical industry working in tandem to bring back my appetite, quell my migraines and nightmares, allow me to regain normal sleeping patterns, and so on. Within a week of taking Prozac (and talk therapy over the next few months) I became relatively functional again. Resuming my normal life was not an option.

I had been a big fan of the movie *Thelma and Louise* in college, and at one point Geena Davis's character, having left her husband and abandoned her pretenses at being a docile housewife, looks over at Susan Sarandon—both trickling with sweat and burnished brown from driving in the sun—and says, "Something has crossed over in me." And that's how I felt, except for not having a tan, convertible, or any intention of driving off a cliff. I just felt different: Maybe it was the fact that my desire to control people's perceptions of me had been finally thwarted (and by none other than myself). Maybe it was the fact that, to my mind, I had tried projecting every image I had been able to come across—adorable moppet; quintessential teen; bohemian chick; feminist activist; femme fatale; intellectual giant—and at some point, had failed at each. The failure, of course, was predestined because those images were simply stock archetypes selected from a dramatis personae. They were ciphers, and so, in a way, was I. In spite of all my incessant coming out, my affliction of being painfully honest about my family, I had done a damn fine job of closeting myself—ignoring the inconsistent, messy paradoxes in order to project something clean and uncomplicated. I had disparaged my Grandma H. for her chameleonic talents and my parents for their identity crises, but the truth—perhaps plain to everyone else—was that I, too, was addicted to the makeover culture that most women contend with. Unlike men, who have only a handful of different images to choose from, there's a veritable plethora of choices for women. Changing yourself is supposed to mean hope, at least according to the self-help books and magazine paradigms, but for me—and I suspect many others—it simply means finding new ways to feel inadequate.

Of course, in those months of recovering from depression, none of this was made manifestly clear to me. I had no moment of clarity or any such fictional moment in which I became a fully integrated person. But slowly, and nearly by accident, I began to embrace the messy parts of myself. I started working at Cleveland's National Public Radio affiliate, and admitted to a coworker that I rushed home after work to watch the entire ABC Daytime lineup. I came clean about not even knowing what dialectics were. Most crucially, I came out to everyone I knew about having depression. It was impossible to try to convey any sort of superwoman image once they knew I had been a drooling, fetal ball for weeks at a time. I found that more liberating than I would have ever expected.

Cleveland, January, February, or March 1996. I was on the Internet researching the long-term effects of psychopharmacological drugs for an NPR report, when I glimpsed a desktop file called "Personal." For some reason, perhaps because Da was a neo-Luddite inclined to archive files on her computer for years at a time without cleaning them out, I was certain this was a wretched short story I'd written back during a college break about a fruit salesman with bowel problems and thought I'd do my father (and myself) the favor of eliminating it from her screen. I got more information than I had bargained for.

Apparently, "Personal" meant "personal ad" for a local alternative paper, and more specifically, the Women Seeking Women section. *There she goes again*, I thought. *Just when I thought we'd run out of family secrets, there's one smacking me in the face.* Da was an out transsexual, and a closeted lesbian. Suddenly, her renewed interest in LGBT intramural volleyball and the annual dyke clambake made some sense.

She was watching pro football in her big comfy chair, and scarfing pistachios when I came into the living room.

I casually mentioned that it seemed like she'd been spending a lot of time with lesbians lately. (For any other family, this might seem like a strange observation to drop into conversation. My family, however, doesn't know the meaning of non sequiturs.)

"Oh geez," she said. "I was going to say something."

"Are we on coming out #3 now, or #7?" I asked. "I've lost count."

She asked if I was angry. She hadn't wanted to saddle me, especially given my delicate emotional state, with any more personal revelations.

I laughed. "You think *this* is going to faze me?" I scoffed. I was relieved that her chances, statistically, of being murdered by her date in a parking lot had dramatically plummeted. Unless she was going to start a relationship with a Valerie Solanas fan, I figured we were safe. Although, since Da hadn't really done any dating in years—a fact that she confirmed during that conversation—this was all pretty much academic, anyway.

But this new piece of info did beg one particular question on my part. I had always assumed, in the back of my mind, that her brusque treatment and sexual neglect of Mom was due to being attracted, as she'd claimed to be, to men. If she truly was interested in women, then how had she really felt about my mother? Blushing, Da muted the TV and cleared her throat. Da said she was attracted to women—that, in fact, she had always been attracted to women. (The fling with heterosexuality a few years back, she explained, was merely an adolescent attempt to seem more "normal" for once.) She paused, and then said that she loved my mother. I already knew that much. She added that my mother was exactly the kind of woman she hoped to meet someday.

"I don't know how to interpret that," I said.

"Let's just say my life is very ironic in certain respects," Da said, in between whole mouthfuls of pistachios.

"I think she's really happy with Michael," I offered, gingerly.

Da nodded, chewing. "That helps," she said, with a sigh. "That's the important thing."

Cleveland, July 6, 1996. During my recovery from depression, I had usurped Da's cookbooks—not so much to play domestic goddess, but simply because the process of chopping, dicing, and sautéeing had turned out to be one of the best ways I'd found to relax. It was vastly more difficult to think ahead, and worry obsessively, when I was slicing a tomato or browning some bacon in a cast-iron skillet.

My new boyfriend, a Canadian toy designer who was significantly more fond of my ever-widening frame than Josh had been, had just sped back to Toronto. I was immersed in prepping my own twenty-fourth birthday dinner for my father and mother, who planned to come by after attending a ball game with her husband.

By the time she arrived, the eggplant-almond enchiladas, the homemade guacamole, margaritas lavishly rimmed in kosher salt, and a host of other Mexican dishes were on the table. My mother exclaimed what a lovely job I'd done, and to their credit, neither of my parents reminded me that they avidly disliked Mexican food. I'm thankful they didn't say anything, because I felt so joyous, truly, from the prospect of feeding them.

Except that it was my birthday, there is no real reason that I remember this evening. There were no arguments, no fallings-out, no passionately felt gestures of admiration and love. It was a simple family dinner—three women: a father, a mother, and a child—and that was the greatest part about it. Despite our own individual journeys and intermittent crises, we had achieved the mundane. I don't mean "normal"—we were still eccentric by most American standards. But we were not a family only by dint of banding together against the world, or uniting to suffer through our own self-imposed dramas. In the end, there was just camaraderie, affection, and what truly counts as unconditional love.

After cake and ice cream, my mother dried her lips with a paper napkin and apologized that she needed to get home to Michael. My father nodded, quietly, perhaps not daring to wince. I kissed my mother good night, and she turned to hug my father.

They paused for a second, just holding each other, and let go.

ACKNOWLEDGMENTS

Writing this book was an awesome task, professionally as well as personally. I owe a debt of gratitude to all those who helped me in all the various and sundry aspects of the process: self-esteem boosts; constructive criticism; occasional karaoke outings.

First of all, I would like to thank my agent and dear friend, Karen Gerwin of the William Morris Agency, for believing in this project from the beginning and nudging me until I eked out a proposal. I am also deeply grateful to Alicia Brooks, my incredible editor at Picador USA, whose intelligent, probing, and critical insights during the writing and revision process enriched this book beyond measure. Her warmth, reassurance, and humor helped steady me through what could have been a stressful time. Additionally, I am indebted to Frances Coady, publisher of Picador USA, for her steadfast encouragement and kind words, and to George Witte, editor-in-chief of St. Martin's Press, for his generous support of this project from the very beginning. I am also grateful to the New York Foundation for the Arts for granting me a nonfiction fellowship, which assisted financially in this process.

There is no way I can repay my trusted friends and readers—who took their time to help me deliver a better story and help quell my worst fears—particularly Lisa Miya-Jervis, Esther Haynes, Gayle Forman, Drs. Leonard and JoAnne Podis, and my frequent collaborator, Ellen Samuels. And certainly there are not enough words (although hopefully 300 pages or so is a good start) to show my appreciation for my parents, Rebecca Christine Howey and Dinah Howey-Mouat. They trusted me to recount some of the most sensitive and painful experiences of their lives and never attempted to censor a word. The hours spent interviewing both of them for this book are ones that I will treasure forever. To my father, Christine, I am indebted for the use of material—both quotes and anecdotes—from her play *Making Faces*, and for use of Grandma Howey's letters. I would also like to thank my mother for use of personal documents and stories once kept private that she kindly allowed me to use in the telling of this story.

Finally, I'd like to thank my husband and best friend, Christopher Healy, who could not have been more supportive of this book, even though it made me cranky, weepy, occasionally unreachable, and eternally preoccupied. He washed all the dishes, did the laundry, massaged my shoulders, read each draft carefully, and generally saved my life over and over again.

ABOUT THE AUTHOR

Noelle Howey is the co-editor of the anthology *Out of the Ordinary: Essays on Growing Up with Gay, Lesbian, and Transgender Parents* (St. Martin's Press), winner of two 2000 Lambda Literary Awards. She has previously written for publications as varied as *Ms., Fortune Small Business, Mother Jones, Teen People, Bitch, Jane, Glamour, Seventeen,* and *Self.* Her work has been nominated for a GLAAD Media Award, and she received a 2001 Nonfiction Fellowship in Nonfiction Literature from the New York Foundation for the Arts. She has lived in Cleveland, Seattle, and New York City, and currently resides in Minneapolis with her husband.